THE EMERGENCE OF FRANK WATERS

A Critical Reader

edited by
Alexander Blackburn and John Nizalowski

IRIE
BOOKS

"This compendium of Frank Waters' visionary literary legacy by a stellar selection of writers, scholars and critics, joyously explores the work of the man who has been called the godfather of Southwestern writing.

Often hailed as the greatest unknown writer in America — despite numerous nominations for the Nobel Prize — this appreciation should go a long way toward advancing the recognition of his place in the pantheon of the world's great writers."

— *Alan Louis Kishbaugh*
Author of *DEEP WATERS: Frank Waters Remembered in Letters and Commentary*

ISBN 978-1-5154-1731-6
Copyright 2020 by Alexander Blackburn and John Nizalowski

Cover design by Mariah Fox, itäl art
Interior design by Nancy R Koucky, NRK Designs

The Emergence of Frank Waters: A Critical Reader
is published by Irie Books, Santa Fe, New Mexico.
For information, contact www.iriebooks.com

IRIE
BOOKS

the prophetick soule,
of the wide world, dreaming on things to come

CONTENTS

V. THE NOVELS

ALEXANDER BLACKBURN
PREFACE

Frank Waters is a major American writer whose life spanned the twentieth century from 1902 to 1995. In his twenty-seven book career, *The Man Who Killed the Deer* and *Book of the Hopi* became and to some extent continue to be best-sellers, and almost all of his works are in print. For all his achievement, however, Waters has yet to be fully and properly recognized. Drawing upon available studies, the editors of *The Emergence of Frank Waters: A Critical Reader* hope to show the greatness in Waters that stands above narrower perfections.

His contemporaries, novelists such as William Faulkner, Ernest Hemingway, John Steinbeck and Thomas Wolfe, are justly celebrated, but the beauty and depth of Waters' novels earn him a place seriously to be considered alongside them. His contemporaries, moreover, were not philosophers with a prophetic vision, whereas Waters was both a novelist and a philosopher, truly a literary phenomenon rarely to be met with either in America or abroad. Waters' contemporaries set out to describe our spiritual disabilities. Waters aimed to cure them.

After the Civil War, Waters' grandfather Joseph Dozier, a North Carolinian and building contractor, headed west and settled in Colorado Springs at the base of Pike's Peak. The little city, founded before the "close" of the frontier, was booming as a health resort and business end of fabulous gold-mining enterprises in nearby Cripple Creek. Prospering as a builder, Dozier invested his small fortune in a search for gold and lost nearly everything, including an auspicious future for Frank. Then in 1914, when Frank was twelve, his father died. Looming before him was a hardscrabble life. Although he studied engineering at The Colorado College, he dropped out before graduating. A future as an engineer seemed sterile. His true vocation as a writer was clarifying itself. Frank decamped from Colorado Springs and took the vast region of the Southwest as his "significant soil." T.S. Eliot's phrase, here attributed to the desert, seems surprisingly right for someone devoted to the interconnectedness of humanity and the wild earth's nobility.

Members of the family, not the Doziers, not Frank's mother, not Frank himself, didn't know much about Frank's father except that he was part-Indian. Perhaps the father kept silent for a reason: those were the days when a "red" n-word could spring from concealment under handlebar mustaches. Or, perhaps, a racial profile in looks and behavior did not invite discrimination. At all events, though Frank was dyed-in-the-wool Anglo, neither an Indian nor an impersonator of an Indian in life and literature, he had a dual heritage to explore and did so profoundly and objectively. He felt at home with Indians, they with him—there's even an element of truth in the proposition that he "grandfathered" modern Native American letters. He wouldn't–because an Anglo couldn't–be Indian, but his quest for what he called "the continental soul" produced stories and studies that confirm an Indian-like sense of rightness with the land. Although this *Reader* gives pride of place to novels such as *The Man Who Killed the Deer* and *The Woman at Otowi Crossing*, not to be overlooked are masterful essays in *Masked Gods, Pumpkin Seed Point, Mexico Mystique* and *Mountain Dialogues*.

In search of the continental soul, Waters did not need to go into exile. It was already here in the wild rivers and abysmal canyons and towering mountains. It was already here in ancient myths that could re-connect us with the most central meanings of life. And in a synecdochal perspective the soul manifested in the Southwest stood for all of America, and all of America stood for the Earth. Unlike his contemporaries, except for a while Faulkner, Waters never went to Europe.

Ages before Darwin's theory of evolution challenged belief in sudden creation, the Amerindian and Mesoamerican myth of Emergence had been helping humankind to understand origins in a process of development of psychic life, primal stages setting the stage for emergence to a new world of consciousness this side of catastrophe. Is there evidence of Emergence in our own time? Although Waters avoided wishful thinking, he had worked at Los Alamos and personally known great nuclear physicists there, so how could he not, as in *Masked Gods* and *The Woman at Otowi Crossing*, confront the possibility of an Earth made uninhabitable by weapons of mass destruction? Clearly, an increased awareness of our peril, a consciousness of what he called "the planetary imperative," had the power to hold humanity together. Pictures of Earth shown to us by astronauts near or on the Moon, pictures inconceivable by most of us a mere half-century ago, have increased awareness. Now we realize more than ever before how fragile is this bright blue and white planet seemingly lost in an infinity of cosmic darkness. Now, as more and more people see themselves as participants in Emergence, a coming world of consciousness looms in reality as a coming world of hope.

Waters was years, perhaps decades, ahead of his time. The main reason for neglect and misinterpretation of his work lies in this fact. James Thomas, editor of *Best of the West*, sums the matter up:

> The Amerindian and Eastern thought which characterizes and forms Waters' fiction has been far from the mind of the literary and cultural establishment these past... years, and ultimately it is hardly a surprise that this author's work should go largely unnoticed except on... a limited regional, ethnocentric, and "cultish" basis. Waters is now, however, on the cutting edge of just about everything we take seriously in this country: the natural environment, our sociopsychological environment (our personal lives, and how we choose to control them), our political relationship with the past, and our political, ecological, and spiritual relationship with the future.

Frank Waters envisioned a future in which humankind, little by little, comes together in an inter-thinking, planetary embrace. The richness and the wonder and the mystery of life that he envisioned are a story of love.

JOHN NIZALOWSKI
PREFACE

In the autumn of 1924, during a decade when many writers of his generation were embarking to Europe, Frank Waters piled his few belongings in
the back of a Star Roadster, got behind the wheel, and headed southwest to
begin a 1,500-mile journey from Casper, Wyoming, to Los Angeles. The car's
owner, a cowboy named Garth, had lived a long and adventurous life as a
trapper, wrangler, and cowhand. He had even served as a guide on one of Ted-
dy Roosevelt's western sojourns. But now in his old age he yearned to replace
the wild Rocky Mountains with southern California's quiet warmth.

Waters, on the other hand, was young and restless, and his reasons for
going to Los Angeles were quite different. A Colorado native and recent college
dropout, he had found the life of a roustabout in the Wyoming gas fields bleak
and unfulfilling. So when Garth, a lousy driver, asked his 22-year-old friend
to take the wheel and guide him to the golden land of oranges and palm trees,
Waters was glad to go. He sensed that in California he could come to grips
with his wayward urges and make a real life for himself (F. Waters, "Notes" 22).

After they left Casper and passed through Cheyenne and Denver, the
duo sped straight south through Colorado, traversing the edge of the prairie
where it meets the Rocky Mountains, a place of rolling hills, weathered buttes,

and high grasses – familiar territory to the young man at the wheel. But after they stayed the night in Colorado Springs at grandfather Dozier's old Shooks Run house, where Waters grew up, and the roadster reached deeper and deeper into the southeastern corner of the state to at last laboriously climb through the 7800-foot-high Raton Pass into New Mexico, Waters was entering an unknown realm.

Paralleling the Santa Fe Trail, they passed through or near towns whose names resonated with western history – Maxwell, Wagon Mound, Las Vegas, and Pecos. Waters knew the stories of these places, and he felt a growing excitement as he journeyed across such fabled lands. Soon after Las Vegas they turned sharply west, passing under the Sangre de Cristo Mountains and over the Glorieta Pass, site of a major Civil War battle.

At last, they descended into the city of Santa Fe.

Waters was amazed by this centuries-old New Mexican capital. In the city's plaza, Indians huddled under their blankets and sold pottery in the portal fronting the Palace of the Governors. Some of its vigas had been cut before Jefferson composed the Declaration of Independence. Up the street stood the gothic cathedral built at the command of Archbishop Lamy in 1875, the tolling of its bells echoing from the city's maze of adobe walls. As if transposed from medieval Spain, donkeys overloaded with firewood clattered down narrow streets. With nightfall drawing near, the travelers decided to stay at the La Fonda Hotel. Built in the Pueblo revival style, it loomed over the plaza like an Anasazi ruin restored to life. That evening, they were the only guests in the hotel's small, four table dining room (F. Waters, "A New Look").

The next morning, Waters and Garth departed Santa Fe, negotiating the torturous turns of the Bajada – the southern wall of the volcanic plateau on which the old capitol city stands. Then they wound past massive cottonwoods, golden in the New Mexican autumn, and the Hispanic communities of Blanco, Algodones, and Bernallio, reaching at last the city of Albuquerque. There they again turned west. The paved road quickly gave way to dirt, and the voyage became a slow crawl beside long red sandstone cliffs and black lava fields. By sundown, the Pueblo Indian village of Laguna came into view, like some medieval Italian mountain redoubt of stone and adobe perched on a mounded hill.

Upon reaching Arizona, the duo ran short of money, so for their evening stops they camped by the roadside, Garth shooting rabbits with a .22 rifle to fill their cooking pot. Sometimes other intrepid wanderers would see their campfire and pull over, seeking company on that dark, lonely highway. In this way the pair made their way across the Painted Desert, through the 19th century brick and stone city of Flagstaff, and down the long descent through the Juniper, Aquarius, and Hualapai Mountains towards their final border crossing.

From the mining camp of Oatman, high in the Black Mountains overlooking the Colorado River, Waters had his first glimpse of California. For someone raised in the shadow of 14,000-foot Pike's Peak, the cactus-strewn expanse of the Mojave Desert struck Waters as very strange and exotic, a feeling that deepened when he glimpsed his first palm tree in Barstow. And when Garth let him out in the midst of Los Angeles' colonial-era plaza, Waters found himself immersed in a world more attuned with old Mexico than modern America (F. Waters, "Notes" 22-23).

So while Hemingway, Pound, and Fitzgerald were, so to say, strolling the Latin Quarter or sipping apéritifs at the Dome, Waters had traversed over 1500 miles of American mountain, prairie, and desert. In this vast landscape, more Mexican and Indian than Euro-American, Waters discovered his literary heartland.

Just as France forms a stark contrast to New Mexico, Waters' writings possess distinct differences from the literary work being done by his American contemporaries. Influenced by Transcendentalism, Jungian psychology, Meso-American mythology, and Asian philosophy, Waters' novels and essays bear more similarity to the writings of Ralph Waldo Emerson, Herman Melville, and Hermann Hesse than to those of Ernest Hemingway or John Dos Passos. Also, unlike most 20th century American writers, Waters' work was centered in the Southwest, and his cultural axis was Mexico City, not Paris (F. Waters, interview).

The excitement and inspiration that Waters experienced during his journey from Wyoming transformed into creative energies when, soon after his arrival in Los Angeles, Waters landed a job as an engineer with the Southern California Telephone Company, a position that would take him to the deserts of the Imperial Valley (F. Waters, "Notes" 24). In 1926 he journeyed by horseback into Lower California's wilderness interior. Its surreal, arid landscape shook his mountain-bred soul so deeply that he felt impelled to write, and when he returned to his cramped two-room shack in El Centro, he began with a passage describing a desert valley in the shape of a lizard with a woman's face. This became the nucleus of his first novel, *Fever Pitch*, published by Horace Liveright in 1930 (F. Waters, *Lizard Woman* vii-viii).

Fever Pitch is a Conradian tale of civil engineer Lee Marston and his fateful plunge off the railroad company's survey map to find gold in an uncharted desert with Arvilla, a mestiza percentage girl. The novel made little impression on critics or the reading public, and Waters himself later dismissed it as an immature work mired in pulp-western conventions (F. Waters, *Lizard Woman* vii-viii). And yet, despite the novel's shortcomings, Waters had struck his vein of literary gold – Mexico and the American Southwest.

Except for a brief sojourn during and just after World War II – when he dwelled in New York City, Washington, D.C., and Jefferson, Texas – Waters would spend his life in a kind of grand circle of the Southwest which included Colorado Springs, Los Angeles, Taos, Santa Fe, Tucson, Las Vegas, and various locales in Mexico, which in *Pike's Peak* Waters named "the motherland of western America" (675). These places and the wealth of experiences they bequeathed to Waters, from riding horseback across the Sierra Madres to witnessing atomic detonations, inspired some of the finest American literature of the 20th century. In the twenty-seven books of fiction and non-fiction – two were published posthumously – he established himself as the leading literary voice of the Southwest, a region that between the world wars possessed its own distinct literary and cultural scene that had a significant place alongside Carmel, Provincetown, Greenwich Village, and Paris in the evolution of 20th century American arts and letters.

In the autumn of 1924, when Waters, on his way to Los Angeles, spent the night in Santa Fe's La Fonda hotel, mere blocks away the poet Witter Bynner was at home in his sprawling adobe dwelling on Buena Vista Street. At this time, Bynner was the author of twelve books, the former fiancé of Edna St. Vincent Millay, and one of America's leading poets. Two years before, Bynner, exhausted by an extended tour of Asia and a relentless lecturing schedule, had arrived in Santa Fe at the invitation of Alice Corbin Henderson, the co-founder of *Poetry* magazine, who had settled in New Mexico to recuperate from tuberculosis. Here Bynner found a land that was both peaceful and inspiring. With its high deserts, adobe structures, and American Indian civilization, it reminded him of his beloved China, and he would remain in Santa Fe until his death in 1968 (Kraft 50-52).

Soon after his arrival, Bynner established a thriving literary salon in

Santa Fe. Many major authors visited him at his Buena Vista home, including D.H. Lawrence, Vachel Lindsay, Carl Sandburg, Yvor Winters, Thornton Wilder, W.H. Auden, and Stephen Spender (Kraft 52). Bynner wrote extensively about New Mexico, as did other Santa Fe authors within Bynner's orbit, including poet Haniel Long, playwright Lynn Riggs, and novelists Paul Horgan, Oliver LaFarge, and Dorothy Hughes.

Meanwhile, seventy miles north in Taos, Mabel Dodge established her own salon patterned after the ones she had previously created in Florence and Greenwich Village. Drawn by its cultural vitality and unspoiled natural beauty, Dodge found in Taos a refuge from what she believed were the sterile materialism and declining artistic energies of urban America (Rudnick 144). In 1923, Mabel Dodge married Antonio Luhan, a Taos Indian from the nearby pueblo. Together, they created Los Gallos, a sprawling adobe mansion on the edge of the Taos Indian pueblo (Rudnick 152-154).

Like Bynner in Santa Fe, Mabel Dodge Luhan in Taos attracted numerous artists and writers of great importance, some of whom would end up making New Mexico their home. Her biggest coup was convincing D.H. Lawrence to live in Taos in the 1920s (Rudnick 195). Other cultural giants associated with Luhan – Georgia O'Keeffe, Ansel Adams, and Robinson Jeffers – all lived for a time at Los Gallos (Rudnick 234, 286). Many significant writers of the West also joined the Taos salon, including essayist Mary Austin, who stayed with Luhan in the early twenties (Rudnick 170), and Montana-born novelist Myron Brinig, who visited Luhan in the mid-thirties and stayed to become a key member of the Taos literary scene for the next decade (Rudnick 302-303).

While Bynner and Luhan were gripped by a sometimes bitter rivalry to make their respective salon the artistic center of the Southwest, they did share a fervent desire to place New Mexico on the international cultural map. To a degree they succeeded, yet they ultimately felt slighted by an American critical establishment that never fully acknowledged their claims for the region's creative prominence.

Possessed by a kind of missionary zeal, Luhan went further than Bynner in these efforts. Once she was established in Taos, she began a quest for the literary voice of the Southwest, a writer who would make the region famous across the planet. Rather than nurture a home-grown literary figure, however, her plan was to lure a major author to Taos, where, Luhan believed, he or she would surely succumb to the region's radiant beauty and spiritual power and remain forever to sing its praises. To accomplish this end, she enticed D.H. Lawrence and, later, Robinson Jeffers to Los Gallos (Rudnick 284-285). Unfortunately for Luhan, Lawrence found Mexico more fertile for his imagination, and Jeffers only wrote one poem about Taos despite his numerous visits to Luhan's estate. Then in 1937, after a dozen years of wandering that had taken him from Los Angeles to Mexico City and back again to his native Colorado Springs, Frank Waters moved to Taos. As novelist and Waters scholar Alexander Blackburn states whimsically in an interview, "Mabel Dodge's long awaited New Mexican literary champion had arrived."

In Taos, Frank Waters joined an established literary community, something that had eluded him in his decade-long writing career. By the early 1940s, Mabel Luhan had embraced Waters as a writer of consequence, and he found a mentor in Myron Brinig. He also became a close associate with *Laughing Horse* editor Spud Johnson and formed vital friendships with Witter Bynner, Andrew Dasburg, Nicolai Fechin, Leon Gaspard, and other important writers and artists. As a result, Waters' work flowered, and he became a mature literary author (F. Waters, *Of Time and Change* 73-76). Between 1938 and 1941 he would compose three of his most enduring novels – *The Dust Within the Rock* (1940), which completed the *Pike's Peak* trilogy; *The People of the Valley* (1941), one of the first major novels to explore Hispanic rural life of the Southwest; and *The Man Who Killed the Deer* (1942), the internationally acclaimed novel of an American Indian's journey from social alienation to tribal connection.

These novels alone are enough to place Frank Waters in the first tier of 20th century American literature, but other essential works were still to come. During the next three decades, Waters lived primarily in Los Angeles, Las Vegas, Sedona, and Arroyo Seco, north of Taos, a place that stood as his psychic axis, his true home. His employment included Hollywood script editor, war era propagandist for the United States government, bilingual newspaper editor, public relations officer at the Nevada Atomic Testing Range, and agricultural laborer.

In the early 1950s, one of the most profound experiences for Waters occurred on the desert basin of Nevada's Frenchman's Flat. There, as a public relations officer for the Atomic Energy Commission, Waters witnessed dozens of atomic detonations, including the infamous shot code-named "Dirty Harry," which spread radioactive debris across eastern Nevada and western Utah (F. Waters, "A New Look"). Waters brought to these experiences a Jungian sense of dualism, and he viewed the atomic enterprise as both a hopeful signal of the progressive transformation of humanity and a warning of possible planetary annihilation.

This sense of dualism, along with his firsthand knowledge of atomic weapons development, informed Waters' writing of *The Woman at Otowi Crossing*, his 1966 novel loosely based on the life of his friend Edith Warner, the owner of a tea house near Los Alamos who became the confidant of J. Robert Oppenheimer, Hans Bethe, Enrico Fermi, and other major players involved in the making of the first atomic bomb.

However, *The Woman at Otowi Crossing* aside, beginning with the 1946 publication of *The Colorado*, Waters' focus turned to non-fiction. The most notable of these works include *Masked Gods* (1950), a study of Navajo and Pueblo Indian myth, ceremony, and history; *The Earp Brothers of Tombstone* (1960), one of the first revisionist histories of the western mythos; *Book of the Hopi* (1963), an ethnography of the Hopi Indians; *Pumpkin Seed Point* (1969), a personal account of the years he spent on the Hopi mesas; *Mexico Mystique* (1975), an esoteric study of pre-Columbian Meso-American cultures; and *Mountain Dialogues* (1981), a collection of essays Waters completed when he was nearing eighty.

By the time *Mountain Dialogues* made its appearance, Waters had married Barbara Hayes, and had settled into his summer home in Arroyo Seco and his winter home in Tucson. Along with this newfound stability, he made the transition from an obscure author laboring away in the American hinterlands to a major figure of western American literature. Reviewers and critics had granted him such laudatory titles as the "godfather of Southwestern writing" and "the Hermann Hesse of the 70's" (Kishbaugh).

Waters attained his strong literary reputation by combining his western heritage and experience with a life-long study of Buddhism, Taoism, mythology, anthropology, psychology, and physics – pursuits that began in childhood under the influence of his grandfather Joseph Dozier, who possessed a surprisingly good metaphysical library (B. Waters). As can be seen from his own writings, Frank Waters found the works of Emerson, Jung, Krishnamurti, and Gurdjieff especially engaging. Waters' work, therefore, has several over-arching philosophical themes. He believed that all people, objects, and energies in the universe are interconnected. Systems of duality – science and mysticism, rationality and intuition, anima and animus – are also deeply connected, even identical. For Waters, humanity is passing through a period of rapid and profound change metaphorically portrayed by the Pueblo Indian myth of Emergence, which depicts humankind's passage through four previous worlds to reach the current Fifth World. Each time we move forwards into a new world, a new reality, our consciousness advances. Waters believed that we are now making the transition into a new, Sixth World, and when we as a species cross over, we will have a deeper understanding of our fundamental connection to each other and to the universe (F. Waters, *Pumpkin* 171-173).

For Waters, the Southwest will be the birthplace of this new world because of its unique mixture of Indian and Euro-American cultures, and this amalgam will answer Jung's call for a balance between the extroverted and the introverted, the rational and the mystical, the Apollonian and Dionysian. As Waters writes in *Masked Gods*:

> Perhaps in no other comparable area on earth are condensed so many contradictions, or manifested so clearly the opposite polarities of all life. The oldest forms of life discovered in this hemisphere, and the newest agent of mass death. The oldest cities in America and the newest. The Sun Temple of Mesa Verde and the nuclear fission laboratories of the Pajarito Plateau. The Indian drum and the atom smasher. Men flying like birds seeding the clouds for rain, while others below them, naked and painted, dance with rattlesnakes in their mouths. Everywhere the future stumbles upon the jutting past, the invisible gives shape to the visible, blind instinct points the way to reason.... For here as nowhere else has the conflict been fought so bitterly, and have the opposing principles approached so closely a fusion. At that fusion there will arise a new faith for which we are crying so desperately. A faith big enough to embrace all of mankind's experiences of the past, all our religious creeds, and all our scientific concepts. (425-426)

Because of this vision of interconnection, and because he lived amongst Hispanics and Indians nearly his entire life, Waters wrote of these cultures when few other authors were doing so. Novels like *People of the Valley* and

The Man Who Killed the Deer anticipate the Chicano and American Indian literary movements that emerged two decades later. In addition, a work like *The Woman at Otowi Crossing* demonstrates Waters' interest in feminist and ecological themes before these concerns entered the mainstream.

Thus, as proclaimed by Sioux author Vine Deloria, Jr., Frank Waters embodies the attributes of a prophet and an explorer, "pointing us towards that inevitable unity of purpose which our species must have if it is to survive" (171-172).

But what about beyond the Southwest?

Despite the fundamental relevance of his literary and philosophical vision to our contemporary global culture, when Frank Waters died in Arroyo Seco on June 3, 1995, most readers and critics outside the Southwest remained unaware of his life and work. This situation, which holds true to this day, is best summed up by Alexander Blackburn in *A Sunrise Brighter Still*: "[C]ontinuously nominated since 1985 for the Nobel Prize for literature, and arguably, on some grounds, as great a novelist as his famous contemporaries William Faulkner, Ernest Hemingway, and John Steinbeck, Waters is nevertheless outside his native Southwest relatively unknown" (xvi).

So, despite being the preeminent author of the American Southwest, why has Waters remained largely unread past the borders of his regional homeland?

To answer this, we must go back to 1924 and that Star Roadster.

When Waters left the natural gas fields of Salt Creek, Wyoming to make the defining journey of his life, he traversed the dusty western roads for Los Angeles. If he had instead gone east, made the expatriate jump to Paris, played the game of polishing his style to a fine modernist sheen, perhaps today Waters would be a widely anthologized author. However, he faced west and embraced the country of his soul – the Hopi Indian carefully winding his way through the labyrinth of a kachina dance, the mestizo farmer tilling his corn beneath the high Sierra Madre peaks, the grit-stained Anglo miner hammering the drill bit home in the granite earth, the exile Russian artist sharing vodka with a British poet under the blue skies of Taos, the Jewish physicist witnessing the first atomic fire in a place called the Journey of Death. These became the worlds from which Frank Waters found his stories; these were the realms that set his creative spirit on fire.

By embracing the full storytelling potential and archetypal depth of the Southwest, Frank Waters wrote some of the finest American literature of the 20th century.

I.
INTRODUCTION

THOMAS J. LYON
INTRODUCTION

Over the course of a twenty-seven-book career, Frank Waters dealt with the most excruciating contradictions of the twentieth century: our heroic technology, concurrent with spiritual impoverishment; our racial and ethnic antagonisms, persisting while we knit the world together mechanically; our declining sense of nature, fading as we gain almost godlike knowledge of the workings of biology. And underneath all this dissonance lies the divided modern self — mostly egoist-accountant-technician, perhaps, but still some part poet. In the face of the general fragmentation, Waters quested lifelong for what heals and unifies.

Unearthing his themes in his own background and life, Frank Waters appears to have sensed early that the world had its correlative in the inward dimension, and that his own narrative, including family background, could be a legitimate point of entry. In a real sense, he wrote his life, but without the obsessive self-centeredness that characterizes so much modern "confessional" literature. More steadily than most writers of his century, he focused not so much on the separate individual as on the idea of the one big picture, the unity.

So it is that nature and the West he lived in — the spare lines of the landscape, the clouds blooming overhead, the scent of pines, the heat of the air on a July day in New Mexico, the companionableness of horses, the mysterious feeling of belonging to the pattern — are Waters' basic reference. The Southwest is where the wholeness touched him. Sense of place in his writing is palpable, and a conduit to all issues. The residue left upon the imagination by a Frank Waters book, above all, is a feeling of where it takes place. This effect is vastly deeper than some sort of local color; it is a sense of being located, and through a particular location, with its lines and shapes and ambient sounds, of having the feel of the totality.

This matter of actual footing is worth emphasizing, because Waters is known as a mystic, and in our culture mysticism usually connotes otherworldliness. Within our dualistic tradition, nature and "the body," as the phrase has it, are thought to be different from, lesser than, perhaps even antagonistic to, spiritual insight. In this tradition, where you are is only a setting, a kind of stage for your drama — you yourself are engaged with more important matters. Any number of spiritual seekers and groups, in the "New Age" as in past times, have dedicated themselves to enlightenment or salvation strictly as a matter of personal sensibility, personal grace. The focus is upon the individual's consciousness or soul, seen separate from trees, wind, and soil. In the dominant paradigm, these are only "the environment," and are, for all intents and purposes, spiritually blank.

Frank Waters was never indifferent to nature and place. Some of his earliest memories, as recorded in his autobiographical fiction, are of the looming presence of Pike's Peak — the landmark by which the way to and from school was navigated surely. The known world was structured on that mountain, a real, present mass of reddish granite rising abruptly and hugely into blue, cloud-decked sky. Just to the west of the Pike's Peak massif itself, at about the age of ten, young Frank Waters had a very strong, direction-setting experience, which he later described in *The Colorado*. As a young man, the autobiographical protagonist "March Cable," depicted in *The Dust within the Rock*, bathed in the pool of a hot spring originating fictionally on Pike's Peak, and while relishing there the sensations of a stormy spring afternoon, again experienced the core feeling of ego-transcendence and oneness with nature — "a brilliant and indestructible illumination," Waters wrote. As it happened, March made a big decision that afternoon. Significantly, Waters' initial foray into the writing of fiction (in 1925, when he was twenty-three) began with a description of an intense, transcendental experience in a desert landscape. Dramatized in his writing over the years, instances of deeply felt experience of place are more than just numerous: they are the armature upon which the writing is built.

It is revealing of the nature of his mind that Waters' delineations of place show simultaneously the particular dimension and the abstract-philosophical. Nature is both close around the body and as big and totalizing as thought can conceive. On the one hand, the leathery leaves of cottonwoods, rustling and clicking in the breeze at Otowi Crossing; on the other, the "wholeness in which every part is interrelated in one vast body of universal Creation" (*Mountain Dialogues*). If there were only the leaves, you might have at best imagism, and the potential for a kind of poetry. If there were only the wholeness, you might have metaphysics, and the potential merely for philosophizing. But Waters' great movement as a writer is to reach toward a full, proportionate expression in which both aspects of any given duality take part.

The specific places which for Waters hold this simultaneous physical-spiritual intensity are in the dry quarter of the country, and it is his connected, reaching-toward-totality consciousness of place that has made him one of the archetypal southwestern writers. There is the sense that a described place is at once out there in the world and deep within ourselves. In his "Introduction" to W. Y. Evans-Wentz's *Cuchama and Sacred Mountains*, Waters indicated his direction succinctly: "We have yet to fully realize that the physical and psychical realms are two aspects of one transcendental unity."

The aura of the Southwest has always been both intensely colored and somewhat rarefied — this has been noted by just about every writer, painter, or historian who has become acquainted with the area. It is gritty and spiritual, both; as mundane as potshards on the ground and as portentous as the future. Waters registers the colorful paradox of "Indian Country" perfectly. Only Mary Austin among writers, or D. H. Lawrence, was as ready as Waters to grant this region universal importance and possible redemptive power. Lawrence averred that it was his experience of New Mexico, "Curious as it may sound . . . that liberated me from the present era of civilization, the great era of material and mechanical development." Austin went so far as to prophesy that the Southwest would generate, as she put it, the "next great and fructifying world culture." And it was not mere random choice, probably, that led Aldous Huxley to locate his "Brave New World's" savage reservation, the dystopic future's one saving remnant of spontaneity and wildness, in New Mexico. Into our consumer era, famously a time of mass media and falseness, when even the Southwest has become a boutique item, Frank Waters' portrayal of the region retains both its authentic detail and its mysterious, beyond-all-markets resonance.

Along with his scrupulously equal regard for the physical reality and spiritual import of landscape, Waters habitually insisted upon overcoming the dualism of rational thought versus intuition, within human psychology. His core idea is that both particle and wave, as it were, are necessary parts of the whole. Although he realized that his own culture was strongly tilted toward the "particle" side of things, mentally, and stood in need of corrective balance, he refused to elevate one aspect of consciousness over the other. In *Pumpkin Seed Point*, he describes a horseback descent to the bottom of the Barranca de Urique in Mexico, one of the deepest gorges on earth and thus a fine symbol for the depths of nonrational consciousness. We need to go down into that canyon — if we never make the journey, we remain superficial. But such a return to "the depths of his [mankind's] archaic past in the fathomless unconscious," as Waters put it, must be combined with the "upper" layers of consciousness to foster genuine growth and a more complete psychic life. Only the whole equals health. The Tarahumara Indians of the deep canyon seemed revealing to Waters: their dark eyes expressed the "wild remoteness of the Barranca itself, the withdrawn look of a people who had not yet emerged from their dark depths; a pleading look, like that of an animal which begs [for] the light of understanding." Clearly, he means to depict them as incomplete, rather than as a model of unspoiledness. Their softness has a certain attraction, but it is not enough.

The Pueblo Indians may offer a different story. According to Waters' portrayal in both *The Man Who Killed the Deer* (1942) and *Masked Gods* (1950), the Pueblo tribes may have recognized humanity's need to integrate the two main dimensions of the mind — a major insight. Thus they would be further along, evolutionarily speaking, than either the mild, intuitive natives of the barranca or the hard-surfaced Anglos of rationalist/mechanist notoriety. In the climactic Deer Dance of *The Man Who Killed the Deer*, there is a ritual involving the polarity of individualism versus unity. Waters' protagonist Martiniano watches the dance with a "hypnotic horror," because what he is seeing is his own story. Individual animals dance toward the outer edge of the circle, particles trying to break free of the center, that deep source of energy connecting all. They dance toward the outside, but always there is the insistent rhythm of the Deer Mothers, at the center, drawing them back into relational unity. This is the dance of life. In the dance, both centripetal and centrifugal forces are at play and, if they are in balance, can create a beautiful pattern.

In human consciousness, the sense of separate selfhood is cognate with what is called rational, or linear, thought. That is one pole of our character, founded in one corner of the mind. The other is the impersonal or nonegoistic sense of embeddedness, deriving from the ability to perceive relation, configuration, pattern. Waters depicts the Pueblo ceremonials as dramas of this polarity. The dance of unity is itself the state of health, the desired, harmonious end of the ritual, and Waters' implication is that a people who have developed such an art form must be well along in the true Emergence. Martiniano, in *The Man Who Killed the Deer*, is slowly and haltingly learning this path, slowly opening up to his birthright range of consciousness. What makes *The Man Who Killed the Deer* one of the great novels of the inner life, and *Masked Gods* one of the farthest-reaching anthropological texts, is that Frank Waters holds so faithfully to the ultimate vision of health. He looks down each attractive byroad, but in the end the inclusive, paradoxical unity of nature is the only satisfying reference and standard. We rational skeptics do not measure up, and the gentle people of the barranca also may not, but the bloom of completeness stands before us as a common human goal. The vision of it probably constitutes our most important element of shared humanity. More than any other characteristic of his writing, it is his concentration on the transcendence of duality, his presentation of such elevation of vision as our shared work in this life, that makes Frank Waters an important writer.

Waters implies that wherever there is duality of some kind, there is also identity, and some degree of conflict. Whites differentiate themselves from Indians; men from women; human beings from the other animals; aliveness (as in a primate, mammal body) from unaliveness (as in a rock or a mountain). There is of course an element of truth in these and similar distinctions: seen by the rationalist side of consciousness, the world simply looks to be divided in this fashion. But if only that limited side of consciousness is working, or if it is excessively dominant, we will not see the complementary part of the big picture. We won't feel the relational pattern, nor, ultimately, the unity within all polarities. Nor will we rightly see the literal place where we are standing; we just don't realize, fully, the nature all around and within. Unseeing in this manner, we are apt to become structurally indifferent to the living quality of nature, to say nothing of its sacredness. Within a dualistically conceived world, stuck in identities, we are compelled to live in conflicts of one kind or another, all the way up to the insanities of racism and nationalism.

Frank Waters' central fictional characters are depicted on this map of consciousness. March Cable, Martiniano, the Woman at Otowi Crossing, and Tai Ling, the Yogi of Cockroach Court, all have at least intimations of the greater view, the hypothetical release from suffering and incompleteness that an integrated consciousness would bring. *The Woman at Otowi Crossing* actually emerges from self-partiality into a weight-free perception unbound by issues of identity. But the others are struggling, learning. Like the rest of us, they live in a culture that prizes self and identity, thinks mountains are spiritually unalive, and believes as an article of faith that all problems can be solved rationally and pragmatically. They have not awakened to the suppressed dimensions of consciousness. These presently hidden, relation-seeking powers, in a state of atrophy from disuse, amount to a kind of shadow country within.

In his major fiction, Waters' plots at their essence are straightforward. There is a movement out of the whole long human background of self, family, tradition, and seeming cultural necessity, toward emergence into compassion-ate, full seeing. His stories are dramas of consciousness and character.

The protagonists are learners, and for the portrayal to be experienceable, democratically available, the author also must be in a state of passionate open-ness, must himself be a learner. We are not talking so much about knowledge here, on the part of these characters and their author, for that is a function of the "thought" side of consciousness, and could be conveyed in a lecture. What is required here, in the fullness of life, is humble, character-opening experience itself, marked by vulnerability. It is perhaps telling that Frank Waters, as late as 1950 and *Masked Gods*, referred to himself as "the boy," as if eschewing the temptations of authority. Apparently he regarded the nondual level of insight as something that needed to be earned, and continually reearned. In a fashion comparable to the yearly rituals of the Pueblo and Hopi people, Waters seemed to reenact the search for the great harmony, the great unity, with each new book.

This focus on the theme of transcendence might appear intellectually simple or even programmatic, considered in isolation as an idea extracted from books, but it seems clear that such a concentration was Frank Waters' own real, life work. Far more complex than a mere idea, the search for integra-tion is heart work, character work.

Following the forthright leads in Waters' autobiographical fiction, we can see some of the origins of this practice in his background and early years. His mother, whose maiden name was May Ione Dozier, came from a solid Colorado Springs family whose standing in the town derived from her father Joseph Dozier's success as a builder. Dozier was one of the early settlers of Colorado Springs and as a trusted contractor had built several public buildings, including the first on the campus of The Colorado College (Cutler Hall, still in use). He was a man whose success was founded on strong will and strong principles. As Joseph Rogier in *The Wild Earth's Nobility* (1935), *Below Grass Roots* (1937), *The Dust within the Rock* (1940), and the decades-later redaction of these works, *Pike's Peak* (1971), this grandfather figure came to epitomize an imposing, mechanically triumphant, rational culture in its early days of glory. But Rogier (and Dozier as well?) also had an "oriental" side, revealed in his reading of Hindu and Buddhist texts and perhaps also in his liking for nonrational intuitions about mountains and treasure. After resisting for years the gold and silver fevers that had animated the life of Colorado Springs, Joseph Rogier gave in to his hunch that gold could be found in unimaginable quantities if only one were to bypass the relatively easy pickings just "below grass roots" and sink a shaft deep into Pike's Peak itself. In the novels, Waters portrays this drive to dig as an obsession, a trope for the search into the unconscious. Rogier/Dozier was not a simple man.

Nevertheless, the Dozier family tradition chiefly embodied mainstream Euro-American mentality and values, and as a typical family in class-conscious Colorado Springs (known at the time as "Little London") the Doziers naturally prized outward appearance. Thus life became more than just economically difficult when Joseph Dozier sunk his fortune into an unprofitable mine called the "Sylvanite," or "our family folly," as Frank Waters later termed it. The mine may have been a deep shaft into the mystery of life, but practically, Waters depicts it as ruinous for the family. The Rogiers/Doziers struggled to maintain some sense of their former status. Ione, called "Ona" in the novels, kept her father's accounts and became increasingly important in holding the family together.

One of the boarders in the big house at 435 East Bijou Street was a dark-complected, quiet man from the midwestern plains of Iowa, a man of a certain mystery. Frank Jonathon Waters ("Jonathon Cable") and Ione Dozier ("Ona Rogier"), described in the novels by their son as psychic opposites, were powerfully attracted to each other. In the books, there are strong hints, and more than hints, that "Jonathon Cable" was at least part Cheyenne. I have not pursued his historical prototype's genealogy, believing that what is of consequence here is that Frank Waters ("March Cable") perceived and was affected by unmistakable differences and oppositions between his parents. With their inherited "White" practicality and rationalism (the hand and the brain, so to speak) and from the other side a "Red" softness of intuition (the heart), Waters' mother and father were the makers of the map of his life.

That the differences between his parents had strong emotional impact on their first-born is shown clearly in *Below Grass Roots*, where Ona and Jonathon compete vigorously with each other for young March's allegiance. Waters describes the boy as "wavering" between them, and in numerous scenes of conflict, or simple lack of communication, there is no doubting the stress of an emotionally divided household. The division begins with the basic one of gender, of course, in this case presumably exacerbated by racial background, with added tension coming from a difficult economic situation. It could not have been an easy or straightforward childhood.

The death of Frank Jonathon Waters in 1914 meant that Ione, with twelve-year-old Frank and his little sister Naomi, had to move back into the Dozier household. Superficially at least, life would now be lived on "White" terms, with the declining and eccentric Grandfather Dozier as the family's central figure. The "Red," of course, would not be effaced entirely; it would become the shadow element, the always looked-for. Waters had already had that profound, consciousness-integrating experience at the age of ten, on the tailings pile at the family mine, and he retained its taste of mysterious fulfillment as a kind of hidden gauge by which to measure what people accepted at home and in town as normal life. That tailings-pile experience probably helped make him a lifelong learner, because it stood glowing in memory as an example of the unexpectable, a refutation of all pat answers and all authorities. Through high school and in his three-year study at Colorado College in the engineering department, Frank Waters tried manfully to play the roles expected of him, but something quite apart from the views of genteel, progressive, material-mechanical society, and in fact from the entire habit of mind of the culture he lived within, was simmering inside.

Soon after he had dropped out of college and left the family house, chance or, more likely, internal gravitation took him southward. He worked on and off for eleven years in El Centro, California, an Imperial Valley location less than ten miles from Mexico. The border region with its mixed-blood population, and then the vast and intimidating desert regions to the south, fascinated Waters. His initial attempts at fiction were set there. But first, it should be noted that this young man, working for the Southern California Telephone Company as an engineer, had indeed become passionately interested in writing. Judging by the content of his earliest efforts, it seems safe to say that he practiced writing as an inner, psychological, perhaps therapeutic exercise. In any case, he began by dramatizing his inward life. *Fever Pitch*, which was finished in 1926 (though not published until 1930), is a short, highly dramatic adventure story, told in a Conrad-like frame, in which a young engineer and a woman friend cross an expanse of wild desert to a gold claim being guarded by an associate of the woman's. The plot itself is almost a throwaway, perhaps embarrassing to Waters in later years — he was opposed to a 1955 paperback reissue of the novel. What is significant is that, by his report, the first fictional scene he ever wrote described the young engineer at a peak of intense experience, in the midst of wild nature. "Lee Marston's" awareness of the rocks and mountains and immense desert playas around him soared beyond rational accounting: "standing there alone in that immensity of creation and alone in the presence of God, he bowed his will to an omnipotent power of nature." "It is at such times," Waters continued, "that a man in an uplift of spirit loses all conception of the present and has removed from him forever that recognition of time and space into which he has been born."

The language of this first novel tries hard to express the inexpressible, perhaps a little too hard. But whatever one may think of the book's artistry, it is clear that Waters began as a writer by sincerely trying to capture the mysterious. In a way, he was occupied with his own Grandfather Dozier-like digging. As further evidence of this kind of motivation, he took up at this time a study of the Buddhist approach to enlightenment, incorporating it into his next piece of writing. This new project would turn out to be a longer, much more complex novel. It described the intermeshed lives of four people in a squalid border town, having as its centerpiece the quest of one of them, a Chinese shopkeeper, for release from all internal contradictions and all entanglements in ego-based, ordinary life. This search is noble, solitary in its intentions, and, as Waters depicts it, oddly self-contradictory. The Chinese man, Tai Ling, has to learn that to seek enlightenment in this way is in effect to be deluded, by reason of having objectified that which cannot be separated from life itself. Tai Ling puts years into his striving, while the life-plots of those around him run their tangled courses. The significance of this ambitious book in Waters' life is shown by his finishing a first draft in 1927, continuing to work on the story for two decades (putting it through several further drafts), and finally publishing it only in 1947. It is unique in American fiction, I believe, in focusing on the paradoxical nature of meditation, or the search for enlightenment. It clearly shows Waters' sense that rationalistic, objectifying consciousness tends to create contradiction. Tai Ling is forced to learn that truth is only experienceable, only totalistic, not something separate arrived at by force of will or intellect. It takes him years to discover this.

Frank Waters was not a writer attracted by Europe — he never went there — nor the wilderness North, certainly not the urban East. His compass always seemed to point toward the magnetic pole of indigenous, Indian life, in the Southwest and Mexico. In 1931, he rode horseback on a solo trip of several hundred miles, down the Sierra Madre Occidental into the heart of back-country Mexico, staying with campesino families, sleeping on the floors of their simple houses, eating the country food, always on the intent lookout, one might imagine, for any hints and clues toward an understanding of what was indigenous in himself. This was neither his first nor last earnest journey southward.

Much of the decade of the nineteen-thirties was occupied by the writing of the family saga-autobiographical trilogy, *The Wild Earth's Nobility* (1935), *Below Grass Roots* (1937), and *The Dust within the Rock* (1940). The project represented, obviously, a venture toward the understanding of self, and was accompanied by a series of significant geographical moves. The first volume was written after the Mexico journey, as if certain understandings had begun to jell down there, in close contact with native people. In 1936, quitting the telephone company, Waters moved to Victor, Colorado, for some months (very near the site of Grandfather Dozier's mine), then to Mora, New Mexico, a small village in the Hispanic hill country. He began writing full-time. In 1937 and 1938, he spent time in Taos, New Mexico, moved back to Mora, and then finally settled in Taos — all the while, during this circling, writing another draft of *The Yogi of Cockroach Court*, a concluding volume of the trilogy, and finally, his first novel really to make a mark, *People of the Valley* (1941). His growing concentration, in the writing, on the theme of integration and transcendence of duality appeared to occur in synergy with his step-by-step zeroing in on the Taos area as his home of choice. The thirties and first couple of years of the forties saw Frank Waters gradually establish both his métier and literal home base as a writer.

Between *The Dust within the Rock* and *People of the Valley*, the narrative voice and locus of perception in Waters' writing shifted from young-white-progressive to ancient-indigenous-mature. This development seemed to be more in the nature of an emergence, to use one of Waters' favorite terms, than a sudden or reactive change. It had much to do, apparently, with coming to emplacement in Taos and with enjoying several friendships among Taoseños, including especially the Taos Pueblo Indian Tony Luhan and his wife Mabel Dodge Luhan, and the trader Ralph Meyers. Waters absorbed Taos intently, in both its community aspect and its spiritual-topographic aura.

People of the Valley represents deepening of Waters' capacities in two main areas: his main character is a woman, and the culture in which the story takes place is long-rooted, folkloric, Hispanic/New Mexican. Remarkable transpositions of consciousness are dramatized with confidence, almost as if from the inside. We believe instantly and completely in brown, fey Maria of the valley and her people, because we see, in detail and particularity, the way the world looks to them, and because their language patterns, smoothly lived into by Waters, give us their mind's rhythms. In the following year, Waters' evocation of the tribal voice in *The Man Who Killed the Deer* has similar authority. The italicized passages, in which the collective, traditional wisdom of the pueblo speaks, ring with a recognizable, sharable inwardness. It seems clear that Waters had "been there," seen enough of the psychological and philosophical territory of the elders to see, at the very least, how their nondualistic approach differed from the mental terrain he had grown up in. That he also intuited the divided and tortured sensibility of the main character Martiniano, and the also divided but somewhat resigned outlook of the trader Rodolfo Byers, as well as the unified, spiritually quickened mind of Martiniano's friend Palemon, altogether demonstrates that he was coming into the identity-entering, compassionate powers of a superior novelist. At the same time, by giving expression to the archaic potency of the landscapes of northern New Mexico, Waters grew in recognition as a voice of his chosen place.

The Colorado (1946) and *Masked Gods* (1950) gave that voice greater range and helped to solidify Waters' position as not only a significant regional writer but a cross-cultural student of humanity at large. In *The Colorado*, a volume in Rinehart's "Rivers of America" series, he gave expression to a powerful landscape notion, depicting the watershed of the Colorado River as an immense and alive pyramid with real connections to the nerves and spirits of all life forms dwelling on it. The land in this book is not merely a setting, it is coparticipant in a living, organismic system. But of course there have been people, even whole cultures, who did not realize this electric oneness, and so the history that has taken place in the watershed is marked by varying and conflicting mentalities. The great measure here is the ability to sense and to see — to have consciousness that ranges beyond the simply rational-mechanical, finally to apperceive the unity we all, land and people together, belong to. Failure to emerge into the greater consciousness would be a genuine human tragedy, a falling-short of global implications. Waters concludes "The Long View," *The Colorado's* next-to-last chapter, with a concise summary:

> For all our technological achievements, our very lives tremble upon the delicate scales of nature. We are as ultimately dependent upon the ancient verities of land and sky as were the prehistoric cliff dwellers. Man has not yet completed the full circle toward a realization that his own laws of life must conform in the long view with those greater laws to which he still and forever owes allegiance. (370)

In Waters' conception of the "full circle," we moderns begin by following our bent toward rational and mechanistic thought as far as it can reach. We go as far as we can in seeing things one at a time. Eventually we begin to see that there must be something beyond the limits of such a procedure, and finally some of us see that what lies outside our favored powers seems in fact to have been intuited millennia ago — by people we commonly regard as less developed than ourselves. According to the outline set forth in *Masked Gods*, this arc toward realization is what many modern physicists traced. Searching with particle-seeing eyes for the ultimately tiny building blocks of matter, they discovered (in one of the great findings of modern science) that particle-seeing is a way of perception with a definite limit. A wider, softer perception would seem to be required for awareness of the shape-shifting between particle and energy-wave, and finally for awareness of the totally relational, unified nature of existence. When the twentieth-century physicists (some of whom, as it happened, worked on the atomic bomb at Los Alamos) came to the end of the road of one-thing-at-a-time thought, they stood in new wonder at the edge of the relativistic universe the Pueblo Indians, among other traditional peoples, had long contemplated. Full circle, indeed. (But it needs to be remembered that at Los Alamos these physicists were making bombs, hardly a holistic, unity-regarding activity. Realization isn't merely intellectual.) Waters finds it interesting that the canyons and plateaus of northern New Mexico should have been the setting in which the drive and power of the "White" rational approach sought security for its work, amid the color and mystic resonance of the "Red" culture's native landscape. But where, in real life on the ground, was the needed synthesis, the real completion of the circle?

Edith Warner, an unusual woman who in the 1930s and '40s ran a small café at the Otowi bridge over the Rio Grande, seemed to comprehend both elements of the needed integration. Poised exactly between the San Ildefonso Pueblo (where she had close friends) and the new, secret installation at Los Alamos, Warner seemed to be ideally placed for the illuminated view of life that in fact came to her. She became acquainted with many of the physicists from "the Hill" during the war, and at the same time maintained her ties with San Ildefonso; and in her inward life she apparently experienced a significant transcendence, so that her sense of place and nature became intense, and her mind — by the written evidence she left — open, still, and creative. She became locally well recognized, among both Indians and certain whites, as "one who knows."

Frank Waters began writing her story in fictional form, with the protagonist as "Helen Chalmers," as early as 1953. At this time he was working as an information specialist with the Atomic Energy Commission, in the course of which assignment he had witnessed dozens of atomic-bomb tests, and had become intimately involved with the most advanced technical project of its time. His work with the AEC had given new scope to his innate rational-technical capacity, and perhaps also intensified the dissonance or discontinuity within the mind that Waters, as a child of the twentieth century, experienced with the rest of us. The same Frank Waters who had freighted his books of the 1930s with detailed exposition on mining now wrote technical reports and information releases for the most ingenious weapons makers on the planet. But he was also, still and ever, the same Frank Waters who like archaic man felt a profound, cellular, mystical connection with the earth.

Two views of existence. But Waters' writings from the 1940s and succeeding years reveal also the beginning of the projection of a third, much larger, in fact overarching, viewpoint. In terms of his contribution to the world, this ultimate or nondualistic view marks the essential Frank Waters. *The Woman at Otowi Crossing*, which after at least four drafts was finally published in 1966, conveys that higher understanding as clearly as any of his works. It tells the story of Helen Chalmers' coming into a timeless, intuitive, regardful view of existence, not dissimilar from that of some of her Indian friends. It also tells the stories of an atomic physicist who comes to the edge of the rational-empirical mentality; an academic careerist who works, sadly enough, to hide her heart; a respected member of the San Ildefonso Pueblo; and finally a bluff and folksy editor of a country weekly. Each has a close connection with Helen. All these characters' points of view are registered in a historically accurate plot involving humanity's development of atomic weapons. (As a race, we take a great and irrevocable step in this book.) Waters the novelist understands this tormented, mid-twentieth-century moment and also, at the individual level, empathizes with each person in the self-partiality of his or her consciousness, without condescension. This objectivity-with-sympathy suggests Waters' own profound, artistic integration.

The realized quality of Waters' viewpoint was apparent in his next two books to focus on issues of mind, *Pumpkin Seed Point* (1969) and *Mexico Mystique* (1975), and became evident as a comprehensive serenity in several of the essays in *Mountain Dialogues* (1981), particularly those dealing with his life in place in Arroyo Seco, New Mexico, just north of Taos. By the early 1980s, Frank Waters had become known (to a steady though comparatively small readership) as a writer with a large, evolutionary view on consciousness and a strongly felt, accessible sense of his home ground. In all three of the books just mentioned, he wrote familiarly from a philosophical synthesis entirely his own. Its elements seem not to have occurred to any other writer, in quite the Frank Waters fashion, yet in combination, in the end, they seem natural, even inevitable. There is, first, an Indian sense of existence, deeply attached to place and "soft," that is, intuitive, non-self-aggrandizing; second, an Eastern understanding of the mind, especially the point that its rational, ego-creating corner constitutes only a fraction of its range; and finally a Jungian approach to psychology and character, emphasizing the need to harmonize seeming opposites within (such as male and female dimensions), and also recognizing that we all share in collective, archetypal patterns at both conscious and unconscious levels. These are the three main influences on Frank Waters' thought, but his determinedly independent, even maverick, reliance on his own truth, and as a continuing influence his chosen southwestern emplacement, also need to be factored in. All of these elements, in a home-made combination, create the distinctive Waters voice.

There are any number of manners-and-morals novelists, and contemporary personal essayists, for whom enlightenment or apperception would perhaps be foreign territory. It took daring, or obsession perhaps, to write *The Yogi of Cockroach Court* at a young age, and to keep at it for two decades. Similarly, it took commitment, years later, to put together a long source study, a personal, Jungian understanding and a home-lover's sense of place and scene and make an anthropology out of these, in *Masked Gods* and *Book of the Hopi* (1963). But these leaps are, one can see, typical. In his long career, Frank Waters followed his intuition of unity faithfully, wherever it might lead and whatever words of rational caution various authorities might have laid down. His life and work represent a dedicated search for integration, and in this moral allegiance, "America's greatest unknown writer," as he is often called, may yet have something to say to our time.

II.
BIOGRAPHICAL

Vine Deloria, Jr.
Frank Waters: Prophet and Explorer

In *The Man Who Killed the Deer*, the elders are in council discussing the use of peyote. "But this peyote. It too creates a faith. That is good, that which creates a faith."[1] The theological basis of decision-making elevates the question to the sublime but it has the slight flaw of exclusiveness, which in turn affects its applicability to the Pueblo because the answer, repeated in a liturgical rhythm, is always: "We are all that we have been." We might have an intellectual/emotional polarity here, and certainly many thinkers in many cultures have posed the question of faith in this manner. But what we really face in this dilemma is the all-encompassing recognition that human beings, individually and communally, travel through many worlds and remain responsible to life as we find it.

In addition to his accomplishments as a talented novelist, a thorough historian, and an excellent essayist, Frank Waters is that rare breed of man who has merged heart and mind early in his life and moved forward to confront ultimate questions. This dilemma of faith and heritage, religion and identity, and commitment and comfort has never been resolved intellectually. Even with profound faith and rigorous discipline of self, mystics have found this dilemma difficult to resolve through action and prayer. Since what we are is a cumulative expression of the soul and includes not only historical experience but those rare moments of the soul when recognitions flash briefly through the mind — never to return — faith cannot give us anything except the resolve to continue searching. I look at the life and writings of Frank Waters as this kind of activity and find, in his religious/historical trilogy — *Masked Gods, Book of the Hopi,* and *Mexico Mystique* — a remarkable journey of inquiry spanning nearly a century and illuminating questions that I did not think possible to formulate.

In order to understand the genius contained in these three books, and follow the subliminal Frank Waters as he ponders questions of supreme importance, we must experience rather than read the books. That is to say, we must participate in the ceremonies and activities of the people as they are described in the books and, thanks to Frank's unerring descriptive talents, it is not difficult to do. Thus *Masked Gods* introduces us to the world of the kiva and sandpainting peoples, Navajo, Zuni, and Pueblo, discusses briefly the historical antecedent experiences of these desert and plateau dwellers, and brings us through turmoil and the crowd of greedy savages surrounding them to the present. In the process we are very gently nudged in the direction of Frank's own personal question that seeks to know the nature, content and structure of reality — what is it that is real?

As the Santo Domingo Corn Dance winds to its conclusion, the description moves dramatically from the objective to the subjective with hardly a pause and we come to know that "these were not men humbly beseeching the gifts of life. They were forces of life made manifest in man as in earth, demanding by the laws that governed both an interchange of the energies potential in each."[2] It is this subtle dimension of understanding that marks the southwestern Indian peoples from other religions and separates tribal peoples from the world's religions. Somewhere in planetary history religious expression changed from participation in the sound, color and rhythm of nature to the abstraction of man outside this context pleading for temporary respite and hoping in the next life to return to the Garden. Waters grasps the essential element — unification — the wholeness of the religious event which has vast implications for the cosmos itself — and brings us right into the vortex of meaning where we *feel* complete whether we understand our feelings intellectually or not.

As we move to the final pages of *Masked Gods,* Waters entertains us with the arrogant assurance of Arnold Toynbee and the suggestion that Christianity is invulnerable to change and decay even if the secular forces of civilization come to naught. "But just at this moment, reassured as we are of the divine impregnability of our Christian-Western ideology, a gust of wind whips down from the Rockies. *A Study of History* is blown from our hands. It hits a gnarled old piñon on the Rim."[3] And Toynbee and twenty-one civilizations fall into the Grand Canyon; the Hopi bids Frank goodbye and heads home to perform his kiva duties. It is not the belief, even with the most compelling logical symmetry, that is real; it is the act, it is assuming the responsible posture whereby cosmic rhythms are maintained that is important.

At the close of *Masked Gods*, Frank Waters poses the question of whether or not the Buddhists are right — is the world some kind of mental construct, no matter how complex and sophisticated, or is it a physical reality, or better yet, "why not a fifth and sixth stage of existence, with their corresponding dimensions?"[4] This question is the only one that need be asked once we have understood and experienced the realities that present themselves to us. And if these other dimensions exist, or if we are responsible to help to create them, we can only discover by moving forward.

In an entirely unexpected way, Frank Waters begins to answer this question in *Book of the Hopi*. Here we have the distilled wisdom of Hopi elders, interpreted partially by White Bear Fredericks and molded very carefully by Frank's continuing search for meaning. *Book of the Hopi* spoke to a generation of Americans searching also for meaning but content for the most part simply to experience new feelings. It is a simple and simply written history of the Hopi people with nods to both prophecy and cultural/historical change. The writing technique here is amazingly precise and subtle so that it takes the reader years after reading the book to come to the message contained therein. The four worlds of Hopi history and the prophecy become the guideposts that validate the present, and in the descriptions of the present, when we discover the abiding spirit of the Hopi, we discover that it has validated the prophecies.

The function of *Book of the Hopi* is to ground our perception of reality — and human experience — in a dimension of cosmic time. We do not need to hypothesize the endless grinding of chronological time with the evolutionary minutia of adaptation as the backdrop of our sense of the historical. Rather we are provided with a solid indigenous tradition to which, if they are able to do it, other beliefs and traditions are invited to become attached. The Hopi understanding of planetary history suggests that our planet might even have been in another galaxy or solar system at one time. The long period of time during which the earth did not revolve on its axis, the people lived underground, and much ice accumulated on the magnetic poles provides an alternative, albeit not an alternative cherished by modern secular science, to current theories of glaciation.

The complexity of Hopi understanding can be illustrated by the fact that spiritual and physical aspects of experience are always closely related if not opposite sides of the same coin. That realization is important because, having intuited this relationship by studying the Hopi, Frank Waters then embarked on an ambitious project to delve deeply into Mexican Indian thought, particularly Aztec theology and cosmology, seeking to create, at least for himself and anyone who had followed his thinking, a credible framework through which the meaning of human life could be assessed.

Mexico Mystique is a terribly complicated book but it is not so much a book as a sketch of a new kind of historical/philosophical understanding. Posing the question of whether or not legends could be understood as real physical happenings *in addition to* their usefulness as psychological structures that enabled our species to orient itself with respect to the whole cosmos, *Mexico Mystique* is a work entirely unique. Waters does not really commit himself on any particular aspect of this thinking, preferring to point out possible connections and relationships that may help the reader gain entrance to the nature of the problem of reconciling spirit and matter.

A good deal of *Mexico Mystique* anticipates the ramblings of the current "New Age" belief in that Waters reaches out to include astrology, Velikovskian celestial theories, and a string of prophets including Nostradamus, Mother Shipstead, and Edgar Cayce. Waters' interpretation of these heretical personalities does not differ much from current New Age understandings either. What distinguishes Waters' view from the New Age is the insistence that spirit and matter have a unity so that what is experienced by one aspect of the universe is mirrored by changes in the other. This form of interpretation is wholly within the American Indian context and is often expressed in the belief that "what is above is also below."

Frank Waters' conclusions may seem a bit naive in view of the persistent rejection of these diverse theories by western intellectual orthodoxy, but it is not. His quest for meaning as illustrated in this religious/historical trilogy marks out the kinds of questions that must be asked — and must have been asked — by countless generations of our species. The current configuration of modern scientific knowledge assumes that we have always had, and will always continue to have, a rather routine and uniform passage of time. Indeed, western civilization assumes that uniformity of time and space are requirements for rational thought. Waters disagrees, feeling that it is in the disruptive unity of a timeless NOW, when it is welded to or manifests itself in a particular place, that life is able to realize itself. Thus when he speaks of cosmic evolution, he is not within the parameters of modern scientific thinking but stands with those solitary souls who have never accepted the easy answer.

Frank Waters is therefore a delightful combination of two of our most cherished archetypal masculine figures: the prophet and the explorer. His life has been dedicated not simply to writing novels and histories but to posing the questions around which new understandings of human emotions, experience and communal activities can be viewed. The initial question of *The Man Who Killed The Deer*, which sought to balance and comprehend the difference between faith and heritage, heritage being the communal expression of the experiences of our species, and groups within our species within a greatly expanded period of time, is definitely resolved in favor of heritage in *Mexico Mystique*. The book ends with the hope that we will recognize our commonality and reach for the maturity that is necessary for us to move forward within the larger movement of cosmic time.

Black Elk, after explaining the origin of the sacred pipe of the Sioux to John Neihardt, paused and then remarked: "This they tell, and whether it happened so or not I do not know; but if you think about it, you can see that is true."[5] The wise men among the Indian tribes did not feel they should know everything at once. Nor did they feel that knowledge for its own sake was valuable. Only knowledge that had applicability to their lives or the lives and welfare of their people was important to them. Theorizing and abstraction were anathema because they created distances between human beings and the rest of creation. So the wisest of the old men remained humbly silent and pondered the great questions. When they were ready to comment on an issue they would quite often formulate their response in the telling of a story. In the interim, they had the Black Elk reflection — "if you think about it, you can see that it is true."

I met Frank Waters when he was in his late seventies, about the age in Indian country when people begin to be appreciated and have worn off the bluster of youth. It seemed to me then, and still impresses me, that Frank had been an explorer in addition to having been a prophet. Explorers push ahead into unknown country, sometimes marking their progress by visible signs and often retaining in their minds the twists and turns and unexpected barriers, later to go back and find a better path. They do not always choose the right path at first, but by reflecting and remembering they are able to suggest the most feasible way of thinking about things and accomplishing tasks.

In reading some of the interviews with Frank conducted by a number of younger scholars it occurred to me that Frank's reflections on questions and comments on modern developments, the changes he has seen in nearly a century of living, have that elusive quality of being both prophetic and exploratory. They reach into the future and reflect on past experiences almost equally. We can learn quite a bit by understanding the accumulated knowledge and experience which enabled Frank to formulate his answers in a particular way and we must also recognize that he continues to call us to take up the task of exploring the world, our fellow human beings, and the cumulative social and historical experiences of our species.

Our faith, if we have one, must be grounded in what and who we are. The passage of time, the belief that age and experience will reveal truth to us, and the recognition that the wisest of us speaks in hushed tones are well stated in *The Man Who Killed the Deer* and can be considered the hallmark of Frank Waters' life. In his ninety-plus years he has made himself, but this accomplishment has been the fulfillment of what he was originally intended to be. We can but hope that another such unique individual will come along and urge, inspire, and teach us to move forward into sixth, seventh, and more worlds of consciousness and become what was intended all along.

Thank you, Frank, for putting this quest within the context of the American Indian tradition and pointing us toward that inevitable unity of purpose which our species must have if it is to survive.

John R. Milton
The Question of Frank Waters' Mysticism

It is no coincidence that the literary reputation of Frank Waters has grown markedly since the beginning in the late 1960s of a parallel growth of interest in the literature and culture of the American Indian. His two non-fiction works on southwestern Indian life and religious ritual (*Masked Gods*, 1950, and *Book of the Hopi*, 1963) were reprinted in paperback editions in 1970 and 1969 respectively, enjoying an immediate popularity not given to the earlier original editions. His Indian novel (*The Man Who Killed the Deer*, 1942), although kept alive by publisher Alan Swallow in this country and reprinted several times in Europe, did not reach the mass market in an inexpensive paperback edition until 1971. Before the advent of recent and sudden exploitation of all things Indian, Waters was relatively unknown except to a small and faithful group of readers, most of them Europeans or scholars of Western American literature. What kept him from a wider acceptance during the 1930s and 1940s was a disinclination on the part of the general reader and most critics to accept his almost mystical view of life. Waters, of course, is not a mystic in the strictest sense of the term because he does not abandon the physical world in which he lives. His reaching out toward something which may well be indefinable is done from a firm rootedness in the earth.

Waters has not set out to be consciously Indian or deliberately Jungian, although his work is increasingly discussed in those terms. He is aware of the conflict between the two worlds represented by the Indians and the European whites, as he must be in light of his own mixed heritage; but he does not establish this conflict as a thesis, to be explained or debated. His method is to describe it, and the conflict is perhaps not so much between white and Indian ways of life as it is between the rational and the instinctual. The emphasis, then, is on a kind of perception, and the white-Indian dichotomy is illustrative rather than autobiographical. What Waters is attempting to get at is primal apperception, which goes beyond normal conceptual words but which must nevertheless be stated as well as possible in normal language. Of necessity, this means a use of stylistic devices which may be misunderstood: not word- iness, but repetitions which allow the idea or feeling to acquire a proximity to what cannot be stated precisely; images which are based on environmental realities but which point to psychic realities; and a purity of language which admits of the crudities and grossness of the objective world of the body while suggesting spiritual conditions whose nature at least borders on the mystical. Waters' style, then, reflects both worlds, sometimes unevenly but often with a clarity that belies the complexities of the relationship. When the latter occurs, polarities or dualities dissolve momentarily and even the uninitiated get a rare glimpse of the ultimate unity of things. Waters' concern is with the harmony between psyche and earth (not land, or nature, although the three words are frequently used synonymously). If such a concern borders on mysticism, we must keep in mind that Waters has insisted that characterization comes first, and if the characters seem to recognize an "ineffable nature," or if they have what seems to be a mystical experience, they do so as characters, as people, not as contrived reflections of the author's personal point of view. The distinction is between novelistic methods and the novelist's persuasions. . . .

Writing entirely about his native Southwest, Waters is unabashedly a regionalist. This label, however, should not prevent anyone from seeing that Waters is concerned with no less than the universe itself, and man's place in it. The Southwest is a fitting stage for such a cosmic pursuit, because in the mountains and on the desert man comes into direct contact with the natural forces and elements which existed long before man emerged and which played a full role in the ancient religious systems. . . . Furthermore, the interplay of three cultures, the intuitive knowledge of the old Indian tribes, and the kind of isolation which not only allows but forces a man to think about himself and his relation to beginnings and endings — these are immediate presences in New Mexico. Waters' journey has taken him back into time, into primitive and nonrational philosophies and religions, and into Jungian racial consciousness. His ultimate concern is not with a selected portion of the historical past but with *all* of the past as it reveals eternal verities. The end of the journey, should it ever be reached, will be a fusion of Oriental thought and perception with European rationalism and linear time. . . .

Waters has been called a visionary and a mystic. This is all right as long as we do not limit those terms to a condition which presupposes a lack of close relationship to the physical world. Waters is not a dreamer, disconnected from the world around him. His mysticism is earth-based, object-based. His visions spring from nature and from those people whose ancestry is traceable to nonwestern origins. The mixture of cultures in his work reveals the similarities in them. In other similarities too, between primitive myths and modern thought, or between such things as creation stories in several major religions, Waters is concerned with common denominators, with the sources which prove essentially the same for all cultures and times. In dealing with sameness, oneness, and the eternal, Waters is therefore deemphasizing the chronology of time, the clocks of the modern western world, and seeking a timelessness and perhaps even an essential form which can ultimately be called formless.

Granted that the Mayas (with whom Waters is involved in *Mexico Mystique*) developed an elaborate system of timekeeping, and that the narrative in the mining trilogy proceeds from one generation to another in sequential order, still the drumbeat in *The Wild Earth's Nobility* serves as an image of blood relationships, not of linear sequences in a form of music. As Rogier listens, the rhythms of the drums hypnotize him, stop him in time, enter his blood stream in a way that is neither gentle nor smooth. The "timeless rhythm" grows in his blood and soon he believes "with his blood more than the capacity of his mind could ever admit." For all this emphasis on blood consciousness, Waters is much closer to Mary Austin than he is to D. H. Lawrence. In "The Woman Who Rode Away" (1928) and in *Apocalypse* (1931), Lawrence leaps past the land and its immediate images directly into human sacrifice and the cosmos itself. Austin, on the other hand, is intimate with the land, its creatures, and the natural rituals of people living close to the land; her attention is therefore focused on rhythms (the same two-handed beat that is basic to the Indian drumming in Waters) and on the achievement of harmony with the earth. The point may seem labored, but it is important.

Lawrence jumps irrationally across the reaches of western thought to find a blood relationship with the undefinable cosmos; Waters and Austin keep their feet on the ground, exploring images which can convey a relationship between intuitive man and the mysteries of nature and, therefore, of life. Blood need not be let, or spilled; its rhythms, or pulse, within the body are akin to the eternal pulse, and the heartbeat, like the drumbeat, is not considered as evidence of the passing of time but as a source, an energy, a vital link between man and nature. Rogier goes into the heart of the mountain in search of this pulse, the secret of life. The Mayas and Aztecs sought this secret in the sun, and it was only in death that they were placed deep inside their mountainlike pyramids, hidden from the sun. The place of death parallels the place of life, yet both are out of the sun which is an obvious source of life, an ancient deity. This is one of the many ambiguities which the intuitive mind recognizes and accepts without subjecting the conflicting parts to rational scrutiny. In this sense, then, Waters is a mystic.

As he notes in *Below Grass Roots*, "not the sorry form, but the splendid substance" in which "the subtle truths" are not known but felt. Waters applies this thought to all of American history: the tales and legends of the West, especially, "stand there, close and touchable, [moving] truthfully with all their faults and without form." And in *The Man Who Killed the Deer* Palemon speaks (in the poetic and italicized words of the language Waters gives to the Indians in the novel) of form as a body. Man is imprisoned in the form which is his physical body but he must have faith in it nevertheless, as well as in the form of life which is his greater body. If he can find this faith he may then be released from his bonds: "That will free your spirit into a formless life without bounds, which will overflow and taste of all life."

This spiritual form may or may not be comparable to a kind of artistic form in the books themselves. Perhaps we are again involved in an ambiguity, saying that faith in form leads to a wholesome formlessness. It occurs to me that Waters is searching for nothing less than the perfect form, the circle, the traditional symbol of unity. In each of his novels he makes progress around the circle but never quite completes it. The circle encompasses space, and the physical space of the American West is difficult to contain, or to frame. Furthermore, it is likely that Waters believes, with others, that the important thing is the journey, not the destination. In the Colorado mining trilogy, in many ways the longest of the Waters journeys, March, out of Boné and

Rogier, travels a long distance, searching for himself, and the conclusion is as open-ended as the land. *The Man Who Killed the Deer* opens with Martiniano in trouble near Blue Lake and closes with an image of a pebble on water, suggesting the completion of a circle (the lake and the rings sent out by the impact are themselves circles). Yet the mass of images throughout the novel and the widening circle of ripples in the metaphorical lake spread to "unguessed shores." And they do so "in the timeless skies of night."

CHARLES L. ADAMS
ON *PIKE'S PEAK*
AND THE LIFE OF FRANK WATERS

A dams: Since my area is not American Lit, I've had to go back and read an awful lot of American Lit to find out what my colleagues and Frank Waters are talking about and make comparisons with other American figures. But I have no compunctions about saying that in Frank Waters I discovered a major writer, a writer of world literature scale, and originally I felt very stupid, to think that I had a doctorate in literature and had never heard the name before. When I read the first Frank Waters' book, I was just embarrassed, and I immediately read another book, and another, and another, and realized that I was going to start teaching him. Then I managed to meet Frank, and we became friends just instantly on that first meeting, and we've been very good friends ever since.

Pike's Peak is a thick book, a big book, but you probably know it was, originally, a trilogy involving three separately published volumes, starting with Joseph Rogier and moving up through the maturity of the grandson, March Cable, and of course Rogier was Frank's grandfather, Dozier, and March is a very thinly disguised Frank Waters.

It's really kind of sad, but there are 800 pages of the original trilogy that are not in *Pike's Peak*, and that's a heck of a lot of material. You think of *Pike's Peak* as a long book, but, when you look at those original three volumes, you realize that for *Pike's Peak* he wrote an awful lot of original material, and then you have an idea of what he could not use. It's the difference between a man in his thirties writing about his life, and a man in his sixties writing about it. He looked back over many of those sections and just said, "That's only about me and I don't need it." Out it went. He cut unmercifully, and most of the stuff that he cut was about Frank Waters growing up in Colorado Springs. I think you will see if you do read the trilogy, there are many things that are immature and wrong with the original version of the story. In many ways Frank is right about what he cut out. He was merciless, he slashed, he cut, he altered, and changed, and he made a *different* story. *Pike's Peak* is really not the same book as you get when you read the original three. It's very different. What's fun is really to read *Pike's Peak* first and get to know the characters, what happens and so forth, and then go back and get all those wonderful little details about the family, to plug in, sort of an expansion, "I wish I knew more about so-and-so," and there it is. You can just enlarge and embroider on all the adventures of the Dozier family.

Audience: I have read those earliest books, but I did not know that this was an autobiography.

Adams: May I interrupt for a moment? He is adamant — this is a novel, not an autobiography.

Audience: I felt it had to be. But I'm interested in knowing what he cut out. I thought he did such an exquisite job of coming back all those years later and picking up such intimate and minute details.

Adam: I agree completely. It's funny, when you ask Frank about *Pike's Peak* and the degree to which it is autobiographical, his reactions range from, "That is fiction" to "Oh, yeah, that's just what happened!" You have to phrase your question very carefully. Let me tell you a secret about Frank I always tell my students. You always get the answer to the question you asked, with Frank. You have to figure out your question very, very carefully, because he answers whatever your question is. That was never brought home to me more violently than one time when I was visiting Frank with a former student of mine. The student had been a conscientious objector during the war. Many times interviewers had asked Frank, in a lot of articles, "Were you in the Service?" and Frank would give a certain answer. This boy said, "Did you have to go to war?" and got a very different answer. There was an interviewer on PBS who said to Frank, "What are you thinking about right now?" And Frank said, "I'm worrying about this party my wife is giving." That's exactly what happens, though.

Audience: Is his sister, Naomi, still alive?

Adams: No, his sister is not. She and her husband died just a few months apart. Interesting: one of them could not be without the other.

Audience: I have a specific question about the book. His mother in it, Ona, was the figure. I'm sure her name was not Ona . . .

Adams: It's close. It was May Ione.

Audience: The encounter she has in the very beginning of the book with the Indians that come into the house, and the one or two that lift her up and sear her bottom on the stove, and this magical-possession kind of hold that they have over her, and later on, he explained in a relatively direct way, that when she marries the part-Indian Cable, that this experience in some way predisposed her for this kind of a husband: I have mulled and mulled that over. Could you explain your interpretation of that or Frank's?

Adams: It's a very strange passage. Funny thing about it, it is absolutely not in the original Frank wrote. It is straight fiction. He wrote it in '65. I think he felt he needed something to explain the initial physical attraction between his mother, who had been raised in this very proud, phoney Southern aristocracy, and a man who was, in the society then, frequently termed a "red nigger." He has "blood" in him. So Frank gave it this psycho-sexual basis in that early scene.

Audience: I found it very strange.

Adams: That's what I mean, because if you could nail one passage like that, and ask him, he will tell you if it was fiction or biography. I remember someone asking him about his experiences with Valerie, his first romance, first sexual experiences. And he says, "Oh, that's just a novel, just like any boy's first romantic involvements." And then one time I was visiting him in Taos, and had a disaster. I had a very strange phone call from my daughter, who was wandering the country on a bus, and was supposed to be in Taos. And the phone rang late at night — Frank had the phone in his bedroom — and he had to call to me in the opposite end of the house to come in and take the call in his room. She told me she missed the bus and would be a day late, but she was coming to Taos, and we made all the arrangements, and I hung up and I said, "Gosh, kids of this age! What did your mother do when you finally announced you quit school and came home and were setting out on your own?" He said, "That's all in *Pike's Peak*." Just like that. So you narrow it down to one incident and you can ask him, fact or fiction?

Audience: I have quite a lot of questions, just while we are talking about Frank's mother. He had come to see a lot of her, I think. Is that correct? In the early 1930s? I wondered if you know anything about whether they talked so much that it reinvigorated his memories of growing up in Colorado Springs, and if that might have been a factor when he undertook to start the trilogy. That's a biographical question. Another question, quite a different kind, is, I think of the book as an epic, whereas he calls it a saga.

Adams: Frank doesn't call it a saga. The publisher did that and Frank hates it. He says it is the story of a man and a mountain on two levels, the *outer* search for gold and the *inner* psychic search. And they called it a "family saga," which throws the readers off.

As far as the mother is concerned, she left Colorado Springs and went to live with her daughter, Naomi, and her husband in Los Angeles. I know Frank visited and stayed with them there quite frequently. That may have had something to do with the detail that went into those first books. Frequently, Naomi and her husband sort of bailed Frank out, when he was penniless, and he could always go and spend six months with them. He began to feel guilty after six months, but he would go there for a while. I think he probably, originally, did plan on starting with grandpa and working down through to his own personal salvation and the resolution of the conflicts in him.

Audience: Along this line somewhat, about female characters, I read a number of reviews about his books, and critics feel that his female characters are done very well, that for a male he paints them very well, from the inside out, so to speak. Would you agree?

Adams: Oh yes, very much so.

Audience: That supposedly was due to his close relationship with his mother?

Adams: I think that's possibly true. Frank himself has pondered this. At one time he said there is so much of the feminine in him: "and yet I did not become a homosexual, I don't understand that at all, though, I don't understand homosexuals, nobody seems to know what makes them tick really." And he said, "I have a lot of the feminine in me and then an awful lot of my father and grandfather." He was just sort of chatting with me back and forth, and I think this is true. I think he has an ability *to use both sides of those dualities* that he recognizes. He can be very aggressive, very hostile, very masculine, if he has to be, and he can be very intuitive, very passive, very sensitive when it's time for that. I know there was one time when some idiotic people in Taos were going to, as part of flood control, chop out the trees that line the stream in front of his house, so they could move in and put down sand bags. Around the house there is a marvelous stand of aspen. And the story is, Frank went out with his deer rifle, and a neighbor came over, too, and eventually the neighbor kept an eye on the workers, while Frank jumped in his car and ran into town and got an order from a judge. In that case there was immediate action and very firm. I think what you see in *Pike's Peak*, in those last sections when March is in Mexico, when he comes to understand that there is a function for adobe, for the soft, yielding patience that can be really in its own way just as masculine as the aggression: it's this Oriental Yin becomes Yang, Yang becomes Yin. You can have passivity that can be a deadly force; as Mahatma Gandhi realized, passive resistance can be tremendously forceful. When Frank was in Mexico in his twenties, he sort of figured out that all these things had a time and a place, and that everything went together for him and his family. Prior to that, I think, he spent many years being kind of torn apart by all these opposites. You may have known this, that almost all of Frank's books in one way or another deal with *resolving conflicts between what look like opposites, that aren't really.* These conflicting dualities on any level, he said once, he had to solve those problems first in his own life. When he went on realizing what he had tapped into, he started seeing that this was the basis of Native American religion, in the ritual of the dance, and so on.

Audience: Why did he feel the need to write *Pike's Peak*? Why couldn't he leave it in the original trilogy?

Adams: Several critics had pointed out flaws, in the original novels, that he eventually came to realize were valid. Some critics that he did respect had suggested that the trilogy, as a unit, ought to be reworked, because the flaws hurt the total and the total deserved to be preserved. So he did eventually go back and do this. If you are familiar with the letters in Tanner's *Frank Waters: A Bibliography with Relevant Selections from His Correspondence*, letters that Tanner has dug up between Frank and editors, Frank and agents, Frank and publishers, whatever, they tell you what he was thinking about at the time of publication and what he thought he was doing with the work. The letters about the original books contain Frank's statements, how "that is not purple prose" and "I should not cut that," that is "absolutely essential," and "I must have those statistics." When the book was first criticized, he defended it with vigor; many years later, he just said, "By George, they were right!" That's how things went with the cuts, not all of them but a lot of them. There are whole pages of mining history and statistics that can drive you crazy. You may think *Pike's Peak* is bad that way, but he was fascinated with the fact that this was a basis of a kind of an American tale that had never been told, that mining was a part of the settlement of the West, and that nobody had dealt with mining in literature. He wanted to make sure that those three books had a really firm American-conquering-the-West mining base. So he threw in everything that he could dig out, and *Pike's Peak* is much better that way.

Audience: What were parts that the critics. . ?

Adams: They said frequently that he wandered away from his story, the main story line, by going into little useless by-ways about things that happened to minor characters. And Frank cut a great number of the minor characters. One of the biggest changes — it's kind of surprising — he took some of the family members and combined them and made just one out of two or three — just compressed them. The names shift, too. Some characters from the original are completely missing, and names move around. One person had a name in the original, that will be completely different in *Pike's Peak*. Some critics have said that *Pike's Peak* is just simply an editing of the original, a shrinking down, but it is not at all. It is a re-telling of a different story about the same family in different lives. It's a strange literary experience to read them both. They are not compatible, frequently. In *The Dust Within the Rock*, which is the third volume, Grandfather Rogier is just a minor character. That is March Cable's book. If you get Rogier at all, the reference is something minor. You see, that's the stuff that he cut. There's a marvelous reference in *Dust* to the attitude of the men in the Wyoming oil fields toward the prostitutes in camp. I think in *Pike's Peak* it's not that big, but in the original, this goes on for pages. Incidentally, this is a true story, too. I asked Frank about that, and over dinner one night he told us exactly what did happen. The men were constantly coming down with venereal disease because of these prostitutes, and they would curse the women that they patronized. But they were the only women available. But there was one we have to elevate to the status of courtesan, a very well-to-do prostitute. She had a very high fee, she was available to people like the town banker, I suppose, and that sort of thing, and Frank came to realize that the men who dreamed of this woman were hungering for a kind of feminine purity and loveliness, because she was unattainable. And they had invested this woman with all the "proper" feminine values. And there is a nice little section where young Frank Waters is practically fixated on this particular woman, whose name is Frisco. On the other hand, he sees he himself has put her up on this pedestal, and she wears these expensive white dresses and lovely jewelry, and she is so dainty and feminine, and then on the other hand he'll think, "What am I doing? She *is* a prostitute." He'll chastise himself, and say, whenever I run into that woman I shall tell her off! Well, it's a true story. Frank was laid off working in the oil fields in rather a brutal way. The men dug ditches and put the pipe in, twelve hours a day, with a minimum wage at the time. When Frank went into supper one night after work, he called his number, and the checker had said, "Sorry, you have been laid off." And that was it. He had no place to sleep, because he slept right there in the company quarters, and he was not fed. He was terminated as of the end of the shift. So he just got his gear together and started hiking into town, which was ten miles away, and this big, black Packard came along the road. Sitting in it was this beautiful woman, and she stopped the car and looked out and said, "Could you use a ride?" Frank said, "Sure can, ma'am." He started to get in the front. She said, "Not there. Get in back." Frank got in and sat down — this is March in the book — and he noticed that she had adjusted the rear view mirror, so that she could keep her eye exactly on him, and that she had a forty-five strapped to the steering column. And she was quite prepared to take her hand off the wheel, whip it out, and blow his brains out if he moved at all. When they got into Casper, she said, "Did they feed you first?" He said, "No." She said, "That figures. Come with me." And as they started walking through the town, the crowds just separated for this woman with her long dress, her parasol, and so forth, and everyone sort of bowed respectfully. And she went into this cafe and signaled people to come and bring him his meal. And he said to me in remembrance, "Boy, what a spread it was, wines and beer and all these dishes!" And she sat with him and talked, and she told him, "You are a funny kind of person, a strange-looking kid, the kind that might pop up anywhere. If you get into Mexico, look up this guy." And she wrote down the name of a bartender. And in the original that is how Frank gets his first job in Mexico. He's just leaving her, had a little too much to drink, and says, "Thanks, lady. Well, what's your name anyway?" And she says, "Frisco will do. So long." Then she orders a couple of guys to take him out of town and make sure he gets a ride and gets on his way. This really was the way Frank left Casper, but in the original book, it's that note. When Frank finally gets down below the Mexican border, he goes to this particular bar, gives the note to the bartender, who befriends him, sees that he has occasional jobs around, and eventually gets him the one big job in mining that leads to all the other Mexican adventures. Of course that is completely slashed out of *Pike's Peak*. He wanted the focus on Grandfather Rogier. And any attention to young Frank Waters was simply extra, and out it went.

Audience: Wasn't it Hemingway who said whoever writes an epic writes a bad book? How would we apply that in evaluating *Pike's Peak*?

Adams: I don't think it's that epic, I think it might be something like *Moby-Dick*. I think maybe the point for emphasis in *Pike's Peak* is Rogier's psychic search and his coming to terms with this thing that he is looking for that he thinks is outside himself, and finally realizes it is inside himself, that he's been looking in the wrong place. It takes him a lifetime, and of course then young March watches this failure, March is the grandson who inherits the problems as set up by his grandfather. In *Dust*, it takes another volume for the grandson to go on and solve these unposed problems. In *Pike's Peak*, March just sort of dribbles off and you go on with Rogier and how he finally comes to terms with himself.

Audience: And was it through reading East Indian philosophies that Rogier does come to terms with himself? It is hinted at the end of *The Wild Earth's Nobility* that he has all this literature around, the East Indian philosophies.

Adams: One of the nice things about *Pike's Peak* is that Frank moved that whole library description up from *Dust* to *Nobility*, to the beginning. By keeping it in that volume, you have a little bit of a clue that grandpa is strange in his reading habits. It's evident that grandpa is searching, but what he finds out is, he can't find the answer in books. He keeps reading to see what the universe all is about, and he tries all these different avenues in literature and finally says, it's not in books. Then he focuses more and more on the idea that it's *gold*, that it's the strange secret heart of the mountain. He probably would never have developed that obsession about gold, if he were a person that had any contact with his own interior at all. You recall how thoroughly undemonstrative he is. He can't show affection to anyone, except his animals; horses, fine, his children or grandchildren, there is just this wall there. He has no sense of his own interior, and he goes mining outside when he should have gone mining inside.

Audience: Could you tell more about Frank's life as he went through it?

Adams: He was living in Taos in '38, and finally settled there after he came back in the forties, after the war.

Audience: That was just a spot in the road in those days.

Adams: Right. And he and Janie bought this wreck of an adobe up in Arroyo Seco. You go through Taos, which at least has a church and a plaza in the middle, stores around it, then you follow the road out of town and around and come to a bend in the road. That is Arroyo Seco, four or five buildings and that's it, and the road turns into a dirt road and starts going up the side of the mountain and you go up, up, and there perched along that road, along the stream, is this little adobe that is Frank's home. He and Janie started fixing it up. Oh, it's a beautiful place! It has a feeling about it. Frank is perfectly at home there in all respects. The place vibrates, it has a rhythm and a spirit of place. I think you can get what he feels about that home in *Mountain Dialogues*. Frank lives very simply. The house has a fireplace in every room, but there is a combination of bedroom and study on one side, and then the living room and you go down one step into a room that they finished, then two steps down a hallway and bathroom on the right, and you go down one more step and you are in what Frank calls the spare room, which they use as a guest room. And they have had to add a second bathroom. The septic tank became a problem; it turned out to be cheaper to add a whole new bathroom than to dig up the septic tank and replace it. It's too [small] a house for two bathrooms, but it came about in an odd way. And the house is overflowing with priceless paintings that have been given to him by people who subsequently became famous, rugs that he picked up, museum quality, Navajo rugs, years ago, pottery: Frank had a natural taste for things picked up along the way, and they all blend together. There's no TV, no phonograph, only a little radio in the kitchen. When he gets up in the morning, he turns on the news, while he starts the morning coffee in an *electric* coffee pot. He is *not* anti-twentieth century. The electric pot keeps coffee hot all day long for him. He has a fascinating schedule still. He wakes up usually with the dawn and never uses an alarm clock. If he is traveling and has to make a plane or something, then he will set an alarm, but otherwise he just wakes up when the birds start twittering. Then he has his breakfast, goes to his desk, begins working, works until noon, breaks, has a sandwich, takes a nap for an hour, and wakes up, goes back to the desk, and works until four o'clock. And he is still on that schedule. Barbara now comes home from work about 4: 30. He quits about four and feeds the birds. And he knows it is four o'clock because the birds raise an awful racket. They feed — this is the Arizona house now — they feed every bird that comes around. He has bird feeders, and he throws some feed on the ground. They have this magnificent array of birds that come in, and the birds are completely dependent upon the feeding. So, four o'clock, they start saying where's our food, and Frank goes out, fills all the feeders, throws grain around, and the birds settle down. Then he watches them for a bit. Barbara comes home, they have maybe one drink, she fixes supper, and they chat and visit for a while. Barbara, you might be interested in knowing, is also a free-lance writer and publishes under the name of Barbara Hayes.

Audience: How long have they been married?

Adams: December 23, 1979.

Audience: One of the things that I found unsatisfying about *Pike's Peak* is that I really didn't get much of a sense of Frank's dissatisfaction. He must have been terribly hurt by what happened to him in Colorado Springs, at Colorado College. I've always suspected, and it's only a suspicion, that to a certain extent he probably became a writer because he was almost so driven into himself by his own unhappiness and by his own alienation from his community. Or by his embarrassment about his grandfather. I don't think he much liked Colorado Springs.

Audience: How would you compare *Pike's Peak* as a literary work with some of the other books?

Adams: I think when it comes to Frank's books, you evaluate each one of them on a different scale. It's funny, because I have had different students like every single one of his books as a favorite, including *Fever Pitch*, the first one. And that is the one Frank called a stumbling, bumbling, immature first attempt, which it is not. You can't compare the non-fiction to the fiction. And I'm not sure you can compare *People of the Valley*, about a Chicano woman, with *Deer* and its Indian protagonist Martiniano. One of Frank's advantages is his not having gone to school with any traditional majors. An engineering curriculum may have been *our* salvation, in terms of getting a major writer. He didn't really major in anything. He has no sense of, "that's outside my field, I can't write about it." If he wants to be interested in a subject, he is interested and he writes about it. Which upsets many people, mostly anthropologists. If he wants to, he'll write about something like ley lines, these land forces something like tides, or, a better illustration, the North-South magnetic current. There is one set of theories that Stonehenge and the like were built on intersecting ley lines. He found the use of ley lines is still prevalent in China. He found them used in central Mexico. So he has a chapter about ley lines in *Mountain Dialogues*, which really bothered some of the critics. Sort of, "Do you *believe* in this?" And if he wants to read up on numerology, or astrology, whatever, he has no sense of, "I can't do that, I'm not supposed to," and then he reads about something and, if he is interested, fine. It can be art history. He published a lovely book on Leon Gaspard. He just gets into everything. It's one reason, I think, that I've been able to have a course on Waters. There is no sameness. We still can't do all of the books. We do a lot of his books, but with tremendous variety, and each work comes as a constant surprise. *The Colorado* is a marvelous book. They are *all* good, I'm not sure how you can compare them. I don't think there is an answer to that.

Audience: What writers were shaping Waters at the time of *Pike's Peak?*

Adams: You ask Frank that, and he says all of them. He says, "Anybody I have ever read. And at any given moment I am a product of anything I have read." As anyone can tell, Joseph Conrad was a big, big influence, and he read all of Conrad. If you look in Frank's house, there are books in every single room, books all over the place. If you look at the kind of things that he's read, you realize that he has not just gone through them once or twice, he has *studied* them. Barbara has put it very nicely. She said, "He paid his dues." He learned his craft. And he read all the great writers. He looked at how they wrote, thinking, "that's a nice technique. How do you get into that? How does he work that transition?" He deliberately studied everyone successful. And I think that it is quite valid for him to say, anybody that I've ever read influenced me. He's very modest. He learned from all of them. And then, since he drew no lines or limitations about what he could read, he had philosophy, astrology, computer graphics, heaven knows what all, all that goes in. Thank heavens for the product! It's unlike anything else. I was at a meeting of the Modern Language Association, once, when a woman spent about twenty minutes saying what really bothered her about Frank Waters was that he didn't fit in to any of the "streams" of American literature. And the poor woman — I didn't want to disillusion her — she couldn't see that this was marvelous, *that he was an original.* She wanted him to be in the "line" from Thoreau, Emerson or something. Or maybe Mark Twain, that way. And the fact that he just was *there* really upset her. That bothers bibliographers too. They go crazy about Frank. And you may know that book stores don't know where to put his books. *Mexico Mystique* in Las Vegas was in the Occult Book section!

Audience: What is the story about the loss of manuscripts by fire? Where did that happen? Where were they kept?

Adams: He had a lot of his early manuscripts under the bed in Naomi's house in California. Naomi did a lot of his typing, and, as I said, he frequently would wind up there. She kept these manuscripts in boxes, and at one time she asked Frank what she was supposed to do with them. He was at a very discouraging time in his life, so he said to throw them all out as worthless. And she did. The manuscript of *Deer* was in that collection.

Audience: In your opinion, is Frank Waters an Anglo writer?

Adams: Yes, an Anglo.

Audience: Frank Waters is an Anglo?

Adams: Because he *is* an Anglo.

Audience: Well, if Frank Waters is March, is March an Anglo?

Adams: Yes. Unfortunately, an Anglo who is all mixed up because he loved his father very much and admired him, and his father had a strong Indian streak in him. And I think March feels this same activity that was in his father in himself. He sympathizes with him and understands it. But he saw his mother opposed to it, and his grandfather opposed to it. And he saw it kill his father. No, there's not enough there. Frank has *never* claimed to be an Indian. He doesn't know even how much of an Indian his father actually was, or what tribe. He thinks possibly Cheyenne, but he doesn't know for sure. Because this was a "disgrace" in his day, and the family would never talk about it. There's a bit more information about that in the original where there is a confrontation between March and Ona, when he says, "Tell me about my father." It's after Father Cable's death. She said, "I don't know anything." He said, "I want to know about his people." And finally, he really lights into her and says, "Come off it! You must know something. I know you have kept this hidden all these years because it is supposed to be a disgrace." They had quite a battle. It's just a young rebellious boy attacking his mother. And of course, the whole thing blows up. And she tells him she honestly doesn't know. She tells him a little tiny bit, that his father was raised by whites, that he had an Indian mother, they think, and he doesn't really remember much, and he himself doesn't know much.

Audience: There's a story in *Masked Gods*, "Daddy, did you kill any Indians?" that I find very interesting.

Adams: The visits that Frank took with his father to the Ute encampment and Navajo country, those were real and very intellectual. Even though his father was wearing suits and celluloid collar and tie, he felt that his father knew he was among his people. And then realizing he could communicate with them. Frank knew that there was something he was cut out of there, that his mother and grandfather knew nothing about.

Audience: Would it have been his great-grandmother who refuses to have anything to do with Cable? Because he is the half-breed. She takes one look at the child and actually calls him that, saying, "You'll be as wild as the March wind," and that's how he gets his name.

Adams: And she spends her later years sitting and gnawing a wart. She gets her comeuppance. Incidentally, there is a kind of cleaning up of *Pike's Peak* that may have been due to social changes. The word "nigger" appears throughout the original frequently. When Frank redid it in '67, he took out those terms. Apparently they had been so common, not just with Frank's family, but with everybody else. The word was just thrown around. Well, for instance, Mrs. Rogier calls her husband, "Big Nigger." Is that a term of endearment? When Frank rewrote in *Pike's Peak*, he went through and constantly avoided that word to clean it up to present social conditions.

Audience: You just answered the question I was going to ask. I believe it is fitting language for Rogier, he being Southern. It's true, writers, from the South particularly, would always say, that's common use, we don't mean anything wrong by that. I'm glad social change has occurred, and that *Pike's Peak* was cleaned up.

Adams: I think every single use of "niggah" in *Pike's Peak* is very carefully considered. Is this right for this character in this context? There is little doubt that Frank would ponder each single usage.

Audience: How did you become interested in Waters?

Adams: It's a funny story. The credit for that goes to a friend of mine, Bob Kostka, an artist. Bob was on a painting grant in Taos; he read some of Frank's books, and he met Frank. One time he was visiting me and said, "You call yourself an English teacher, but you have never even read a book by this guy." I said, "Well, I'll read him sometime." I assumed Waters wrote "Westerns." A year or so went by. Bob said, "Have you read any Waters yet?" I said, "No, I'll think about it sometime." And a couple more years went by, and this kept happening, and finally Bob in frustration said, "If I give you a Frank Waters book, will you read it?" I said, "Sure, sure." So he sent me a copy, a very nice hard-cover British edition, signed by Frank.

Audience: What book?

Adams: "*The Deer* of course. I put it in the book case, and I think another whole year went by, and finally one summer I was going to lie out in the sun, and I didn't have anything to read, so I looked through the book case, and here is one with a hard-cover that wouldn't fall apart in the sun, so I took it out, started reading it, and my mind was blown. I felt so dumb. Here I am a Ph.D and I had never heard of this guy. He's a living *great* man. I went from there to *People of the Valley*. The top of my head went off.

Audience: One last question, just to get back to the book. Again, I've read some reviews of this book. One claims *Pike's Peak* doesn't work because Rogier's character is flawed, but also the book is flawed in the sense that even with this cutting of a book supposedly twice this size, it is still too long and it's didactic in the sense that it does not allow the reader to develop any sympathy for Rogier. Waters tells and tells us and goes on and on about mining and Rogier's feelings, instead of letting Rogier act for himself. Now, these are not my words. I am paraphrasing some critic. Would you agree?

Adams: No. I think maybe the book is too long. I think maybe there are too many passages of mining information, that could be narrowed down. As far as Rogier is concerned, I personally felt sympathy for him, with him, from my first reading. I think maybe the business about didacticism, that is a very modern kind of criticism, that the author can't tell you what he thinks, that he has got to show you, there's got to be action, action, action. But it is not always true in the twentieth century. I don't think it's necessarily some golden precept.

Audience: My reaction is, I found Rogier early is a very sympathic figure, a fact which to a certain extent works against him, what Frank wanted to do with the book. I just liked that crazy old man digging his tunnel, and all kinds of crazy things.

Audience: In the end when that tunnel finally caved in in the yard and the neighbors mock Rogier, I had to put the book down. I couldn't read any more; I almost cried. That was so touching.

Audience: I got a little upset with March, because he didn't understand his grandfather better. He was always kind of ashamed of him, was running away from him, trying to forget.

Adams: In the original it really hits March in a different way. He is coming down the mountain from that first night with Valerie, when the green-house tunnel collapses. He has just left Valerie, and he runs, because the crowds are all around his front yard, and sees what is going on. He has this tremendous emotional upheaval from his first sexual experience and the collapse of his grandfather's mine, and of the family. It was a gruesome thing. Much too rough, I think, in the original. But, yes, poor old grandpa.

Audience: Did that really happen to Grandpa Dozier?

Adams: No, the tunnel business where Rogier goes insane trying to dig a tunnel from his greenhouse all the way under Pike's Peak is completely made up. That's straight fiction. As for grandpa Dozier losing his fortune in the mine called the Sylvanite, yes, that happened. I was sitting in an easy chair in the Taos house one time, and I looked over the table and picked up this piece of rock mounted on a piece of wood. I said, "Nice. What's this?" "Sylvanite from that damn mine," Frank replied. It was an ore sample of Dozier's.

QUAY GRIGG
MASKING THE SELF

"How is Paul Bowles these days?" I asked. The question leapt off the page of a new book in Barnes & Noble. "And *where*?" I said aloud without losing a beat. The woman next to me edged away. For Paul Bowles' generation and the one before his, the primary question is always "where?," not "how." The answer might be Paris, Rome, or Tangier, but our first thought is where have these American writers fled to. Following "And *where*?" my internal discourse continued: so many people have hung onto Frank Waters' words that many have inquired as to "when" the next book will be out but neither "where" nor "how" has been a real question. If he had been in Tangier, both would have been on our lips.

But he wasn't. This fact is the defining difference for those American writers who stayed in America, declining the expatriate escape. Along with William Faulkner, Waters and other writers about the West stayed home. Sinclair Lewis' crucial gestation occurred in France. Even William Carlos Williams, the quintessential American poet, hungered for Paris and managed a crucial year's sabbatical from his cultural roots. Back in New Jersey, his cultural claustrophobia was allayed by those who had fled Europe for New York, whether as refugees themselves or as returning prodigal children. Frank Waters' natural habitat is the West. Even though he found the golden drafts of Asia a necessary nourishment, he found "Asia" in the American West and recognized it as akin to the native strain brought in ancient times by the earliest settlers. Waters seemed to feel no need to reassure us all that the sun also rises, that roses are repetitively roses, that black skin is less a sign of evil in Europe. Though he hasn't lived out his life in the house where he was born, he has embraced his birthright. His desert, his arid West, is not for him a wasteland.

Staying in his region of birth and of context has given Waters a direct apprehension of life in his place that fades with the onset of flight. Paul Bowles found his arid region in the Middle East, and wonderful it is, with many affinities for Waters' own sheltering sky in *Fever Pitch*. The difference is the spiritual desiccation that pervades the existential writings of Camus, Sartre, and Bowles. A defining difference between Bowles and Waters is that Bowles' desert wanderers were the peak of his writing. Frank Waters' desert wanderers led him within ten years or so to a series of books hard to match by any American writer: *People of the Valley, The Man Who Killed the Deer, The Yogi of Cockroach Court,* and *The Colorado.* The series is one of the triumphs of those who stayed home; the comparable sequence would be that of William Faulkner during the same period.

"And how is William Faulkner these days?" My impression is that his novels are still blue chip, but around the edges tending toward sky blue, perhaps. Novels from the past are always an endangered species. Both Faulkner and Waters have had dry professional periods when their books were less available. Some writers' books are retrieved from the cultural trash heap by publishers who are able to create a new reading public. Faulkner's books had gone out of print until an academic critic revived them. Waters did not ever have just that experience so that his availability has never been so completely owed to anyone except the reading public. It has made a difference in his work, and in the way in which he is read. Waters like other Western writers has complained about "New York publishers," but his alternative, regional publishers have kept his work available. How many writers find almost all their work in print at the age of ninety? Waters has not had the experience of having his work brought back into print solely due to the efforts of an academic critic, but in recent years academic critics (notably Robert Kostka, John Milton, and Charles Adams) have added an academic campus audience to the more underground movement of sixties' campus readers focused on the Southwest and Native American literature. Waters may complain about publishers, but he is discreet about academics — who knows what he thinks of all the pointy-headed essays his work inspires? Nevertheless they have indisputably added readers who help assure that his work remains in print. That in itself is a measure of a survivor's strength. The fact that only a few novels survive the decades through appeals to popular readers indeed produces odd bedfellows. It's a good sign that Waters has not yet needed rescue to remain in print, as did Faulkner, who got it, and Melville, who did not.

"And how is Herman Melville?" Fine, last year had a chic cafe named after him in the building in the West Village where he worked for several decades after he gave up his writing career because the public abandoned him. The careers of both Melville and Waters began with a series of blockbuster books that are the heart of their appeals today. Melville's career faltered after his big book fizzled, in spite of his being in New York at the center of what was becoming the publishing center of the country. Henry D. Thoreau had moved to New York to break into publishing, but found proximity little help in establishing a career as a professional writer. Waters was far from a publishing center and suffered some problems for being from the West instead, but he did not give up publishing as a career, and hasn't yet. Melville did give up and his books remained unavailable for two decades after his death. Keeping a book in print now requires at least as much staying power — and luck — as it did in 1860; but there the books of Frank Waters are, at our fingertips.

"And how is Frank Waters?" Just fine. He is in his home region, where he seems naturally to belong, avoiding the existential alienation that led his and the preceding generation of writers abroad. As a result — or as a cause — the places in his work have a reality for readers that is hard to forget. Cardboard backdrops, common in both unsuccessful fiction and in "mythic" fiction, are not his thing. Exotic places, not in Morocco but in the more-than-mythic part of our own country, are. Not for him the naked, hallucinogenic lunch; Frank Waters' well-clothed lunches are garbed in the kind of mythic robes that are at once to us strikingly original and intimately known as though they had been pulled out of our own deeper selves where they had hidden for long times. His places are exotic, and deeply our own. That's what the West is: the foreign and exotic, the intimately familiar — our own place, not where we really are but a more meaningful place that Frank Waters led us to deep inside ourselves. His places have become ours too, or were ours before he created them for us. I need only mention certain mountains, valleys, adobe buildings, restaurants, rivers, kivas, stores, each a mundane object in itself but endowed with highly-charged meanings when they become images from his books that light up in the mind.

The sense of place in Waters' books has qualities that could come only from immersion, as well as birth — immersion in the earth he is part of but also in the age-old culture that still flourishes there. He is one of the writers who is not only superhumanly sensitive to places battered by alien, invading cultures but also able to find in words signs that unloose in readers a recovered sense of the unspoiled character of a place. In T. S. Eliot, even though he removed to the most civilized city in Europe, the landscape remains a wasteland, albeit one with rumblings of a from-the-dead revival of a culture whose valence is positive. The native piece of earth, riddled with valleys, kivas, rising into monumental adobe structures, gave strength that expatriate vistas rarely provided.

Hawthorne wrote his body of novels before he moved abroad. Henry James became the expatriate model, producing his major work outside his homeplace. Edith Wharton, Gertrude Stein, Stephen Crane, and the others wrote back from abroad. It made the difference: they wrote from a Europe that was the home of the traditional novel. That novel genre had become rigidly wedded to character development. How alive do the characters seem? How long do they live in the reader's mind? These became the hallmarks of Edwardian criticism of the novel. As much as he tried to go beyond it, Henry James never fully escaped the straitjacket of "the realistic novel," that nineteenth-century genre. The great tradition of the novel lived in Europe in its world of manners and morals, as Hawthorne and lots of others lamented. That "great tradition" lived especially in the commitment to the supremacy of the individual self. It followed that the fine points of the novel would become questions of individualized vs. stereotyped characters. The individual's relationship to self and to society became the binding trap of the traditional novel. Henry James did not escape it.

What an irony for the democracy of democracies to be inhospitable to the great genre dedicated to individualism! Expatriate novelists were left to worship at the altar of the personal self. One avenue of escape became the reportorial novel, that "realism" still enshrined in the classroom. It has become apparent that realistic novels aren't real at all — they merely seem real, a technique of illusion and delusion useful to any cultural power wishing to reproduce itself. One success was Walt Whitman, who stayed at home and who became marginally a professional writer and explorer of new materials and new forms. Whitman's places — the streets of New York, the battlefields, the seclusion of Timber Creek — have some of the original strengths Frank Waters' places have. There are other affinities, too, especially Whitman's intense longing for the West, which he finally visited after he had been invalided by strokes. The culture had exacted its price in Whitman's debilitating stroke at the peak of his career [. . .].

[Frank Waters] was able to plunge deeply into the traditions of the novel and to alter them — especially in regard to character and narration as they function in narrative.

First, Waters' contribution to the development of the modern narrative: the narrating voice. His treatment of the narrator ("Author") declared war on "the great tradition" by restructuring it to signify new cultural values. The content, yoking a lesbian together with a Yoga theme, is innovative, but Waters' treatment of the narrative point of view—playing with the voice that speaks the discourse and also with the "seeing," literally the point of view. The speaker through much of *The Yogi of Cockroach Court* seems to be the traditional, authoritative Author. A second, competing discourse (the Yogi's discourse, his perspective in things, sometimes even in phrasing that might be partially the Yogi's) is fed to us also through the narrating voice of the Author. As the narrative progresses, the Yogi's "seeing" predominates; the Author recedes. All well and good, except that the Yogi — who is on the road to obliteration of self — does eventually explode in a bomb blast. Where then is the "seeing"? A voice is left but it has little discourse of its own left to offer. The "ultimate truth" (or at least the last assertion) is left to folklore and the mass media's penchant for stories it is familiar with. The reader knows what this story has been but only because the reader has been taught by Waters to survive the death not only of the Author but of the perceiving character within the action (as invented by Spanish writers of the sixteenth century and reinvented by Jane Austen and Henry James). The central narrating, structuring function of the novel seems to have been deconstructed by Frank Waters in the late 1920s. As of then, the psychological novel of the early part of this century was dead. The Jane Austen/Henry James/Kate Chopin validation of "reality" as the individual consciousness and its perceptions went up in smoke as the body of the novel's perceiver exploded, leaving no individual self in charge of "reality."

Waters' treatment of character has also been revolutionary, growing out of the validating self in the narration. Up to a point the usual academic critical tools work: Is the character three-dimensional enough to come alive in the reader's imagination? Is the character intended to be flat? Or — for variation — is there a mythic quality, an archetypal figure? We settled for this discrimination earlier in discussing Waters' characters. They do indeed have qualities we can call mythic. So do Joyce's Stephen and Bloom and Mann's Dr. Faustus. Waters' folk seem somehow different. They do not comfortably accept labels of individual, type, or myth.

People in his great series of books into the 1940s have a "collective" quality that replaces the self more traditional characters were made of, but they go beyond the usual stereotypes and myths. One way they go beyond stereotypes is in their timelessness, or their encompassing elements of the past as well as the present. It is as if they are products of the past living in the present. Thus they more easily seem to be mythic archetypes. Are Martiniano, Maria, and the woman at Otowi Crossing merely expressions of archetypes? Not exactly. They might be called archetypes with deep imprint of the place and culture they derive from. They seem to me precisely to have a "kachina" quality, to be more like kachina figures than like typical "characters" or "social types" or "archetypes." Frank Waters could have created important examples of all three of these types of characters even had he lived in Tangier — this flashed into my mind as I stood in Barnes & Noble absorbing the question "How is Paul Bowles these days?" What could not have developed there is the place- and culture-specific kachina quality that distinguishes some of Waters' major creations: Martiniano, Maria, the Colorado River.

I have looked back at the first printed words I published about Frank Waters' work in 1973 in *South Dakota Review*. I had immersed myself in Hopi Arizona, returning by Window Rock to Gallup, where a dust storm pinned me down for two days. In an elderly motel there it came to me: Each of Frank Waters' novels is an energy field in which a single kachina figure dances toward us, in line with all the others. At supreme moments they seem to be the kachina; more often they are more like the masked impersonators of kachinas. As the massiveness of Waters' early trio of Rocky Mountain novels eroded by half into a new, less massive *Pike's Peak*, half as long as the original three novels, it seemed that the chief character, Rogier's kachina-like mountain psyche, was being joined by the very physical form of the novel/mountain itself. In

People of the Valley Doña Maria is known to the valley people as one of the agents of the earth's power because of her kachina-like relation with earth in this place about to be submerged by a proposed dam. She is the source of good seeds, the mediator along life's journey between the folk and the forces of nature. A more accurate title to describe *The Man Who Killed the Deer* might be "the man who killed part of himself, the deer-man," so kachina-like is the chief character. Martiniano is distinctly a man whose spirit is closely connected with a specific deer, which causes him to be a troublemaker, but which also then warns of danger along the Peyote Road. The deer guides his human life as the spirit controls a kachina dancer. Martiniano's wife Flowers Playing has not been cut off from the animal kachina but gradually becomes its impersonator as she dances the sacred role of Deer Mother.

Waters' prose-poem *The Colorado* is at once an offering to this god and instructions for white America to find "the way" to regeneration and life. This red dancing god, so like the dancing Indians in immemorial ritual, is Frank Waters' "tao." In spite of his dancing movement downstream, the Colorado is the reverse of a restless being because its course is inevitable. *The Colorado* is therefore our explicit key to Waters' technical treatment of "character" in the novel and to his philosophical and religious view of human kind as well. For him humans in their social relations, as described by George Eliot, are of secondary interest to humans in their natural relations. For in nature — that part of it outside himself and that part of it inside himself — is our energy source. White and black as well as red can relate to the major deity Earth through the lesser gods, these kachinas: the instrument of passage, of interconnection, of transfer of energy, and of union. It is as figures of passage, filling a role similar to that of the kachinas, that we should view Marston, Rogier, Doña Maria, Martiniano, Helen Chalmers, and — larger than mere life — the Colorado River. Rather than creating "realistic" portraits of human individuals, or generalized mythic representations, Frank Waters has created a kind of fictional character who, remaining masked and separate, can mediate between the individual self and the collective self.

III.
GEOGRAPHICAL

ALEXANDER BLACKBURN
THE INTERIOR COUNTRY

"Beautiful my desire, and the place of my desire,"[1] wrote Theodore Roethke in "North American Sequence," a series of poems depicting the soul's journey spatially into the interior of the continent, temporally into the interior of the past to effect redemption through acceptance, and spiritually into self-transcending depths of interior landscape. It is through place that one exceeds place. One comes to stand outside self with a heightened awareness obtained by relationship with the external world and to the mystery of life, itself. The what and the how of Roethke's poetry of place, then, may serve to introduce the serious literature of the various "wests" of the modern American West — truly the heartland, truly the interior country. For the literature of this region is a genuine literature of place, of a real place or series of places inhabited by real people, neither a mythical "country of the mind" (as Archibald MacLeish dismissed it) nor a cultural province existing for the sake of national fantasies or of historical exploitation. The interior country is in fact a place of beautiful desire, a symbolic landscape with a power to revitalize the continental soul.

To approach this interior country, we must first remove the shrubbery of capital-W "Western" literature and film that stands between us and the truth that is beautiful. The shrubbery is not easily cut down. It is stubbornly rooted in morality plays about cowboys and Indians and in stereotyped chivalric romances about hard-riding, fast-shooting heroes who have a kind of messianic ego-identity. Fabulous as the West may have been from the time of the Spanish conquistadors to, roughly, the start of the present century, serious writers want little of this Buffalo Billing. In *Pike's Peak*, an authentic novelistic epic first completed as a trilogy in the 1930s, Frank Waters told the story of New Westerners struggling and failing to attune their psyches to a rightness with the land. In this novel, comparable to Herman Melville's nineteenth-century classic novel *Moby Dick*, the protagonist's materialistic egotism turns to madness as he seeks the heart of a Great White Mountain.[2] Here, the legendary virtues of western pioneers disintegrate when not balanced with nature's living mystery. Then in *The Ox-Bow Incident*, Walter Van Tilburg Clark's novel published in 1940, the stripping down of frontier fakelore continued in earnest as, behind the façade of retributive justice, the tragic consequences of wrong-minded self-reliance and mob violence lay exposed. And so it has been since then, western writers continuing to feel the need of making a clearing, of turning stereotyped characters and situations on their often nakedly imperialistic heads, without at the same time discarding the real achievements of individualism, the lingering authenticity of innocence, and the possibilities still for realizing the American dream in a land that likes to live in the shape of tomorrow. Whereas some of this effort has been and is the result of a "mock-Western," negative stance, the commitment of anger, like as not, yields a positive force in the attitude of love and respect for a land long-violated yet magnificent and capable of touching us at the core of being. For this reason, the classic capital-W "Western" hero such as Jack Schaefer's Shane, who is solid and separate and alone in his sense of individuality, cannot be brought down merely by social humiliation — society in the West being still in process of formation, Native American and Hispanic communities aside. The fabulous Western hero has to be humbled in his whole relationship with the universe, that his egoistic will-to-power may be brought into balance with nature and humanity, not asserted too far, not seeking to possess the land or to extract from the world of nature more than nature will allow.

The antiromantic and realistic approach to the interior country has led some western writers of fiction to a conception of personality different from the one found in traditional European and Eastern American literature with its centuries-old emphasis upon the subtle nuances of manners and morals. To be sure, that traditional perspective, often expressed in satirical vein, has not gone dry. Today's Californian and Sun Belt culture called forth the steady gaze of such powerful moralists as Wallace Stegner in the Pulitzer Prize-winning novel, *Angle of Repose*, and Edward Abbey in the hilariously fulminating novel, *The Monkey-Wrench Gang*. But the traditional perspective may not serve the western writer out in the metaphorical lunar landscape beyond the Sun Belt. So he or she may not be writing traditionally at all, a view championed by such contemporary scholars as Thomas J. Lyon, for many years editor of *Western American Literature*. The reader who approaches all western fiction from the traditional perspective will argue that western writers, overpowered by landscape, neglect the complexity, depth, and realism of characterization one should expect, and create, instead of subtle fiction, something akin to moral fables. In other words, inferior fiction. And, it is true, western stories often have an ethical and philosophical import that suggests a regional imperative. However, where some of the greatest of western writers are concerned, there is apt to be *more*, not less, subtlety of characterization than one finds in manners-and-morals fiction. To view character as weighed in the balance between the sense of the individual self and the sense of its being a part of nature, of the timeless and indivisible whole, demands skill of the highest order.[3]

Whereas European and Eastern and (usually) Southern American fiction has flourished in hierarchic society and tends to rest its case upon individual action in the social sphere, western fiction sometimes goes beyond the social nuances of interpersonal relationships to the nuances of the interior life, where true subtlety lies. It is as if a western writer has to envision something like the whole range of our lives in society, in history, and in nature and to dramatize the effect, like that of ever-widening ripples on a pool, of the microcosmic individual on the macrocosm at every level from the family to social group to the land and, ultimately, to the cosmos itself. Out West, where the individual consciousness is spatially forced to come to terms with a macrocosmic universe oblivious to its presence, the personality may be formed between polarities of reason and intuition, between conscious and unconscious forces. If the polarization prove constructive, a fictionalized character may become attuned to place and discover at-one-ness with it and with humanity. On the other hand, if the polarization prove destructive, a character may destroy the land, its ancient inhabitants, community, and his own humanity. Western fiction at its best is a call for living within the emerging process of creation.

A western writer, far from being artistically limited by place, may move through it and from it in a kind of ritual catharsis to therapeutic vision.[4]

What, then, is the West? It comprises the region beyond the 100th meridian, an arid region fragile both socially and ecologically. The West is principally the Rockies — New Mexico, Colorado, Wyoming, Montana, Arizona, Utah, Nevada, Idaho, and the eastern areas of California, Oregon, and Washington — with subregional borders from West Texas to the Dakota Badlands and from Baja California to Puget Sound. This region represents more than half of the continental United States. It is sparsely populated save for patches of wildly growing cities, especially along the Pacific littoral, and aridity limits future population growth. A region half-owned and not infrequently exploited by the federal government, the West has wilderness areas into which urban civilization has been allowed to expand, but the social and economic structure of major cities is likely to remain tentative and shifting.

Wallace Stegner calls the West "an oasis civilization,"[5] its history since the arrival of New Westerners one of the importation of humid-land habits into a dry land that will not tolerate them, of the indulgence of personal liberty in a country that experience says can only be successfully tamed and lived in by a high degree of cooperation. In short, the West lives precariously close to a reality that warns of the collapse of its eco-systems and of the consequent physical and psychical impoverishment of its inhabitants. The sheer beauty and mystery of the West are vulnerable indeed.

Yet vulnerability elicits the response of cherishing, as if the West is a child requiring constant care and protection. When this child-like land and the children of it are, unremittingly, raped by the forces of materialism — and metaphors of rape, violence, and mutilation are strongly present in stories of the modern West — then it is easy to understand why western writers often reveal their love through outrage. Here, though, is some explanation of a surprising fact: writers need not be native to the West nor long resident in it to care about it, to derive actual substance from it, and to write about it at depth of import. The same literary phenomenon is less true, if true at all, about other regions. Southern literature, for example, reflects a special historical experience of land and people and of a language shared from the Carolinas to Mississippi. Consequently, nonsouthern writers have contributed little to the South's letters. By contrast, Spanish and Native American languages excepted, "western" English has few deeply shared meanings, and its vernacular is in part a fabrication of popular culture, in part an importation from other regions and nations. Freed of linguistic restraint, the newcomer may feel and express solidarity with native writers born with wild rivers, lonely plains, and towering mountains in their blood. This freemasonry among new and native writers may be accounted for, too, by the nature of experience of the interior country: the subtleties not always being traditionally social, they may come readily to the soul's grasp and the heart's concern. A correct compassion, in sum, may be sufficient credentials for a writer to become western and to participate in the West's history.

It may be argued that the West has no history, or rather, as Gerald Haslam puts it, it has been assigned "a permanent, ossified past without a present."[6] Where, indeed, are the connections, and how to recover them? The problem is a serious one for western writers, whatever their racial and cultural backgrounds. Anglos of the dominant culture may yet be nostalgic about the "winning of the West" in the past century, whereas Hispanics and Native Americans feel victimized by this conquest, their traditions enervated. Meanwhile, as eastern assumptions persist that the West is a historical vacuum, nuclear devices will be detonated in the deserts, water and mineral resources will be exploited regardless of human needs, and wilderness will suffer urban encroachment. Because these events have already happened, a restored and properly focused history is a concern for all writers in the modern West. From such restorations as are currently available, a picture emerges not only of relentless plunder but also of the past and continuing genocide against the Indians.[7] In other words, there is a *burden* to western history with profoundly tragic implications, a tragic awareness opening up on two fronts: that of the attempt of New Westerners to comprehend the land psychically, failing which comprehension they subdue it to European and Eastern American patterns; and that of encounter with the Indian, whose enduring presence undermines notions of a heroic Manifest Destiny. As Dee Brown shows in *Bury My Heart at Wounded Knee: An Indian History of the West*, the West was not won but *lost*. This sense of burdensome history continues in Peter Matthiessen's *In the Spirit of Crazy Horse*, an analysis of how a defiant group of Indians has been "neutralized" since the early 1970s by government forces working to clear the way for progress — that is, for multinational energy corporations that will mine the vast mineral resources and pump down water resources from reservation lands as well as from public lands. Once Americans understand the true nature of western history, writers of the modern West will have found their audience.

Western writers often share in and express tragic vision. Tragedy, which is the inevitable result of taking a complete view of the human situation, makes the richness and beauty of life depend on a balance. The basic tenet of this world-view is that all life is maintained by observance of the natural order, that is, perception that what goes on in one sphere affects what goes on in other spheres. Both Greek and Shakespearean literary tragedy reveal that a disorder in the human system is symbolically paralleled by a disorder in the social system and by a disorder in the cosmic system. The core of tragedy's idea of order, by contrast, is the sacredness of the bonds which hold human beings together and establish mutuality between their lives and the natural order.[8] It is at this juncture that western experience and the idea of tragedy are apt to meet. The experience of the New West — a civilization largely made possible through technological achievements such as construction of Hoover Dam in the mid-1930s — is that the power of tragedy's destructive principle has been admitted and constitutes a general threat. Although the industrial, military, agribusiness, and governmental infrastructure has now stretched western development to the breaking point, particularly in terms of resources and of the problems associated with "instant cities,"[9] the Great Western Boom continues with visions of projects larger than the pyramids, of excavations rivaling the Panama Canal, of trillion-dollar military projects, of Sun Belt expansions, and of forced relocations of Indians from ancestral lands. Thus at the very moment of the region's greatest rise to power, unless there is a dramatic return to the ethics of balance, a hubristic civilization of the New West may be headed into decadence, catastrophe, and silence.

Part of the evidence of a tragic vision in western writers lies in their questioning of the ideology of individualism, which has had a heyday in the West. The historian Frederick Jackson Turner was its most influential and enthusiastic proponent. The West, he wrote in 1920 in *The Frontier in American History*,

> was another name for opportunity. Here were mines to be seized, fertile valleys to be preempted, all the natural resources open to the shrewdest and the boldest. . . . The self-made man was the Western man's ideal, was the kind of man that all men might become. Out of his wilderness experience, out of the freedom of his opportunities, he fashioned a formula for social regeneration — the freedom of the individual to seek his own.[10]

Well, that thesis rings a historical freedom bell all right. But its peal is increasingly hollow now that a metropolitan West is destroying what's left of the frontier. The national, indeed international, myth of a West of rugged individualism triumphing over a decaying East has proven itself, in part, a denial of humanity. In terms of tragic vision, the ideology of individualism throws the natural order out of balance, negating tragedy's complete view of the human situation by vesting authority in the atomic individual regardless of the effects on the social system and the cosmic system. Of course, the great open spaces of the West may still enforce an isolation that can make people independent and resourceful; may call forth a saving, intuitive reluctance to surrender themselves to the blind ethics of an imperfectly formed, excessively masculine society; may make it possible to escape from the moral claustrophobia of ideology, and to open emotional doors to forces of the natural order that can nurture western civilization without demanding that it be repudiated altogether.

Journeying to the interior of historical experiences in the full light of tragic consciousness, Anglo, Hispanic, and Native American writers may and sometimes do discover that the connections between past and present are to be found not in a span of centuries, but in millennia. At the Sun Temple at Mesa Verde in southwestern Colorado we begin to comprehend the antiquity of the heartland; and in witnessing the unique mystery plays enacted in Hopi, Pueblo, and Navajo ceremonies we may realize that an ancient American civilization is a living presence — and more. The symbols of this civilization are pertinent to the future survival of the human species. Historical orientation locates the pulse of the heartland in pre-Columbian Mexico among Mayan and Aztec cultures, the center being the sacred city of Teotihuacán, at the mythic heart of which lies the Temple of Quetzalcoatl, the "plumed serpent," symbol of the union of heaven and earth, matter and spirit, a self-sacrificing God-Redeemer who taught that the Road of Life is within man, himself. An ethic based upon regard for all forms of life, the Road is a psychological affirmation of an evolutionary emergence of mankind to a new stage of increased awareness of our responsibility in the cosmic plan. Astonishing as this deep meaning of western history may seem, it is true to say that Ancient America has power stored up for the redemption of Modern America. Accordingly, some writers of the West, among whom there is the genius of Frank Waters, are able to render the modern world spiritually significant and to fulfill the prime task of mythology, which is to carry the human spirit forward.[11]

The West is a region of myth vitalized by the relationship of peoples to the land. For Native Americans especially that relationship is sacred. Other westerners, drawn to similar regard, move spiritually from the damaged terrain of exterior landscape to the interior country where place is important because it is timeless and self-transcending — where, in Roethke's mystical vision, "all finite things reveal infinitude."[12]

The modern West is the modern world. This beautiful country, though, is not as benighted or as chaotic as a Waste-Land, its special poignancy being that it remains a place of the soul's desire. Western writers confront with urgency and insight and with remembered anguish some of the most tortured racial, moral, and spiritual questions of our time, and some find answers to them. Waters envisions a coming world of consciousness of the timeless essence of both the exterior and the interior country. Stegner calls for an ordering principle that will allow modern culture to stop its drift toward decadence. Other writers assert our needs for less willfulness and for a return to humanity, to love and community. Still others remind us that, our earthly tenure being brief if not illusory, we should not take the world too seriously, but take it nonetheless, honestly, responsibly, and wholeheartedly. And even when the world seems to have lost all meaning — when, like Edward Abbey's Will Gatlin, we have descended in our quest for meaning to the very pit of the Grand Canyon of our microcosmic selves — there spreads before us the prospect of endurance and the knowledge that we could not imagine doing anything else, any less.[13] In the final analysis, stories of the modern West have the power to lift the gaze of our hearts to a larger sky. "Everything is held together with stories," concludes Barry Lopez in one of his stories. "That is all that is holding us together, stories and compassion."[14]

Joseph Gordon
Shining Mountains

When I learned from Barbara Waters we'd meet at the Waters' home this morning, high on the western flank of the legendary Sangre de Cristo Mountains, I thought it would be appropriate to share a few thoughts on the importance of mountains in Frank's life and work. Thinking about Frank's mountains reminded me of a memorable conversation I once had with a student. Knowing he was a fan, I asked what he enjoyed most about Frank's books. Without hesitation he replied that when he "hunkered down" with one of Frank's books, he felt he could "chuck a hunk of granite" in any direction and hit a mountain, and that all those mountains made him feel right at home. I should mention here that the young man was an accomplished mountaineer, who was born and raised in and on top of the San Juan Mountains of southern Colorado. I say "on top" because he was an intrepid climber.

Some time later I was visiting with Frank and our conversation reminded me of my former student's remarks. I told Frank the story. We agreed my student was a penetrating critic of good literature, knowing what he liked and why, and that he had a memorable and admirable way of expressing himself and should become a writer, but he was probably destined to become a field geologist. I don't know if he became a writer or a geologist, but I'll bet he's still reading Frank's books. At any rate, he had one thing right: "Shining Mountains," a term Frank borrowed from the description of the Rockies by early French explorers, are a very dynamic and important part of almost everything Frank wrote.

Writers have a fondness for landscape. They might use their environment to set a scene, create atmosphere, or delineate a character. We all remember stories opening on a cold and stormy night, or with the cowboy hero pulling his six-shooter, the ominous mountains rising threateningly behind him. Why is it always raining when John gets his separation papers from the lovely and long-gone Jane? Frank often used his mountains for these reasons. In *People of the Valley* we read, "Winter crept down the mountains. The valley paled from a lake of blue to a lake of white. Cold clutched and throttled it. And then its white turned blue again with the reflection of the peaks upon its icy crusts."[1] In *The Man Who Killed the Deer* he begins a chapter in the traditional way, using the landscape to prepare the reader for what is to come.

> The indentation on the breast of the mountain began to overflow, and the viscous white crept down the cañon trails. Below, under the great cottonwoods, the deep still pools ringed with white. Rime covered the withered squash vines each morning. The roads rang hard and dry. Under a flurry of snow the desert beyond spread out bleak and illimitable as the sky overhead; one could scarcely distinguish where they met. The tone of land, sky, and people was a somber gray. Its mood was a frosty silence. Even the voice of the white-blanketed figure on the house-tops seems strangely muted.[2]

As readers, our imaginations slide down the frozen mountainside to the frozen men in white silhouetted against the mountain. The icy scene is set. A chilling atmosphere is created. Action. People enter from the right and left. The narrator, like a camera, follows the movement of the entering characters.

A more typical use of landscape in Frank's work is to present scenes filtered through the eyes of a character other than the narrator, as they are in the above examples. In this way the author not only sets the scene, but intimates the state of mind of the beholder, his character. Jack Turner, for example, a figure not unlike Frank in many ways, while driving home contemplates the mountains in *The Woman at Otowi Crossing*.

> Early that morning after leaving Otowi Crossing, Turner drove home to La Oreja. It lay about fifty miles north, on a high

wind-swept plateau that stretched almost unbroken from the
deep gorge of the Rio Grande to the curving wall of the Sangre
de Cristos. The horizontal plane of the sage-gray desert structurally counterbalanced by the vertical mass of spruce-blue
mountains rising abruptly into the turquoise sky, the constant
subtle shifting of light and color, the miraculous clarity of the
air — all these composed a landscape incomparably beautiful
and justly famous.[3]

Notice how the scene is structured, ordered in the mind of Turner. In the
story he is a newspaper man. He prides himself on his objectivity, and so his
landscape must have shape, recognizable form, and perspective. He admires
what he sees, but only after he is able to confront it in his terms of reference.
The horizontal planes and vertical masses, all structurally counterbalanced,
are indicators of his world view, of his personality. The scene, in other words,
develops character.

A third way that Frank integrates mountains into his stories is more
subtle, and, I feel, the most dramatic. Helen Chalmers, who is the woman at
Otowi Crossing in the book of the same name, goes high into the mountains
above her home to cut wood for the winter. Mysteriously she is drawn to a
pile of debris, the remains of an ancient dwelling. "Feverishly," we are told, she
reaches down and discovers "a smooth round edge which carefully scooped
out became the rim of a large perfectly formed bowl. . . . In this Helen now
saw the clear imprint of a woman's thumb."[4] Alone, high on the mountain,
Helen is about to achieve an insight that will change her life. She realizes that
everything around her is "one undivided, living whole."[5] To dramatize her
epiphany Frank brings the mountain landscape — past and present — to life.

> She was still standing on the ledge, tremblingly clutching her
> discovery, when she heard the faint, familiar honk of wild geese
> flying south. In a moment she could detect the undulating V
> sweeping toward her, high in the mist. Always she had believed
> the flocks followed the course of the river below. Now she knew
> that some of them used the plateau to mark their high road.
> That ancient Navawi'i woman, thumb pressing into the wet
> clay stuck to her cooking pot, must have watched their passage
> too, as she prepared for winter.[6]

The geese give the mountain landscape sound and motion; and Frank adds, "The mountain peaks stood firm against time. Eternity flowed in the river below."[7] Such revelations occur to other characters in Frank's work: Martiniano in *The Man Who Killed the Deer*, Maria del Valle in *People of the Valley*, and, as we shall see, March Cable in *Pike's Peak*. All these characters come to an understanding of the inter-relatedness of all life. Always, this message is transmitted to them when they are in the mountains.

In *Pike's Peak*, Frank's semiautobiographical novel, he pushes the message of landscape even further. Joseph Rogier, the dominant figure in the first half of the novel, becomes obsessed by the mountain that has mysteriously drawn him to itself. He broods over it; he talks to it. In the passage which follows, the narrator begins by standing outside Rogier's consciousness and describes for the reader what he sees when he looks at the mountain. Then he moves us inside Rogier to realize his angle of vision.

> In geologic time it stood there, a monstrous volcano belching fire and smoke upon a world that had sunk beneath forgotten seas. It had stood there in organic time, a lofty snow-crowned peak looking upon a virgin continent yet unraped by greedy man. . . . And now at last in their moment of truth and fruition they [Rogier and Pike's Peak] faced each other like two adversaries bound together in a common selfhood. Over them both a common golden sun rose and set. . . . And in each of them glowed the reflection of the one great sun, the golden sun that was the heart of all.[8]

The passage begins in geology and ends in mysticism. The transition happens with the "peak looking upon a virgin continent." Mountains don't look. Characters do. Is this an example of what is called the "pathetic fallacy," granting nature human capacity, attributing to a mountain human emotions? I don't think so. By the end of the passage, we have moved into the feverish imagination of Rogier. He sees the mountain as his "adversary," and assumes the mountain retaliates by hating him. He imposes human passions on the mountain, and by so doing makes Pike's Peak a character, his antagonist, if you will. In the end Rogier is destroyed, not by Pike's Peak, but by his delusional perception of nature — his own misconception of the mountain. Of course, this is Frank's way of suggesting the tragedy of the American experience in the West.

"I suppose that at heart I'm a Mountain Man,"[9] Frank wrote in *Mountain Dialogues*. By "Mountain Man," Frank explained, he meant those first Europeans who came west to trap beaver. In *The Colorado*, published more than thirty years before *Mountain Dialogues*, he explained that trappers were the first "Westerners." The trapper walked into the wilderness and "saw before him something he had never seen before, something that would haunt him always, something of which forever after he would be an unalienable part. The mountains! The great front wall of the Rockies looming into the clouds above him, extending to each side as far as he could see, from Canada to Chihuahua."[10] The mountain experience changed the trapper forever. He became a new breed of man, "European on the outside and Indian inside, men neither wholly white nor wholly red."[11] Frank was cautious about calling himself a "Mountain Man" in capitals, so he qualified with the opening "I suppose." He was right to do so, because historically he didn't qualify, at least not physically. But spiritually Frank was a mountain man, even without capitalization. Reading what he says of the trapper, I am struck with how it applies to Frank, for he, too, was stamped with "the great spirit-of-place."[12] He, too, was haunted by Shining Mountains.

There is another breed of men whom Frank admired for many of the same reasons he respected the trapper. In *Midas of the Rockies*, his biography of Winfield Scott Stratton, Frank was more fascinated by Stratton's lonely seventeen-year search for gold than he was by his discovery and development of the Independence, the richest mine in Cripple Creek, Colorado. Stratton left no record of the seventeen years he wandered alone in the San Juan Mountains. Lacking specific information, and knowing only that Stratton disappeared into the mountains, Frank followed him, and others like him, in his imagination.

> The prospector, for all his age and misfortune, remains the eternally youthful fellow long after his white beard turns yellow and his rheumy blue eyes grow dim to all but the distant horizon. And when in a forgotten gulch, a lonely hillside, one comes upon his bleached bones, his upturning skull seems still fixed in a derisive grin. Of a strange and incomprehensible breed of men to whom nothing, neither success, failure, riches nor fame, means anything compared to his never ending search — the prospector remains of them all America's wayward child.[13]

If it is true that you can tell a man by the company he keeps, if only imaginatively, we learn much of Frank's values by knowing his spiritual predecessors, mountain men all. Lonely, restless, courageous men, prospectors as well as trappers were, according to Frank, our original "Westerners." They all walked into the wilderness, and the wilderness took them in. "All non-conformists and discontents isolated from the mainstream of life. The wilderness insured their isolation and ingrownness, a certain wildness, and a peculiar psychic response to the tremendous forces of nature which enclosed them. They became mountain people."[14] Not a perfect fit for Frank, but close in many ways. He was a mountain man.

The Colorado, first published in 1946, is important here for several reasons. In addition to being a first-rate natural history, in the tradition of Henry David Thoreau's *Walden*, it contains information about Frank's early life. The book is the story of his journey down the Colorado River, and his discovery and description of the place, the people, the past, and the present. Fortunately for us it is also his journey of personal discovery. Both journeys begin in the Rocky Mountains of Colorado. He begins the chapter, titled appropriately "High Country,"

> Next time by hook or crook, make sure you're born with a mountain in your front yard. It comes in mighty handy all the way around.
>
> When you're no bigger than *that* you can hang on to the grimy window curtains and watch it hour after hour. Then you know it best with all its moods and mutations, its sternness, dignity and immeasurable depth. . . . [15]

In the same chapter he recalls how, when he was young, his whole day was shaped by Pike's Peak, the mountain in his "front yard." He watched it for signs of coming storms, and in the evening the "sun snags on the rimrock and the hollows fill up with red and lilac, damson blue and purple."[16] Here, as in all his scenic descriptions, Frank was a good observer of nature, the first qualification of a competent naturalist, and he was an especially good watcher of mountains.

Mountain people always know where they are. Frank was always conscious of space and place, a feat he accomplished by his relation to mountains.

When he was a child going to Columbia School in Colorado Springs, he never worried about getting lost; he always kept his eye on Pike's Peak. The same was true of camping when he grew older. "But besides being a compass the peak is a timekeeper and weather prophet too. . . . A mountain peak, all in all, is about the handiest thing to have around and strike up friends with. Our mountain was a whopper, a beaut of a peak. We got along fine."[17]

He never lost his sense of space and place. Even when he grew older, he still centered himself by relating to the mountains around him. In *Mountain Dialogues*, he knows exactly where he is, physically and spiritually, when he sees ". . . the snow-tipped peaks of Jicarita and the Truchas to the south, down toward Santa Fe, rise sharply into the blue. Beyond the slit of the Rio Grande to the west, the upland desert rises to the southern thrust of the Colorado Rockies. And to the east and north, directly behind me, the Sangre de Cristos curve in their great semi-circle."[18]

When he was a boy, Frank tells us in *The Colorado*, he often helped his grandfather at the family mine, high on the far side of Pike's Peak. One day as he watched his grandfather and his two helpers, Abe and Jake, he realized they saw the mountain as "merely dead stone."[19] That was the way most people saw the mountain, the way he was taught to view nature.

> Then suddenly it happened, the boy did not know how. All this dead stone became intensely, vibrantly alive. Playing on the dump one morning after he had washed the breakfast dishes, he happened to pick up a pinch. In the bright sunlight he saw with microscopic clarity the infinitesimal shapes and colors, the monstrous and miraculous complexity of that single thimbleful of sand. In that instant the world about him took on a new, great, and terrifying meaning. Every stone, every enormous boulder fitted into a close-knit unity similar to the one in his sweaty palm. For the first time he saw their own queer and individual shapes, their subtle colors, knew their textures, felt their weight, their strain and stress. It was is if in one instant the whole mountain had become alive and known.[20]

This startling revelation, so contrary to everything the boy had been taught about innate matter, was a central event in Frank's personal and creative life.

It becomes a central thesis in much of his writing. I find it interesting that in this most important scene he uses the third person "he," as if he were not writing about himself, but witnessing the experience of another. Yet it is clear from the content of the story that he is writing about himself, recalling his own childhood experience. Perhaps his vision here is so intense, so central to the core of his personal and creative life, he needed to step back, to distance himself from what is clearly a mystical experience.

Certainly the boy is the father of the man here. Frank never forgot what he learned, nor where he learned it, high on Pike's Peak. In the preface to the 1974 edition of *The Colorado*, he writes that "[all Mother Earth's] children are alive — the living stones, the great breathing mountains, plants and trees, as well as birds and animals and man."[21] Much later in *Mountain Dialogues* he writes that it is from the mountains, "the high places that saints, prophets, and law givers throughout the world have brought down spiritual teachings which have enriched civilizations."[22] Perhaps he should have included boys, too.

Finally, I don't want to leave the impression that Frank's awareness of the mountains was only emotional or spiritual. He knew a great deal about mountain ecology. He acquired this knowledge through the years by close observation and careful study. I think an important reason we enjoy Frank's nature descriptions so much is because they are not vague mumblings about beauty, serenity, or majesty. Rather, they are specific and detailed. Let me give you some examples, the first from *The Colorado*. The scene is of a pack trip he was taking in the Rockies.

> We started out one warm morning in early September. Burro and rabbit brush scraped our stirrups. Chokecherry bushes and hedges of wild plum were loaded with fruit. Soon the air became edged with the sharp clean smell of sage. There rose a low dark growth of piñon, juniper and Rocky Mountain red cedar.[23]

Later on the same trip, he points out that they were climbing through "the Upper Sonoran, Transition, Canadian, and Hudsonian plant zones, we had reached timberline, the boundary of High Country, whose frozen tundra duplicated that of the Arctic."[24]

In addition to his awareness of botany, his knowledge of mountain geology is impressive, especially mining geology. Here is a passage from *Pike's Peak*:

During the great eruption a mass of volcanic material had burst through the granite in aqueo-igneous condition. Cooling, solidification, and contraction followed, resulting in the formation of fissures. Hot water ascended with great velocity from the depths of volcano, and nearing the surface spread slowly through the fissures. As it stagnated, deposition and chemical action changed the composition of the solution and gold ore was precipitated. The principle volcanic rock was andesite breccia, more commonly known as porphyry from its deep purple color.[25]

Now we know where purple mountain majesty comes from. Katherine Lee Bates was standing on top of Pike's Peak when the idea of "America the Beautiful" came to her. Frank was incapable "of purple mountain's majesty." Too vague and misty. He gives us details that add depth and perspective to his descriptions of the mountains; at the same time they balance his mysticism.

Well, this was a great deal of work to prove one student was a good reader of Frank's books. I don't even know where the rascal is today. Of course, he's a grown man now. I hope he's climbing a mountain. But if he ever reads this, he'll remember, and maybe I'll hear from him. I thank Barbara Waters for the honor of being a part of this celebration. I would also like to thank her for all she meant to Frank, the man and the writer, past, present, and future. I close with a favorite passage from *Mountain Dialogues*. It seems appropriate on this day and at this place.

> Here I stand, sniffing the early morning breeze and spying out the vast landscape like an old coyote, as if to assure myself I am in the center flow of its invisible, magnetic currents. To the sun, and to the two oppositely polarized peaks, El Cuchillo and the Sacred Mountain, I offer my morning prayers. Then, letting the bright warming rays of the sun engulf me, I give myself up to a thoughtless silence.[26]

May Frank's Shining Mountains haunt you forever, as they do me.

IV.
CRITICAL OVERVIEWS

John Nizalowski
Frank Waters:
Prophet of the Sixth World Consciousness

In 1950, a little-known author living and working deep in America's southwestern hinterlands dared to challenge the established cultural paradigms of a nation still euphoric from its Second World War triumphs. The author, Frank Waters, had published eight novels and two works of nonfiction set mostly in the American Southwest and Mexico. The most successful of these, *The Man Who Killed the Deer*, is a novel about a young Pueblo Indian torn by the conflict between his Euroamerican education and his Pueblo traditions. While reviewers praised the book, its readership at the time was slight, due partly to its remote setting and to its appearance in 1942, when America's gaze turned outward to a world in crisis rather than inward to its own social contradictions and alienated races.

By 1950, when Waters voiced his challenge to American culture in *Masked Gods*, a study of Pueblo and Navajo ceremonialism, most critics and readers had consigned its author to the dust bin of regionalism. However, Waters did not let this unjustified image deter him from making important and controversial philosophical observations in *Masked Gods*. An initiate to the secrets of both Pueblo kiva rites and the technology of nuclear weaponry, he possessed the foresight and wisdom to proclaim from his small adobe home

north of Taos, New Mexico, that Western civilization had essentially reached
its end:

> Thus the wheel has turned full circle. The introversive city-
> states of the Pueblos, like the ancient civilizations of the Maya,
> Aztecs and Incas, have given way to the rationally extroverted
> civilization of Euro-America. And we in turn have reached
> the summit of our mechanistic-material-mental advance. Like
> Indo-America, Euro-America has completed this phase of its
> destiny.
>
> The struggle is over. We each have died a death whose
> causes were inherent in our very natures from the beginning.
> A rebirth is necessary.
>
> To what? And how? (402)[1]

A half century later, this stance has become widely accepted — at least in
scholarly circles — as the cracks in Euroamerican social and cultural structures
have grown. However, we still ponder Waters' questions: What is the direction of our metamorphosis? How will it come about?

In *Masked Gods*, Waters argues that returning to a pre-Enlightenment
past is not an answer to these questions, a belief he expresses through another
challenge, this one to a major literary figure who lived in Taos a decade before
Waters — D. H. Lawrence. While appreciating Lawrence's stylistic genius,
Waters deeply questions his understanding of American Indian philosophy
and mysticism, finding it incomplete and ultimately dangerous. Waters fires
his sharpest attacks at *The Plumed Serpent* (1926), Lawrence's portrayal of
a fictional uprising against Mexico's Catholic- and European-centered so-
cial-political structure. The revolution's leader is Don Ramon, an upper-class,
Columbia-educated adventurer who revives the faith in Quetzalcoatl, the
Plumed Serpent of Mesoamerican myth. This faith then becomes the political
and cultural heart of a transformed Mexico returned to its deep Indian past.

The problem, according to Waters, is that this kind of regressive transformation results in only violence and terror. It is clearly not a remedy for
Western civilization's crisis of stifling materialism and sterility. Waters finds
close parallels between Don Ramon and Adolf Hitler. While Ramon appeals
to Indian blood identity and Aztec myth, Hitler appealed to Aryan purity and
Teutonic legends. Thus Waters concludes, "There was only one thing wrong

with Lawrence's evocation. He did not know enough about Indian ceremonialism. It would have taught him that the Road of Life is a one-way road. No,
we cannot minimize the tragic falsity of the Lawrencian cult which urges us,
even individually, to regress to the impulses of instinct" (408).

Instead, Waters proposes that our cultural rebirth will come by moving
forward along the Indian Path of Life. In *Masked Gods*, Waters evokes Jungian
psychology to explain how a crisis acts as a crucible, pushing an individual to
discover in his or her collective unconscious the reconciling archetypal symbol
that will heal the illusory duality between instinct and rationality, thus solving
the crisis. Waters calls this moment an Emergence, after the Pueblo and Navajo
belief in humanity's Emergence along the Path of Life into four successive
worlds — five worlds in Aztec belief — each one more advanced in consciousness. For the Hopi, humanity is on the verge of entering the Fifth World; for
the Aztec, it is the Sixth World. The Hopi and Aztec Seventh world will be the
climax of humanity's ascension, for then we will join with the Sun, the Creator.

Waters explains that just as with an individual, the entire human species
can experience a planetary crisis followed by a unified Emergence:

> The problem of humanity at various stages of its development
> is the same as for the individual during his growth to maturity:
> relief from the ruthless tyranny of the instincts, or from the
> exclusive dominion of the conscious ego. And in the past such
> reconciling symbols have arisen from the collective unconscious
> of mankind to lead whole races, nations, and civilizations in
> great bursts of creative energy to another Emergence, a new
> stage of consciousness. (410)

Waters' belief in this global transformation — or, in accordance to Pueblo
mythology, an Emergence — is a thread that runs throughout most of the
twenty-five books of his six-decade literary career (two more books were published posthumously). Waters conceived of an Emergence as a unifying of the
great dualities — male and female, Occident and Orient, Euroamerican and
American Indian, rational and instinctive, material and spiritual — combined
with a deep understanding of the interconnection of humans with nature and
a fusion of ancient and modern wisdom. When enough individuals have integrated these dualities, humanity will move higher in its evolutionary journey
toward universal enlightenment.

As Alexander Blackburn states in his study of Waters' visionary novels: "By contrast with writers of his own generation, Waters may be seriously considered as the twentieth-century American writer who in searching the meaning of his experience through the mode of mythic consciousness has reconciled the dualities of male and female awareness, reason and intuition, and has come upon a world view that is tantamount to an affirmation of faith" (5).[2]

The roots of Waters' faith reside in his mixed Euroamerican and American Indian ancestry. On his Anglo maternal side, his grandfather, Joseph Dozier, a hard-rock miner and a Colorado Springs pioneer, provided Waters with an appreciation for technical ingenuity and knowledge, which would lead Waters to become an engineer for Bell Telephone in the 1920s and an information specialist for the Atomic Energy Commission in the 1950s. On the other hand, his father, who was probably part Cheyenne, had embraced an American Indian vision of life, and from him Waters gained a deep love for the earth and American Indian spirituality. As Thomas J. Lyon notes, "Waters' mother and father came, then, from different worlds; and, in a very real sense, it has been the life quest of their son to unite those worlds. . . . When Waters talks of syncretism, it is from the inside" (17).[3]

Waters found a way to merge the dual aspects of his Anglo and American Indian soul when he learned of the Mesoamerican concept of Emergence. This mythic idea would guide him throughout his life (Blackburn 138).

The Navajo and Pueblo believe in a succession of worlds. Each world has suffered destruction when its inhabitants, becoming greedy and imbalanced, lose their connection with the Sun Father. These worlds exist in a rising succession, layers in a psychic universe. As the survivors of each world climb to the next, they also climb higher in consciousness and spiritual development, thereby furthering humanity's evolution. Waters realized that this Emergence myth has a personal dimension, for each of us ascends through levels of awareness as we discover the connections between spirit and matter and reach for total integration with the universe. And there are those rare individuals, like Walt Whitman or Saint Francis, who even have a moment of ecstatic, enlightened revelation, a direct experience of their absolute harmony with the universe.

Waters experienced such a moment when lightning struck a hot springs cave he was soaking in while he was in Valle Grande in the Jémez Mountains of New Mexico (2).[4] Waters "transplants" this awakening to the Pike's Peak foothills in Colorado Springs in *The Dust Within the Rock* (1940) through the experiences of March Cable, the novel's autobiographical character:

> At that moment it happened. It was as if that flash of lightning had gone through him. He felt like a flame, as if lit up from within. And all about him remained this brilliant and indestructible illumination. In a moment it passed. He heaved up from the pool, flung himself upon the rock, weeping.
>
> He was not sad or frightened. He was cleansed, fused, made whole, happy and joyously alive. It was as though he had passed, in one moment, through a resurrection of the spirit. . . .
>
> And so he stood there high above the world of men, in pride and humility, and with a compassionate love for all that moved and breathed . . . (326)[5]

This vision's unifying power did much to heal Waters' torn soul, and he began to see in his blood dilemma a new definition of American identity that combined the strengths and deep perceptions of both Indian and European cultures. A similar, though less pyrotechnic, moment of healing occurs in the revised version of *The Dust Within the Rock* that appears in the 1971 single volume edition of the *Pike's Peak* trilogy. As March Cable, now in his mid-20s, stands before the graves of his Euroamerican grandfather and his American Indian father, he hears a voice on the wind proclaim that the grandfather has turned into the granite he mined for gold and that the father has returned to the adobe earth from which he came: "And now they both lie before you, intermingled, even as the rising plains merge into the rocky mountains. . . . What is adobe and what is granite but the mingled flesh of all flesh, the earth eternal?" (741).[6] Thus, March Cable, as did Frank Waters at a comparable age, perceives the European and Indian races merging in an earth-centered alchemical transmutation into a third, new race.

By the late 1930s, before writing *The Dust Within the Rock*, Waters had become deeply immersed in American Indian and Mesoamerican mythology, as well as Taoism and Tibetan Buddhism (Blackburn 138). These studies enriched his understanding of the Emergence concept, thus informing March Cable's mystical transformation with a broad cultural and metaphysical context. These same sources also inform Waters' next novel, *People of the Valley*.

In it Waters traces the life of Maria del Valle, a mestizo dwelling in a remote valley on the eastern slope of New Mexico's Sangre de Cristo Mountains.

Maria is the valley's archetypal mother, a goddess figure dispensing healing and wisdom. When she turns eighty, a dam threatens to bring rapid technological and social disruption to a locale that has remained essentially unchanged from the day the Mexican settlers first arrived. Maria sees the dam as a crow's shadow, a harbinger of imperialistic progress. Since it is not based on faith, its lack of soul will wipe out all its good intentions. "The dam too would cast a shadow. This misfortune of men who would lose their land would not stop it. It would flit across their lives with fear and suffering, anger and evil. All shadows of the shadow of the dam itself" (134).[7]

However, as Matthias Schubnell observes, Maria realizes she lives in an era of transition, and a day will arrive when "the machine age will generate its own faith, when the inner world of the spirit and the outer world are harmonized" (15).[8] This new faith — with its merging of an earth-centered culture with one based upon technology and rationality — finds a spokesperson in Don Eliseo, the valley's district judge, a man born to poor Mexican farmers who has attained a university education. He is one of the few characters whom Maria treats with deference. In describing Don Aliseo's wisdom, Maria evokes the dawn of a new world based upon the merging of intuition and rationality: "These Anglo-Americans . . . are ignorant of some things as we are ignorant of others. So do not condemn them unjustly. When we both see all, then there will be no difference between us. There is little now. The good judge, was he not a ragged little chamaco? Is he not respected now by the Anglos perhaps more than by us? Simply because his eyes, through learning, have seen both ways?" (*People of the Valley* 163).

Don Eliseo, who "sees both ways," understands that the dam is inevitable because it has emerged from what the Pueblo call the Road of Life, from humanity's own evolutionary spiral: "The dam cannot be stopped. . . . It is not a dam alone. It is new roads, new food and clothing, new customs to add to the old, education for all; it is the progress of the world which sweeps all nations, all valleys of men. No man can stop it, for it is of man himself" (164-165).

As Don Eliseo predicts, the dam is victorious. Maria finds another valley for those displaced by the dam, even higher and more remote than their current home, but like Moses she dies before the exodus to this "promised land." This new valley may simply be a last redoubt for Maria's earth-centered faith, a mere holding action before the "Maquina of progress" reaches it as well, sweeping it into the past. However, Schubnell finds in Maria's new valley the seeds of planetary change: "There is a danger in taking the novel's ending too literally, for the force of Waters' imagery suggests that the higher valley is not merely a geographic location, but a new plateau of human consciousness, where the present forces of obstruction will have been transcended" (17).

In Waters' next novel, *The Man Who Killed the Deer* (1942), the novel's protagonist, Martiniano, also faces the disruptive forces of Euroamerican "progress."[9] Martiniano is a member of La Oreja Pueblo, a fictionalized version of Taos Pueblo. He spends his youth in an "away school," one of the federally sponsored schools that for decades trained American Indian children to reject their own culture and acquire Euroamerican ways. Indian people called these institutions "away schools" because they were often hundreds of miles away from tribal lands, and each year the government forced a certain number of Indian children to attend them. Thus "away schools" created several generations of Indians severely alienated from their own people. Martiniano is one of them.

When Martiniano returns to the pueblo, he does not have a place in its intricate social structure because he has missed the all-important time of kiva training. Therefore, he has failed to become initiated in one of the pueblo's sacred societies and is, from a spiritual standpoint, not a fully mature Pueblo man. However, Martiniano also finds himself too Pueblo to fit into the Euroamerican world. Cut off from both societies, Martiniano is deeply bitter — a classic example of modern dislocation.

Yet Martiniano possesses the potential to attain the next world's fusion of Indian and Anglo ways. Martiniano's friend Palemon, who never left the pueblo and is therefore fully integrated into its life patterns, tries to explain this to Martiniano. Though Palemon lacks the abstract terms to do so, he shares a spiritual bond with Martiniano, an unspoken communion of heart and spirit, which Waters "translates" into text: "Forgive me, my friend. Do you see what you lack? Not a form of life, for there are three for you to choose from: our old ways, the white man's new ways, or your own which may be part of both or newer still. You lack only faith in one of them" (65). Palemon's explanation echoes Maria's declaration that the world will someday have its own faith and, with it, a more enlightened humanity.

Another friend of Martiniano's is Rudolfo Byers, an Anglo trading-post owner. He, too, responds to Martiniano's situation with silence, and his silence is also tantalizing with possibilities. Martiniano and Byers build a new room for the trading post, and as they carve a pine viga for the ceiling, Waters compares the two men's contrasting views of the pine log. Byers sees it as a dead object without consciousness, to be used however its owner deems fit; Martiniano believes the log possesses spirit and that one must pray for its permission before cutting it. Waters then reveals the moment's aching potential for a planetary Emergence: "The brotherhood of man! It will always be a dreary phrase, a futile hope, until each man, all men, realize that they themselves are but different reflections and insubstantial images of a greater invisible whole. . . . A means, a tongue, a bridge to span the wordless chasm that separates us all; it is the cry of every human heart. And Byers looked at Martiniano but neither spoke" (244).

Ultimately, like Maria's followers escaping to a higher valley to continue the old ways, Martiniano heals his crisis by returning to the traditional Pueblo pattern of life. However, when the people of La Oreja Pueblo win back their sacred Dawn Lake from the federal government — a decades-old demand paralleling the Taos Pueblo's struggle for the return of their sacred Blue Lake from National Forest holdings — Byers connects the victory with the transformation of all humanity: "But perhaps there would still be time, thought Byers, to learn from these people before they pass from this earth which was theirs and shall be all men's — the simple and monstrous truth of mankind's solidarity with all that breathes and does not breathe . . ." (261).

Alexander Blackburn proposes that Martiniano's Emergence from alienation to reconnection is a metaphor for every individual's Emergence, regardless of race. Blackburn states, "[T]he allegory of Emergence, formulated in Deer as the redeeming necessity of a return to the unconscious, creates a new sense of wonder out of the mystery that lies buried, apparently, in us all" (iii). Thomas J. Lyon goes one step further by asserting that Martiniano's Emergence is planetary in nature: "Martiniano was microcosmic; he reflected and manifested nothing less than our whole world, which in Waters' view is changing. The world and Martiniano are and were in a state of process . . ." (21)[10]

While Martiniano's Emergence may be a metaphor of universal awakening, Helen Chalmers of The Woman at Otowi Crossing is unambiguously a pioneer of the coming new world consciousness. Thirteen years in the writing,

The Woman at Otowi Crossing bears the influences of Waters' enriched experiences and expanded learning — his studies in Carl Jung and in quantum physics, his witnessing of nuclear weapon tests as an information specialist at Los Alamos, and his three years spent living on the Hopi Mesas researching their myth, ceremony, and history.

Waters based *The Woman at Otowi Crossing* on Edith Warner, who in the 1930s and 1940s owned a small teahouse where the road to Los Alamos crosses the Rio Grande. She befriended both the major physicists who patronized her teahouse and the people from nearby San Ildefonso Pueblo. Thus Warner was a unique link between the contemporary world of nuclear physics and the ancient world of Pueblo civilization, a living example of Waters' Emergence concept.

Helen Chalmers, Waters' fictional version of Edith Warner, has a spiritual awakening that closely parallels March Cable's in *The Dust Within the Rock*. In Chalmers' case, the discovery of a malignant breast tumor triggers the awakening. Chalmers' Emergence produces complementary pairs of visions. One pair confirms Pueblo mysticism — a dream of humanity's evolutionary journey through multiple worlds (60) and a waking revelation during which a flock of geese metamorphose into the plumed serpent, the Mesoamerican god Quetzalcoatl (124-125).[11]

The other visions are far more disturbing. The first, a waking dream, occurs when Chalmers' former lover, Jack Turner, kicks a mushroom in the canyons below Los Alamos. As Chalmers watches the shattered mushroom rise into the air, it expands into a vast cloud from which billions of poisonous spores bring death to the earth below (173). Then, mere days before the atomic bombing of Hiroshima, she dreams of a candle that detonates the world "in one brilliant apocalyptic burst of fire" (204).

The mushroom and candle are prescient symbols for the atomic and hydrogen bombs, and, as Frances M. Malpezzi notes, they connect Chalmers' spiritual Emergence with a world Emergence (109).[12] Just as cancer triggered Chalmers' transformation, atomic weaponry will inspire planetary metamorphosis: "What had happened to her had now been manifested in the outer world. Like her, mankind would suffer a period of fear and guilt. Then this would pass, and the world would face a new age with a new power to use for good" (*Otowi Crossing* 207).

Two events deepen Chalmers' connection with the Pueblo Emergence myth. The first is when Chalmers is on her deathbed and seven deer mysteriously appear to witness her passing. Blackburn notes that these seven deer correspond to the seven worlds of the Pueblo Emergence story (131). Then, in the novel's epilogue, an investigator of psychic phenomena named Mr. Meru examines Chalmers' Emergence journal. He proclaims her experience to be the makings of a true contemporary myth responding to the modern world's sterility: "We ourselves created it — we of a new age, desperately crying for a new faith or merely a new form that will model old truths to a useful purpose. Helen Chalmers affirms our mistrust of the neuter and negative materialism of our time" (313). As Malpezzi observes, Mount Meru is a sacred mountain in Buddhist and Hindu mythology, the world axis that is the center of faith, the connection between heaven and earth. Thus Mr. Meru's pronouncements are the deepest possible validation of Chalmers' mystical experiences, and an indication that, in Malpezzi's words, "Helen's inner journey is a representative one, the evolutionary road of every individual" (29).[13]

Therefore, Waters has created in Helen Chalmers a guide for personal change and planetary evolution. Blackburn declares, "By counterpointing the myth of the [atomic bomb] Project and the myth of the Woman at Otowi Crossing and unifying these in the myth of Emergence, Waters shapes for those who can respond to it a vision for the future, in which world crisis is resolved on a higher plane of at-one-ment with the cosmos" (115).

Many of Waters' major nonfiction works have examined this Emergence theme as well, but with a key difference. Whereas novels like *People of the Valley* and *The Man Who Killed the Deer* develop the Emergence myth and its connection to humanity through imaginative constructs, Waters' nonfiction develops the concept from the actual heart of his own experiences. In *The Colorado*, for example, Waters examines the Colorado River basin as a crucible where the cultural collision between the Euroamerican and American Indian worlds produces a new and unique people shaped by the American earth and sharing in both viewpoints — a continentwide version of March Cable's revelation of racial unity as he stood before the graves of his grandfather and father (267-268).[14]

As noted, *Masked Gods* was Waters' first major declaration of his Emergence belief. In it he states that the book's purpose is to discover the direction of our planetary evolution:

We are concerned with the subjective record of the evolutionary development of man through successive, well-defined
stages. Through these stages each individual, each race and
civilization, evolves alike. At each stage, tremendous conflicts
take place. In the individual it is the inner conflict between
instinct and ego. Between the Indians and the Anglos, as races
and cultures, it has been the same basic psychological conflict
objectified and extroverted on the field of war, economics, and
politics. (160)

A new element that enters Waters' Emergence concept in *Masked Gods* is the
warning that humanity cannot go back in its spiritual and evolutionary development. To return to a preindustrial culture, to turn away from our outward
spiral life path, will lead only to chaos and self-destruction, but to remain in
our present extreme materialism will result in psychic and ecological death.
Waters' answer is to move forward and merge European ego-driven materialism and American Indian instinctive spirituality in a Jungian symbol of reconciliation. For Waters, humanity will find this potent symbol by combining
quantum physics, American Indian ceremonialism, Jungian psychology, and
Tibetan metaphysics in a syncretic triumph of spirit and heart.

In *Mexico Mystique: The Coming Sixth World of Consciousness,* Waters
looked to the esoteric wisdom of ancient Mesoamerican civilizations — the
Mayan, Toltec, and Aztec — to further elaborate his Emergence concept.
Probably Waters' most difficult and controversial book, *Mexico Mystique* examines the end of the current 5,200-year Mayan Great Cycle on December 24,
2011. While some scholars and mystics believe this end will bring planetary
cataclysm, Waters, with his deep-seated faith in Emergence, gives a hopeful
interpretation to Mesoamerican apocalyptic myths, finding in them archetypal
symbols for a rapid transformation of consciousness (282).[15]

These ideas on the connection between humanity and the cosmos are
summed up in the collection of essays, *Mountain Dialogues,* which begins with
a child holding a fistful of earth and asking Waters, "How does this dirt make
our garden grow?" (3).[16] From here, Waters launches into a voyage that ranges from the beauty and mythology of his Taos neighborhood to a discussion
of Jung, Bhagavan Sri Maharshi, Plains Indian metaphysics, and humanity's
coming Emergence. But clearly Waters' most personal examination of the

Emergence concept occurs in *Pumpkin Seed Point*, an account of the three years he spent on the Hopi Mesas researching *Book of the Hopi*, a landmark study of Hopi myth, ceremony, and history. Thomas J. Lyon notes the central place of *Pumpkin Seed Point* in the body of Waters' work: "In its totality, this short but complex book is perhaps meant to stand as a kind of morning star. A summation of Frank Waters' inward journey, it contains a declaration of what he has found" (*Frank Waters* 67).

The text opens with a description of Waters walking to his Hopi Mesa home at Pumpkin Seed Point during a bitterly cold winter night. All is dark in the village of New Oraibi, the only light coming from the feeble glow of a single bulb behind the trading post's barred windows. For Waters, this light becomes a metaphor of his quest for enlightenment among the Hopis, the enlightenment all humanity is striving for, consciously or unconsciously, in order to make the transition into the next world paradigm (13).[17] As in *Masked Gods*, Waters proposes that humanity is at a critical junction in history when it must rise to a higher consciousness by reconciling the duality of instinct and reason.

In *Pumpkin Seed Point*, Waters dramatizes the necessity of unifying this duality with his descent into Mexico's Barranca del Cobre, a vast network of canyons deeper and more extensive than the Grand Canyon. These canyons remain largely unexplored except by the Tarahumara Indians who live there, and to this day few non-Indians have attained Barranca del Cobre's floor.

What Waters discovered there was a powerful symbol of the unconscious and of the Mother Goddess: "The looming cliffs blotted out the sun, and the world suddenly became a shadowy womb-cavern deep in the immortal, maternal earth" (152). When a crescent moon appears above the canyon's rim, Waters has a revelatory moment that confirms the need to transcend the instinctive level while never losing touch with it: "For consciousness, having once broken free from the maternal unconscious, cannot sink back defeated into the maw of its devouring mother. It must continue to climb forward to a higher level. But man cannot cut himself off from the one great pool of life without losing all he has gained" (153). How are we to maintain this connection between our higher consciousness and our deep unconscious memory? Waters calls on us to keep listening to our interior world — the world of myth and the collective unconscious — which he believes ultimately shapes history and culture (103). For the people of the Western Hemisphere, that myth is largely Indian.

To illustrate, Waters relates the story of a Catholic church in the far mountains of Michoacan. The local Indians attended this church in unusually high numbers and with an uncharacteristic outpouring of devotion, a situation that mystified the parish priest until an earthquake toppled the Catholic altar to reveal an Aztec statue underneath. As Waters writes, "[T]he altar signifies a religion made rationally conscious, under which lies the mythological content of the unconscious, that one great pool of life and time" (108).

This, for Waters, is the meaning of the Hopi legend of the Pahana, the lost white brother who will someday return to the Hopi with the missing piece of their sacred tablet that grants them sovereignty over the Hopi Mesas. For the Hopi, when the Pahana returns, we will be ushered into the coming Fifth World transformation. For Waters, the Pahana represents, in the words of Shawnee Chief Tecumseh, "the Being within, communing with the past ages" (167). The Pahana is therefore every Euroamerican transformed by the "psychic and even anatomical changes that the secret forces of the land have worked upon us." According to Waters, these changes are "slowly integrating tribes, races and nations the world over" (171).

Waters was silent on the exact social, political, and cultural details of this new age, as Tom Tarbet discovered in a 1973 interview: "Well, what exactly lies ahead — as far as actual living conditions — will take a better man than me to even make a guess" (59).[18] In a truly existential manner, Waters has left the exact outlines of the future to each of us who will dwell in it. As he states in *Pumpkin Seed Point*, "The mass is made up of individuals and it is in the individual, both red and white, where the conflict [of duality] must be resolved" (xii).

Still, Waters' legacy is clear. Vine Deloria, Jr., the author of *God is Red*, describes Waters as "a delightful combination of two of our most cherished archetypal masculine figures: the prophet and the explorer" (170-171).[19] Novelist Rudolfo Anaya also believes Waters is a prophet vital to our era, stating, "We are living at the end of an age, and we look desperately around for men like Frank Waters to point the way into a new cycle of time" (36).[20]

From the crisis of his own troubled soul, torn between the American Indian and Anglo bloodlines of his father and mother, Waters discovered a vision of wholeness, a unity of opposites, both racial and metaphysical. From this awakening, he went on to write twenty-five books that charted a way, a Path of Life, for the rest of us to follow. In essence, Waters brought the Pueblo and Navajo myth of Emergence to the rest of humanity to guide us in our difficult global transition. As Alexander Blackburn states, "Waters' quest through the dimensions of the [Mesoamerican] heartland has yielded a creative mythology, Emergence, and this myth is the heartland's answer to wasteland" (3).

Matthias Schubnell
Toward the Sixth World: Frank Waters and the New Environmental Consciousness

Frank Waters' concern for an appropriate relationship between people and their environment has dominated much of his writing. Given our present global ecologic crisis, his thoughts on this issue become increasingly relevant. Even though Waters has consistently attacked the rapacity and materialism of Western culture from the vantage point of Native American and Mexican American land ethics, he, until recently, has received little attention for his contributions as an environmental thinker. In his novels *People of the Valley* and *The Man Who Killed the Deer*, Waters celebrates the reciprocal relationship between people who have tenure in the land and the natural world around them. While both works suggest that the destructive onslaught of the industrial, technological world cannot be stemmed, Waters already indicates in these texts that a fundamental change in attitude is not only necessary if the human species is to survive, but indeed possible.

Forty years after *People of the Valley*, Waters laid out in *Mountain Dialogues* his detailed hypothesis that humanity is on the verge of an evolutionary leap to a new environmental consciousness. This vision places Waters at the forefront of contemporary environmental thought, and specifically in the company of Thomas Berry, a major figure in the current ecologic debate, who articulates ideas essentially akin to those of Waters in his recent work, *The Dream of the Earth* (1988). Both men believe that if we listen to the earth itself, we shall escape the looming destruction of our planet. If we allow ourselves to be guided by the powerful influences of our planet, indeed of the cosmos at large, we shall enter a new world where all entities are fully integrated and balanced. To illustrate this notion, Waters draws on ancient Native American thought. According to the Hopis and Mayas, these tribes have ascended through successive underground worlds — the Hopi recall four, the Maya five — to their present homes. If we can learn from them to exist in physical and spiritual harmony with the rest of creation, Waters foresees the possibility that we shall have a place in the "coming Sixth World of Consciousness" (*Mountain Dialogues* 134), predicted in the Mayan prophecies.

In *People of the Valley* Waters reveals the hidden costs of progress and technological advancement by bringing into conflict a traditional earthbound, oral community with the emissaries of a modern, bureaucratic, industrialized society. The construction of the dam emerges as a symbol of divisiveness: it separates people from their land, divides them against each other, undermines timeless traditions which celebrate the people's connectedness to natural cycles, and ultimately forces the remnants of the uprooted community into deeper isolation in a more remote valley. Waters' own comment in the "Water" chapter of *Mountain Dialogues* sums up the essence of this early novel: " . . . it seems obvious that by damming, straightening, and contaminating rivers, as well as despoiling the land and polluting the air, we are destroying the vital coherence of the whole circular ecosystem of nature *both outside and within us*" (63; italics added). What is significant here is Waters' contention that we cannot damage the environment without damaging ourselves, physically and spiritually.

The novel's protagonist, Maria del Valle, personifies the geography that has shaped her and her ancestors. Part Indian, she is keenly aware of the valley's spirit of place. Her personal development mirrors the changes in the valley, and her opposition to the construction of the dam is as much a protest against the dispossession of people and the disruption of the ecology as it is an act of self-preservation. For it is the internal, spiritual damage the technological assault is threatening to bring upon her community which motivates Maria to fight against it. "There is no philosophy of value," she reflects, "which would deny the earth below" (135). The damming of the water, then, is not only an unacceptable interference in nature's fragile web of life and an attempt to exploit nature's resources while eliminating her destructive potential, but also a threat to Maria's and her people's identities which rest on their faith in nature's integrity and order.

Early in the novel, when the community considers the proposed land sale and construction plan, one unidentified voice asserts, "No doubt it is wrong to stop [the floods]" (5). This pronouncement, made in full knowledge of the local river's destructiveness and the substantial property payments offered by the developers to build "a dam de checks!" (5), reflects the deeply held belief that nature's workings should remain inviolate, that a mysterious, intuitively sensed spiritual force in nature protects those who protect the land. The recurrent metaphor for this intimate physical and spiritual nexus between people and their environment is "the timeless and changeless pulse" (18) emanating from the heart of the universe. This metaphor, which is also central to Waters' next novel, *The Man Who Killed the Deer*, signifies an all-pervasive life force.

Maria is particularly susceptible to its influence as she awaits the birth of her first child:

> The pulse beats throbbed through [Maria] and through the
> earth below, they shook the mountains and the evening star
> in its socket above. It was her time and another's too, and all
> to which they were bound in unbroken sequence by the one
> pulsing beat which echoes dreamily and powerfully through the
> earth of the flesh and the flesh of the earth alike. (25)

In contrast, Waters suggests, modern civilization is no longer attuned to this rhythm and displaces those societies which still are. In its insistence on rationality and its equation of progress with growing material well-being, Western culture is uncoupling itself from the spiritual dimension of the universe, which, according to Waters, has guided us through the course of evolution.

In *People of the Valley*, then, Waters questions the idea of progress by examining its relation to the imperatives of ecological responsibilities. It is this aspect of the novel which continues to make a fresh contribution to the ongoing environmental debate. Starting with the premise that progress is inevitable, Waters examines the options of those who choose not to be a party to it. Early in the novel, Maria flees in terror from the sounds of a music box, a technical wonder she has never heard before. She runs away because "she had not yet learned that there are things one cannot escape" (37). Later, however, she learns that retreating in a spirit of solidarity with likeminded people can preserve dignity and integrity. In her reply to Judge Don Eliseo, who tries to talk Maria out of her opposition to the dam, the old woman agrees that the sweep of progress cannot be dropped and adds:

> I do not oppose the dam, new customs, a new vision of life; I oppose nothing. But I uphold the old ways because they are good too. I awaken in men their love for their land for they are a people of the land. It is their faith. And so I place that faith above all the lesser benefits they might derive from that which would oppose it. (166)

Progress at the expense of Maria's faith in the mystery of nature is unacceptable, and any reconciliation between the two appears to be still a long way off.

Nevertheless, Maria offers the possibility of such a reconciliation, which anticipates the idea of a new ecologic consciousness that Waters spells out in greater detail in more recent writings and interviews. Maria's belief that the machine age is ultimately doomed unless it can generate a faith of its own, and her trust in a unified vision of life, symbolized by the mystical white stone, manifest an early version of Waters' conviction that our current world must undergo radical changes before mankind can evolve to a higher plateau, the sixth world of Mayan philosophy.

In one of the central passages of the novel, Maria refers to water not only as a symbol of the life force, but also as a metaphor for man's faith "in the one living mystery of everflowing life . . . [which] must be renewed as life itself is ever renewed" (177). Any civilization which cuts itself off from this process of renewal is ultimately doomed:

> This is the meaning of the dam, that it would obstruct the free flow of faith which renews and refreshes life and gives it its only meaning. It is self-enclosing. It means stagnation. It means death.
>
> Faith is not to be dammed. It is not to be measured and meted out when timely. It must be free to penetrate every cell

and germ of the whole. For it is the obstructed whole that
finally bursts the dam, rings destruction and misery, swaps the
temporal benefits of the past (177).

This, however, is not to say that there may not come a time when the machine
age will generate its own faith, when the inner world of the spirit and the outer, material world are harmonized. Having conceded defeat to the technological age which supersedes the age of the land, Maria affirms not only a sense
of personal liberation, but also her conviction that the technological era will
become acceptable in due course: "But the time of the Maquina has *yet* no
faith, and so we must refuse it. . . . [The dam] has no faith behind it to give it
meaning. And so we must accept our own time which has a faith *until the new
time has also given rise to a faith,* and you are ready for it" (184; italics added).
This implies, of course, that Maria's defeat is only temporary. Hers is the long
outwaiting of a period leading to a new age of integration between land and
machine.

   The image of the "great white stone" (150), the symbol of life, also con-
jures up a time when we shall have arrived at a unified vision of reality. Waters'
point here is that in order to comprehend reality in its totality, we have to
view it from every conceivable angle and from great distance:

   Then you see it: how it has many different sides and shapes
   and patterns, some smooth, some rough, but still the one great
   white stone: how all these sides merge into one another, in-
   distinguishable: the past into the present, the present into the
   future, the future again into the past. (159)

Alas, the civilization which encroaches on Maria and the people of the valley
is still far from embracing this vision of integration, and instead pursues its
policy of cultural and environmental hegemony. Therefore, Maria must face
her final tasks of preparing the remnants of her traditional community, under
the guidance of her grand-daughter, Piedad, for their withdrawal to a higher,
more remote valley, and of ensuring that her personal pledge never to see this
new dam is realized.

   The imagery surrounding both these concluding actions is further evidence that the novel does not end on a note of defeat, but rather of hope for
the future, however uncertain it may be. As Piedad and her followers prepare

for their departure to the new valley, Maria admonishes them to keep faith in the enduring universe. As Thomas J. Lyon points out, the passage in which Maria bids farewell to the travelers anticipates her own impending departure from life and return to the earth (103):

> The sun poked through the fir above her and shone on hair gray and rumpled as the dead moss she leaned against. Her dirty black rebozo seemed streaked and rusty as the oxidized iron in the rock. She wiggled a bare toe in the green grass. A beetle crawled across her leg. A robin chirped. (196)

These images suggest that Maria's death takes the form of a transformation, a translation back into the non-human manifestations of nature.

Equally telling are the sun images at the end of the novel. The description of the final sunset before Maria's death appears to signify finality, without the promise for a rekindling of life's flame.

> The sun was sinking behind the Sangre de Cristo. The snow-capped picachos were red as blood. This blood was ebbing swiftly. The peaks grew anemic; a slow pallor beclouded their faces. Then suddenly a strange effulgence lighted up the dusk — a light that came from nowhere, but as if from within, like a brief resurgence of life flickering up in a dying candle. (199)

But when Waters allows a final glimpse of the dying woman, he reassures us that the values she stands for will prevail, that they are in fact already on their way to the new valley, stored safely on the wagon which rolls on toward life, if only squeakingly (198). In the novel's closing scene, Waters affirms his trust in the community's survival by focusing on Maria's "steadily gleaming eyes that burned through time with a faith which could not be dammed, and with a gaze which saw neither the darkness of the day nor the brightness of the morrow, but behind these illusions the enduring reality that makes of one sunset a prelude to a sunrise brighter still" (201). Maria makes good on her promise never to see the dam, but this victory is more than a personal evasion of the forces of progress, just as the community's exodus to higher ground in advance of the machine age is more than a "pathetic" (103) spectacle, as Lyon puts it. There is a danger in taking the novel's ending too literally, for the force of Waters' imagery suggests that the higher valley is not merely a geographic location, but a new plateau of human consciousness, where the present forces of obstruction will have been transcended.

This idea has been expounded in several of Waters' more recent nonfictional contributions to our environmental debate. In an interview with Charles L. Adams, Waters repeatedly expressed his pessimism about the future of Western civilization. At the same time he contends that we have reached a crucial evolutionary threshold leading to a new level of consciousness where the material and the spiritual aspects of the universe coexist in harmony:

> . . . as the Hopis say, I think that we are already beginning our emergence to a new world. I am not really too pessimistic. . . . But . . . to attain that feeling of unity, of solidarity, we must recognize our oneness with all nature. Not only with all of mankind, but with the plant and the vegetable and the animal kingdoms, with the earth itself, and with the planetary bodies which exert an influence on us too. ("Frank Waters: Interview by Charles Adams" 25)

In order to cross this threshold we need to rediscover our spiritual links to the cosmos, a task for which we must rely on the power of intuition rather than reason. Waters points, as a viable model, to the ceremonies of the Rio Grande Pueblos which "express the intuitive recognition that everything in nature possesses a spiritual essence as well as material form, and all is interconnected in one vast body of universal life. We cannot needlessly destroy one part without injuring ourselves and disrupting the harmonious whole" ("This Sacred Land" 44).

Perhaps the most provocative aspect of Waters' theory is that the evolution of the human species is determined by the earth itself: ". . . we must believe that the living earth itself was endowed with a basic threshold of consciousness by the universal consciousness to ever higher levels, being necessary accompaniments to the geological states of the earth" (*Mountain Dialogues* 6). Waters uses C. G. Jung's concept of the collective unconscious as an analogy to the rise of a universal consciousness. Just as archetypes emerge from the unconscious to become accessible to human awareness, so the planetary consciousness has evolved to find its highest articulation in the human mind

(*Mountain Dialogues* 6). Having postulated the theory that evolution has both a material and a spiritual component, Waters concludes his considerations by pointing to the mutual dependence of earth and the human species for survival:

> What makes the question [of the earth's destiny] significant is that its answer may lie beyond the context of life on this planet, even beyond our comprehension. If so, our earth is but striving through mankind, its highest level of consciousness yet developed, to comprehend the purpose of its role in the universal order of creation. *The earth is as dependent upon us as we are upon it.* (*Mountain Dialogues* 6; italics added)

These ideas, formulated before 1981, are virtually identical to those in Thomas Berry's environmental philosophy, published in 1988 in his widely read book, *The Dream of the Earth*. While the following summary of Berry's central ideas does not suggest any dependence — Berry, incidentally, makes no mention of Waters — it does illustrate how advanced Waters' ideas have been in view of recent environmental thinking. Like Waters, Berry calls for a new, "affective relationship" (3) to the earth, a reawakening to the "divine presence" (8) in the cosmos. Berry also believes that "the human is . . . a mode of being of the universe as well as a distinctive being in the universe," an idea he refers to as the "anthropic principle" (16). In our current situation, the channels of communication between the greater whole and the individual have been obstructed. Berry calls for the reversal of this "autistic situation" (16) and the beginning of a new "entrancement with the natural world" (17). Like Waters, Berry looks to the Native Americans for guidance, pointing especially to their awe of the sacred in the natural order (184) and their close contact to the collective unconscious (186). In order to advance to a higher order of consciousness, we first need to step back and salvage the wisdom of our tribal past. We need to develop "the shamanistic personality" (211) which assures an intimate relationship to our spontaneities within and our connectedness to the universe.

Perhaps most remarkable is Waters' and Berry's agreement that the human species is on the verge of an evolutionary leap. Berry sees the current crisis as a transition from a crumbling industrial economy and a polluted environment to a new existence integrated into a cosmic scheme (31). It is a "groping phase" (47) in which we learn to reattune ourselves to the "deep spontaneities, . . . the psychic energies deep in the very structure of reality itself" (48). These energies are, according to Berry, integral to our genetic coding and can be tapped through the unconscious. The antagonism between genetic and cultural coding in the industrial phase of human history has led us to the brink of disaster, because our industrial coding and the creation of an anthropocentric society violate what Berry calls "the primary law of the universe, the law of the integrity of the universe" (202). Berry adds that "to remain viable a species must establish a niche for itself that is beneficial both for itself and for the surrounding community" (208). Only by realigning our genetic and cultural coding can we hope to arrive at the new earth-consciousness and build a biocentric society.

Berry also concurs with Waters when he insists that this consciousness will be the outcome of "an intuitive, non-rational process" (211), an "inscendence" (208) into the unconscious in order to read the blueprint for survival, which is part of our genetic coding. He is confident that the earth will protect itself through us: "The earth . . . seems now to be entering a phase of conscious decision through its human expression. This is the ultimate daring venture for the earth, this confiding its destiny to human decision. . . ." (19). Berry echoes here Waters' contention that "our earth is but striving through mankind, its highest level of consciousness yet developed, to comprehend the purpose of its role in a universal order of creation," and both would agree that in our struggle to stabilize the precarious condition of our planet, "the earth is as dependent on us as we are upon it" (*Mountain Dialogues* 6).

Clearly, Frank Waters' concern for the land and his philosophy of an integrated, earth-conscious existence are central aspects of his work, expressed over a period of more than half a century. They constitute major contributions to our environmental debate, and given the increasing urgency to find solutions to the present ecologic crisis, they deserve a much larger audience. After all, Frank Waters may well be one of Thomas Berry's shamanistic voices who can lead us toward a new existence in the sixth world.

Vine Deloria, Jr.
Reflections from a Dusty Road:
Frank Waters, Time, and the Indians

Too many topics suggest themselves when one is asked to write a paper on Frank Waters. The breadth of his writing discourages any ordinary mortal from picking a theme and proclaiming it definitive. Thus it is with great trepidation that I undertake an examination of Frank's writings on Indians.

The books one most associates with him in this regard are *Masked Gods*, *Book of the Hopi*, and *Mexico Mystique*. All three are historical/philosophical presentations of the beliefs and practices of the Southwestern Indians. There is also his autobiographical *Pumpkin Seed Point*, the story of his years spent at Hopi. Finally, the early classic novel *The Man Who Killed the Deer* presents in narrative form many of the themes that appear in later writings. This body of work is a formidable corpus to confront; thus if some favorite theme is not mentioned, it is because I am unable to integrate everything into this short paper.

Upon examination of Frank's books, I find that separating them into fiction and nonfiction is useless. The novel contains as much philosophy and history as do the nonfiction books, and the latter are presented in an entertaining and informing narrative. There is no good way to step into Frank's literary tapestry and extricate a clear notion of what he felt and how he thought, for the weave is seamless. Frank is well-known in many intellectual circles today: literature, religion, western and Indian history. People in each field see entirely different things in his writings. Literary critics see the novels as containing probing, developing personalities and universal human conflict. Historians count the nonfiction books as major contributions to our understanding of the frontier experiences that made us what we are today. Religious thinkers rely on Frank's books for a clear and concise explanation of a major cultural tradition. From this complex web of insights about his ideas, I will examine his concept of time since it is key to his view of Indians.

After a quick rereading of Frank's major Indian works, it occurs to me that *The Man Who Killed the Deer* stands as his definitive book on Indians even though *Masked Gods, Book of the Hopi*, and *Mexico Mystique* provide an amazing amount of specific material about Indians. *Deer*, although a novel, is clearly philosophical and empirical in ways that many novels are not. Through reflective descriptions of the dilemmas in which the characters find themselves, we find our nuggets of understanding; and since we are seeking to understand how Frank understood time, it is well to lay some groundwork first and to glance at some related subjects.

Who were the Indians and why did people think they were different? Was it their colorful clothing and jewelry or the many ceremonials they performed? Was it simply that they were rural people? Or people who had come long before the Europeans and therefore had precedent as inhabitants of the area? In *Deer* we have a concise and insightful explanation. After he has paid the fine for Martiniano, the Indian trader Rodolfo Byers in his frustration describes the dilemma Indians pose for others:

> They couldn't be thought about intelligently. They had to be either dismissed or taken on their own ground. And their premises of life were based not on the rational, the reasoning, evaluating approach, but wholly on the instinctive and intuitive. Things came or they didn't; they didn't proceed logically from point to point. So you had to take them or leave them as they were in fact, not theory.[1]

At first blush this reflection appears to deal primarily with the difference in philosophy and epistemology between Indians and other people. How they understand the world. But isn't there something more involved here? The driving force in the novel is the relationship between Martiniano and the deer. Not simply the deer he has killed but the deer as an initiating presence in the small universe of Taos Pueblo. The deer seems to know far more than Martiniano about the deeper movement of cosmic process since its appearance, in many guises, provides the pivot around which events develop. The deer is the guiding spirit of the universe that leads everyone forward to seemingly predetermined realizations of the potential of their lives. It introduces us to those occasions when the specificity of our personal lives must join the larger whole in such a way that we are able to participate in creating the future.

The deer leads us back to ground zero, away from the anticipated turmoil of our daily lives, and initiates a process whereby we can shuck off our personal chaos and stand at the beginning of time and space once again. We see this happen when the council must confront Martiniano's deed and deal with the ripples of response it has triggered in the life of the Pueblo. Frank takes us deep within the kiva and describes the elements set in motion. No longer are we dealing with the requirements of two different cultures. We are now wholly within one culture and we hear:

> A silence so heavy and profound that it squashes the kernel of
> truth out of his words, and leaves the meaningless husks merci-
> lessly exposed. And still no man speaks. Each waits courteously
> for another. And the silence grows round the walls, handed
> from one to another, until all the silence is one silence, and
> that silence has meaning of all. So the individuals vanish. It
> is all one heart. It is the soul of the tribe. A soul that is linked
> by that other silence with all the souls of all the tribal councils
> which have sat here in the memory of man.[2]

Is this a profound, cosmic silence or merely an embarrassing interlude between speakers? Frank was not to know for two decades how powerful a scene he had created. The burden of silence that makes modern people nervous reminds one of the moments before the creation when everything possible was in wait for the process to begin. Here we have an important dichotomy: silence and sound. It takes us forward to the creation story in *Book of the Hopi*, where we find:

. . . Palongawhoya traveling throughout the earth, sounded out his call as he was bidden. All the vibratory centers along earth's axis from pole to pole resounded his call; the whole earth trembled; the universe quivered in tune. Thus he made the whole world an instrument of sound, and the sound an instrument for carrying the messages, resounding praise to the Creator of all.[3]

Prior to sound was, of course, silence. A silence so gripping that it did not allow for individuality and particularity. This state of being was re-experienced in the kiva, and its purpose was obvious.

One cannot accurately identify the point in time when any specific thing begins. Historians and poets may offer insights and suggest credible themes to interpret human experience. Yet there is always the nagging "but what if" aspect to analysis; and since everything is related, who can tell where anything originates? Thus the speeches and gestures within the kiva seek to create the primordial conditions within which the question can be understood. The silence enables people to arrange their minds so that the question can run its course in cosmic process; answers will be given in the events to follow. The kiva scene, then, involves many dimensions of time that must all run their courses in the events to follow. The decision of the council becomes a later practical choice but does not follow directly from the kiva to the actions of the people. Rather, people leave the kiva in anticipation of future developments.

In *Masked Gods* Frank offers an important insight into the movement of time. We believe we understand time, but what we understand is the passage of time. "In fact," he reminds us, "with every step that we are moving through the Present, we are converting some of it into the Future and some of it into the Past."[4] This idea sounds simple enough except that we have no present way of knowing *which* parts of the present are to be allocated to past and future. We try to hang on to precious moments, hoping they will not end.

In crisis and sorrow we seek to put part of the present behind us in a past we wish would disappear. While we believe these efforts are a product of our will, in *Deer* we come to understand that the relationships we have with others largely determine how we process the present and create both future and past. It was not taking the deer out of season that created the turmoil. When the forest rangers disrupted Martiniano's hunting by preventing him from performing a thanksgiving ritual by placing the deer's head to the east, a path of development opens that changes the course of many lives. Appearing in many guises the cosmos/deer suggests a larger pattern of growth — and time — than we have been taught to understand.

Is there a short cut in cosmic process? People always think there is. Such a choice is offered to those who must deal with the question of peyote. This religious tradition is offered to Martiniano and for a while he finds it attractive. Then the question comes to a head. The council debates the question of adopting peyote. An Indian of great prestige, Manuel Rena, presents the new religion and stresses that it is not an imported religion like Catholicism but rather an ancient practice used by many tribes. Tribes in Mexico and the United States to which, in some way, the Pueblos must have been related. Rena, we have been informed, has already violated certain customs of the people but invoked little response from tribal elders. He is something of a bridge between the old ways and the new, between two possible paths to cosmic enlightenment. This introduction of peyote as a serious religious alternative, however, calls into question how religion is to be received in the future. Rena's advocacy of peyote is a path of dissent not unlike that already chosen by Martiniano, who has refused to participate in ceremonies or to follow traditionally approved customs such as cutting the seat from pants and knocking off heels of shoes and boots.

The response of the council can easily be anticipated since the council represents the most steadfast traditional people in the community. But it is described in language reaching back to primordial time through the respective worlds in which the people have lived:

> Through all our previous arisings we have slowly emerged from
> formlessness to separateness. Now we must return again to the
> formless, to the boundless, to the undivided. From the worlds
> of the physical to the world of the spirit which transcends
> them. But with the consciousness of their non-separateness. . . .
> That is our new emergence. We are all that we shall be.[5]

Again we have a partially hidden sense of time. We must fulfill our destiny in this life, but this life is a part of a larger process in which the spirit reshapes us so that we can continue our journey and become what we are supposed to be.

Here I think we find the best articulation of the idea of the endless cosmic cycles bringing us through many different worlds. We, as spirit, always continue on. The contemporary conditions in each world in which we find ourselves enable us to deal with the specificity of ideas that any creation must have. This process is a sophisticated explanation of cosmic reincarnation. Without question, some version of reincarnation was central to understanding their universe for many tribes. None is as sophisticated as the Taos concept of returning to the formlessness. Reincarnation may have been plainly apparent to some Indians in the physical resemblance of their children to deceased relatives. It can be seen in the belief that twins were souls close in a previous life who want to be even closer in this one. It may even have manifested itself physically in the ready acceptance of the Ghost Dance, where the earth itself is transformed. In *Masked Gods* Frank presents his understanding of the idea:

> There is not much more difference between the man when he dies and the child when he is reborn. Death breaks the identity of personality — because he may have another name, live in another civilization — but this causal nexus is still maintained. The continuity of consciousness remains unbroken too; all the memories of his past lives are stored in the unconscious which one day will release them to his conscious mind.[6]

This phrasing of an old belief suggests that we can clearly identify both a soul and a personality. We also respond to the empirical data of our lives on two levels: the immediate experience; and the gnawing, nagging feeling that we have of a far deeper reality behind the events of our lives. On two levels, therefore, we must find our pathway through the succession of worlds that eventually coalesce into the profound silence of creation. We might even believe, as some do, that all possibilities of creation will eventually be realized and everything that has happened or ever will happen can be found in an Akashic Record Book. There are, consequently, times within times and yet more times.

In one scene Martiniano lies awake, his pregnant wife sleeping beside him, and contemplates the several dimensions of time that have taken over his life.

> And lying alone at night, feeling the world rushing with him through space and time, he knew how necessary and precious was this time of waiting for the thing that was to come upon him.[7]

One is tempted to say that we can understand the time of waiting as part of our own makeup; but we live in a world that measures and allocates time, reducing it to a commodity. In *Deer*, Waters uses the interminable sense of waiting to show us that time, if we consider it as a steadily moving progression within which we live, does not determine our lives. Instead, our relationships seize chronological time and subdivide it into a series of special moments. Waiting, emotionally standing still, is often a more sophisticated use of time — or how time uses us, perhaps.

Throughout *Deer* we see the instinctive and intuitive use of time by Indians. Although ceremonials mark the annual calendar, it is apparent that Indians "feel" their way through the day. Thus one of the standard jokes among Indians is the idea of "Indian time": the complete avoidance of following an artificial measurement of time, and arriving or beginning as the event requires. If Indians are not rational and logical but rather instinctive and intuitive, then can we argue that they attach themselves to a different sense of time continuously? Or do they reserve these mystical senses for important things, using ceremonials to give them an objective framework within which they live virtually quantum existences? Western thinking has encouraged us to think in logical sequence, in dualities: before and after, up and down, hot and cold. But there remains a constant feeling inside us that we are moving through periods of intense waiting for the moment of consummation.

Ceremonials, as Frank points out in his nonfiction books, allow deeper cycles of cosmic time to become manifest and reorder our participation in the world. Ceremonials are events experienced by the community through its participation. They orient the group toward the powers of the universe. In so doing, ceremonials provide a counterbalance to the physical entropy ruling the physical world. In a world of increasing randomness, the ceremonial provides a focus, thereby reducing chaos so that the proper pathways are renewed. We go back into the formlessness and allow new forms to begin to manifest themselves.

Of importance here is that the best explanations of these ideas are already well represented in *The Man Who Killed the Deer*, written long before Frank spent time with the Hopi, and before their elders could tutor him. His intuitive sense of what was happening in the Pueblo and Navajo ceremonials was later confirmed during his two years of living among the Hopi. Thus *Deer* is a remarkable achievement in that it comes from Frank at a time when no one would have expected him to have such insights. Too, his nonfiction books provide historical and empirical data arranged according to the spirit insight he had intuitively grasped many years before.

Masked Gods holds up well after more than a half-century of change and development, and it records scenes that cannot now be repeated. *Book of the Hopi*, immensely popular with readers, also continues to be the most comprehensive presentation of Hopi traditions. Again, it describes ceremonies and behavior that can never be repeated. Time and change have moved Indians beyond the simple ceremonial life they once knew and many religious activities have now become merely social gatherings.

Mexico Mystique represents a different situation altogether. This book was Frank's daring effort to connect the emerging new world view of science with the age-old myths of Mexico and Central America. The display of scholarship and erudition in it is daunting and at times overwhelming. Early mythology of the peoples of Mexico and Central America is unfamiliar to most of us, and even with the best of authors it requires immense and intense study. Here Frank was caught, as are so many of us today, between a desire to explore the unstructured world of spirit and a driving motive to know what has gone on before us in the purely historical physical sense.

Taking the "worlds" of the peoples of the Southwest and Mexico, Frank suggests that the mass of new materials now being given us by science, which will surely produce a completely new view of planetary history, continues to have a hidden internal dimension. He is quite right in suggesting that if there is a physical, chronological story of our planet, there must be a corresponding psychic counterpart. We are just now realizing that instead of a steady, reliable, eternal solar system, we live on the bull's eye of a planet that seems to collect more than its share of cosmic collisions. Our ancestors witnessed spectacular cosmic events that we can only vaguely imagine. We will some day look at the destruction of previous physical worlds as a haphazard and possibly cyclic process. We will learn that out of the utter formlessness of planetary catastrophe some sentient beings survived and were perhaps physically and psychically reformed. How else can we explain the complete biotic systems we find in each geological age when we know that the previous age experienced extinction of eighty to ninety percent of existing biota? The genius of kiva ritual is its ability to use and understand formlessness so that we can renew the spiritual path and for a brief instant renew all possibilities.

After first reading *Mexico Mystique* when it came out, I wrote to Frank and asked him whether the catastrophic interpretation of earth history was not so fundamentally sound in principle that it must be regarded as a real alternative history of our planet. His response was that it could well be true but that his interest was in matching the physical and spiritual to see if the spiritual/ psychological interpretation could also be true. He was certainly correct in maintaining that whatever physical experiences our ancestors might have had, they most certainly had to integrate those experiences into a body of knowledge allowing them to make sense of what had happened to the earth and to continue living.

In rereading the book to prepare this paper, I was surprised to see that so many of the specific things Frank cited in his discussions of catastrophism have long since been voided by later developments and scenarios. The geologic time scale is rapidly being revised, and in a radically shorter period of time. An asteroid hit can do in three days what endless eras of mythical geologic time once purported to do. Indeed, scenarios are being offered for solar system history that are becoming more and more precise, and they are reconciling astronomical data that were formerly discarded as anomalies.

Western hemisphere history is also experiencing this great change. Dates are being pushed back continually for human presence on all continents. The possibility that there were many expeditions from other continents exploring the western hemisphere at a very early date looms large in our eyes today.

Yet Frank's sense of catastrophic change both physically and psychologically seems to have been correct. In many ways we are experiencing today what the people of Taos Pueblo must have felt at the time Frank wrote *The Man Who Killed the Deer*. Our familiar institutional and emotional landscape is suffering disastrous disruptions. As did Martiniano, we often find ourselves victims of unreasonable restrictions and mindless prohibitions.

Is this a time of waiting or must we take some kind of action? Do we have a community that can go back into the silence and find a proper path to follow? Can we find a deer that will guide us; and if so, will we have the sense and patience to recognize this deer when it comes to us? Frank Waters' books represent the deepest philosophical struggles of a thinker who lives by instinct and intuition and who suggests a way to adopt this mode of living. In experiencing and understanding time, he brings to literature the essence of the Indian.

Alexander Blackburn
The Mythology of the Planet

"The only mythology that is valid today is the mythology of the planet–and we don't have such a mythology."[1] This is what Joseph Campbell said to a television audience of millions in his series of talks subsequently published in 1988 in a book called *The Power of Myth*. While I agree that the only valid mythology today is the mythology of the planet, I must disagree with Campbell's peremptory thesis that we don't have (because we can't enforce) such a mythology.

Admittedly, modern man has not yet fully awakened from the shock of dread: he has persuaded himself that he is an ant in an ant heap and that the earth is nothing more than a speck of sidereal dust. A myth to live by, however, has already made its appearance. Like the impact of a pebble cast upon the shallow waters of our civilization, it is causing ripples that will eventually beat upon all shores. Two stone-throwers in particular concern me here, the one a priest-scientist, Pierre Teilhard de Chardin, the other a novelist-philosopher, Frank Waters. Their visions, I believe, meet the requirements for global unity based upon mankind's system of awareness–in other words, for myth. If we are not prepared to identify its presence, it is because we are creatures of habit.

The power of habit was very well understood, Montaigne tells us, by the man who first forged the tale of a village woman who had grown used to cuddling a calf and carrying it about from the time it was born. She grew so accustomed to doing so that she was able to carry it when a fully grown bull. Comparing Habit to a violent and treacherous school-teacher, Montaigne says she gradually and stealthily slides her authoritative foot into us, "then, having by this gentle and humble beginning planted it firmly within us, helped by times she later discloses an angry tyrannous countenance, against which we are no longer allowed even to lift up our eyes."[2]

Like the village woman, we are today accustomed to lugging around a lot of fully grown bulls, only they are more violent and treacherous than ever and infinitely larger; they are enormities of the cosmos. We feel crushed by them. Although it seems to us incredible that men could have lived for thousands of years without suspecting that the stars above us are hundreds of light years away, or that the universe is formed of galaxies whose distance apart runs into hundreds of thousands of light years, or that the contours of life stretch out millions of years behind us, our immediate forebears nevertheless felt perfectly at ease in a space-time where the stars turned round the earth and had been doing so for less than six thousand years. This illusion of proximity remains on the menu of habit for people who still live in Jurassic Park. The conviction of historical, as opposed to spiritual, truth in scriptures more than two thousand years old is the faith-based diet of hundreds of millions of people. And yet, when such firmly planted habits are uprooted, the ones that take their place are often so burdensome that we feel threatened by a loss of the very taste for life. Is there no progress, no suitable outcome for life in the future, no prospect of an emergent divinity? Is all thought now doomed to be stillborn in an absurd universe? What assures us that tomorrow exists? What is human density in relation to the movement of time? What is our proper place as individuals among the suddenly swarming populations of the earth? Are we shut in at a dead end?

Any mythology of the planet inevitably encounters the obstinacy of habit. For instance—and here Joseph Campbell was for the most part intensely right—even as the hour of socialization seems to have sounded for mankind, those who speak through their myths of love, brotherhood, and solidarity reserve their pieties for an in-group or bounded community, projecting aggression outward upon the Other because it is our habit to divide up our human world according to tribes, nations, races, religions, and ideologies.

Although boundaries no longer exist, the habit persists. Besides, we are accustomed to regard an individual as diametrically opposed to a collective.

When an individual finds himself involved in a group or lost in a crowd, he or she experiences a disagreeable sense of loss and constraint. Any agglomeration, he or she believes, stifles and neutralizes the elements that compose it. For those habituated to egocentricity and to the cult of isolated individualism, there in no satisfying model of collectivity.

Finally, we are addicted to materialism and excessive rationalism. Accustomed to old, dying myths that condemn nature as evil, we feel justified in accelerating attempts to subdue the planet, including genocidal erasure of native peoples. In spite of the new physics that breaks down the separation of man and nature, mind and matter, we continue to think of the planet as an object to be exploited. As for rationalism, that is, the identification of "mind" with reason to the exclusion of intuitive and emotional avenues to truth, we continue to deploy this seventeenth-century Cartesian delusion as an excuse for male dominance, for technological hubris, and for the political and economic plunder of so-called "third world" peoples and races. We ignore the evidence of a bicameral mind whereby intuition and emotion earn prestige. In puritanical cultures such as that of the United States we relegate imagination to the shadows, treating artists as if they are cockroaches.

So it seems as if all the king's horses and all the king's men are immobilized in any attempts to put our Humpty-Dumpty world of bits and pieces back together again. It seems as if we might as well resign ourselves to a planet without joy or supportable weight. Or are we simply so bored and afraid that we cannot look the tyrannous countenance of Habit straight in the eye?

Suppose evolution is not only movement but direction or, better, is directed. Suppose that there is a constantly rising tide of life with an expanding and deepening of human consciousness as its culminating thrust. Suppose that we, ourselves, are part of vast and continuous processes and that nature demands the true union of mankind in an association that promotes instead of eliminates the differences of its separate elements. Let us try to picture the union of heart and spirit as a phenomenon on a terrestrial scale. Frank Waters said:

> Today I believe we are beginning to experience another periodic
> expansion toward a psychic, universal consciousness which will
> supersede our rational, terrestrial mode of thinking: a quan-
> tum leap... toward a new perspective inspired by a planetary
> imperative.[3]

Pierre Teilhard de Chardin said:

> True union, the union of heart and spirit, does not enslave,
> nor does it neutralize the individuals which it brings together.
> It super-personalizes them.... Imagine men awakening at last,
> under the influence of the ever-tightening planetary embrace,
> to a sense of universal solidarity based on their profound com-
> munity, evolutionary in its nature and purpose. The nightmares
> of brutalization and mechanization which are conjured up to
> terrify us and prevent our advance are at once dispelled. It is
> not harshness or hatred, but a new kind of love, not yet expe-
> rienced by man, which we much learn to look for as it is borne
> to us on the rising tide of planetization.[4]

Born in Auvergne in 1881, Teilhard was sent to a Jesuit College at the age of
ten and ordained a priest in 1912. He then embarked on a geological career,
with special emphasis on paleontology, later synthesizing these studies with
biology. Having spent most of his career in China and there completing the
manuscript of *Le Phénomène Humain* in 1938, he returned to France in 1946
only to encounter difficulty: in 1948 he was forbidden to put forward his
Professorship in the Collège de France, and in 1950 his application to publish
his philosophical work was refused in Rome. At the invitation of the Wen-
ner-Gren Foundation, he moved to New York in 1951; he died there in 1955.
Le Phénomène Humain, his great work, was published in French that year.
The English translation, *The Phenomenon of Man*, appeared in 1959 with an
introduction by Sir Julian Huxley, who had independently envisaged human
evolution and biological evolution as two phases of a single process.

According to Huxley, Teilhard had already by 1919,

> ... reached a point where the entire phenomenal universe,
> including man, was revealed as a process of evolution, and he
> found himself impelled to build up a generalized theory or
> philosophy of evolutionary process which could take account of
> human history and human personality as well as of biology, and
> from which one could draw conclusions as to the future evolu-
> tion of man on earth.[5]

It was imperative for Teilhard, Huxley continues, "to try to reconcile Christian theology with this evolutionary philosophy, to relate the facts of religious experience to those of natural science."[6]

In the following summary some statements and phrases from Teilhard and Huxley are mingled in my text without inverted commas. I hope that my ignorance of science will permit me to be indulged on the gentle side of a charge of plagiarism. Teilhard's key terms are *emergence* and *convergence*. As we will see later, Waters uses a single term, *Emergence*, to convey both concepts.

Emergence in Teilhard's philosophy denotes the increasingly elaborate organization of life in its passage from sub-atomic units to atoms, from atoms to inorganic and later to organic molecules, thence to the first sub-cellular living units of self-replicating assemblages of molecules, and then to cells, to multi-cellular individuals, to cephalized metazoa with brains, to primitive man, and now to civilized societies. Emergence also denotes an original imprisonment in the matter of earth of a certain mass of elementary consciousness. It too has been in process, but it leaped forward with cephalization, that is, with the differentiation of the head as the dominant guiding region of the body.

The emergence of human beings with their power of reflective thought—a consciousness no longer merely knowing but knowing itself—has given them in a flash the capacity to raise themselves to a new sphere of increased awareness and thus to a future on the planet.

First, the man alone constitutes the last-born, the freshest, and the most complicated of all the successive layers of life. Second, man's augmenting consciousness is nothing less than the substance and heart of life in process of evolution. Third, the direction of life is irreversible and ineluctable. The road ahead is not only open to individual fulfillment, but also, as regards the choices and responsibilities of our activity, open to the unanimous construction of a spirit of earth.

Convergence denotes the tendency of mankind during his evolution to incorporate in an organized and unified pattern the fragmentations that have enervated the progress of other species. Convergence has prevented humankind from diverging into separated species even though there is differentiation in races and cultures. In natural fact it is convergence that has led to an accelerating process of psychosocial union of the whole human species into a single interthinking group. Especially in our own times with the dramatic increase of human numbers, convergence necessitates the kind of integrated mental activity that can guide our species to high levels—integration of the self with the outer world of men and nature, and integration of the separate elements of the self with each other.

The essence of Teilhard's philosophy is the "noosphere" (a word he coined in 1925). Now convergence tends to a final state where interthinking humanity may be considered a new type of organism, a "thinking layer" spread over and above the earth as an enveloping consciousness. Teilhard invokes the authority of a natural law to support his thesis, namely, that no element can move or grow except with and by all the others with itself.

The plurality of individual reflections grouping themselves together in a mega-synthesis is a grand and enabling vision. Under the influence of a supremely autonomous focus of unanimity the more Other we become in conjunction, the more depth we have as parts of an organized whole. Here, of course, we must be on our guard: modern attempts at collective organization have ended up in totalitarianism, a lowering and enslavement of consciousness.

Therefore human beings must be united by what is deepest in themselves into a sort of super-consciousness, by love, not by forced coalescence. We must come together inwardly and in entire freedom. As a corollary to this proposition, we must recognize that egocentricity is against nature and is a blind alley. Of man's future, Teilhard writes:

> The life-giving coming together of mankind… links those who love in bonds that unite but do not confound, causing them to discover in their mutual contact an exaltation, capable incomparably more than any arrogance of solitude, of arousing in the heart of their being all that they possess of uniqueness and creative power.[7]

Human nobility, in sum, consists in our serving the work of an ultimate reality proceeding in the universe.

The Phenomenon of Man, written in 1938 but not published in English until 1959, could not have exercised an influence on Waters' *The Man Who Killed the Deer*, written in 1941 and published in 1942. Working independently and coming to similar conclusions almost simultaneously, Teilhard and Waters give us a glimpse of what seems to be the genesis of a myth. These very circumstances support the feeling that a fresh spirit is at large and is coming to birth–or rather, to rebirth through the synthesis of ancient religion and modern science.

The life of Frank Waters personifies the loneliness of the long-distance mystic. Early experiences of an infinite existence, an Ultimate Reality underlying all forms and manifesting itself in us as we are in it, isolated him in the modern wasteland. Along the way, though, he found congenial and corroboratory myths (Amerindian, Mesoamerican, Buddhist, Hindu, quantum physics) and minds (Evans-Wentz, Gurdjieff, Einstein, Maharshi, Jung, and eventually Teilhard) to ease the burden of his quest.

Although Waters is in general agreement with Teilhard about evolutionary process, particularly with respect to an enlargement of consciousness that enlarges humanity, Waters does not project our inward coming together as a utopian construction of the future. Planetization, in fact, is not to be sought after by acts of individual or collective will: the ego obstructs such seeking. Integration is actually already here, already inherent. We are already the Other. Man is essentially related to, merged with, or embodied with all living entities, including mankind. As Waters says in *Mexico Mystique*:

> In the supreme law governing both external and internal re-
> alities, there seems to be a factor of cohesiveness that links in
> one great process the evolving life of every microscopic cell and
> giant star. Plants, animals, man, the Earth itself, may be but
> microcosmic reflections of that macrocosmic life which also
> informs all planets in our solar system and the farthest galaxies
> in a universe too great to be conceived by the human mind. All
> are embodied in the same cosmic process of the whole.[8]

In other words, the emergent divinity that gives power to myth is immanent in all, relating them. We have but to be awakened to these relationships. Thus the realization of the dream of brotherhood with the peoples and races of all continents depends upon awareness of the universal capital-S Self embodied in all our lesser worldly selves. The nature, meaning, and final goal of man is to lose his individual identity and personal consciousness and to merge into that supreme Self.

If we look at the planet in a way new to those of us habituated to separating man and nature, look with this holistic, cosmological perspective, we discover that the physical structure of man is akin to that of the earth. His body is composed of the same four living elements of the global entity: earth, air, water and fire. Waters argues in *Mountain Dialogues* as follows:

> The earth pulsates in an almost imperceptible but ordered rhythm. Water in man and on earth moves in tune with the phases of the moon, as reflected by the tides of the sea, the rises of sap in trees, the female menstrual periods. Air circulates through both bodies, ascending over warm land areas and descending over cool areas, constituting the "breathing of the continents." And our common life energy of light and heat relates us to the sun.[9]

Waters continues:

> [Man] breathes 18 times a minute, 25,920 times a day. Hence, he is connected with the sun, for it takes 25,920 years for the vernal equinox to move through the great Precession of the Equinoxes. Air also relates man to the element of water. For every 18 breaths there are 72 beats of the pulse, a ratio of 1:4 for the circulation of the blood. This confirms the fact that propagation of sound is four times faster in water than in air, blood being the archetypal organ of liquid flow in man as water is throughout the earth.[10]

As I interpret the Waters canon, its dominant idea is capital-E Emergence, a term that incorporates from natural science the concepts of emergence and convergence and from religion the concept of embodiment in a supreme power. Waters' Emergence rests more or less tranquilly on the pillow of such Teilhardian terms as "noosphere" and planetization, but Waters, unlike Teilhard, explores psychological rather than biological approaches to a new world of the mind. Capital-E Emergence represents a stage of human consciousness that reconciles the duality of reason and instinct and supersedes these on a numinous plane of intuition. This plane is an effulgence of an immanent power that relates the inner world of man to the living universe, itself composed of expanding psychic as well as physical energies. From this perspective, which is above all evolutionary, the long journey of mankind has been through successive states of ever-expanding consciousness.

From complete polarization to the instinctive or unconscious mentation, man has emerged to his present state of rational consciousness and must not surrender this advantage over the lower forms of life or sink back into the unconscious. Modern man, however, has become excessively rationalistic and consequently alienated from the source of life. Suffering a loss of relationship to nature and to mankind, he has reached a spiritual and ethical dead end. Now his task is to live in harmonious relationship with all the emergent life forces of Creation. Once he recognizes on the plane of increased awareness his indebtedness to these forces and his responsibility for them, his fulfillment is assured.

Human conscience, though it may be local and tribal in orientation and enforcement, serves all humanity in a world culture because conscience pulls individuals back from ego-centeredness into harmonic relationships at all levels: family, tribe, society, all peoples, all living things, the universe itself. The individual is pulled forward on the path of Emergence.

Joseph Campbell, especially in *Creative Mythology*, discerns four functions of a mythology: mystical, cosmological, sociological, and psychological. The first function is to reconcile waking consciousness to the mystery of the universe as it is. The second function is to render an interpretive total image of the same. The third is to shape the individual to the requirements of his social group. And the fourth is to foster the centering and unfolding of the individual in integrity, in accord with himself, his culture, the universe, and the "ultimate mystery which is both beyond and within himself and all things."[11]

According to Campbell the failure in modern centuries of the third, sociological function of a mythology has put the individual on his own, and consequently it is lived experience, not tribal or dogmatic authority, which leads to "creative symbolization" and "restores to existence the quality of adventure, at once shattering and reinterpreting the fixed, already known, in the sacrificial fire of the becoming thing that is no thing at all but life... as it is, in depth, in process, *here and now*, inside and out."[12]

A synthesis of science and religion such as we find in Teilhard and in Waters opens out in back to eternity, to the structuring laws and forces interior to the earthly being that is man, here and now, and so has the value of living myth. The survival problems now facing us are collective rather than individual: how to prevent destruction of the earth, and how to relate and understand diverse ideas, doctrines, and peoples. The concept of a coming world of consciousness refers to a view of reality in which individual actions combine into something more organized.

Undertaking conscious evolution may be easier, closer at hand, and more liberating than we might normally think. It is for this reason that I have disagreed with Campbell, who saw little contemporary promise of a socialization of mankind. The myth of planetization or Emergence, I believe is already in place. Teilhard de Chardin and Frank Waters perceived our power for embracing the totality of men and of the earth. We could call this power a new kind of love. We could call it the mythology of the planet.

V.
THE NOVELS

John Nizalowski
Borderlands and Transfiguration:
Desert Mysticism in Frank Waters'
The Lizard Woman

The author of nearly thirty books of fiction and non-fiction, most of them set in Colorado or New Mexico, Frank Waters is best known for his novel of Taos Pueblo, *The Man Who Killed the Deer,* and his ethnographic study, *Book of the Hopi*. However, his first two novels, *The Lizard Woman* (published in 1930 as *Fever Pitch*) and *The Yogi of Cockroach Court* (written in 1927 and published in 1947), use the Mexican-American border as their settings. While *Yogi* explores the tragic and futile lives of Mexicali's mixed-blood inhabitants, Waters' first novel, *The Lizard Woman*, examines the transformational power of the Sonoran Desert on the rare adventurer who makes his or her way into one of the most desolate and terrifyingly beautiful landscapes on the planet. Lee Marston, the protagonist of *The Lizard Woman*, undergoes a profound, transcendental metamorphosis in the remote stretches of the Mexican-American border region, and his transfiguration anticipates a literary motif found in works by John Steinbeck, Jack Kerouac, Edward Abbey, Cormac McCarthy, Craig Childs, and others.

Frank Waters was born in Colorado Springs in 1902, the son of a part-Indian father and the grandson of Joseph Dozier, a contractor who helped build the city and then lost his fortune in a series of poorly producing Cripple Creek mines. Despite this, Waters studied mine engineering at Colorado College until he dropped out his junior year in 1924. Footloose, he made his way to the oil fields of Salt Creek, Wyoming, where he worked as a roustabout. A few months later, Waters ditched Wyoming for Los Angeles, accepted a position as a junior engineer for the Pacific Bell Telephone Company, and was soon supervising phone-line construction in the Imperial Valley (Waters, "Changing" 202-205).

It was here that the mountain-bred Frank Waters first explored true desert — the surreal vastness of the Mojave and the Sonoran basins — an encounter that would singe his soul and inspire him to write. As Waters himself states in the preface to the 1995 Swallow Press edition of *The Lizard Woman*:

> The novel was begun in 1925, when I was twenty-three years old and working as a telephone engineer in Imperial Valley, on the California-Baja California border. During my stay there I made a horseback trip down into the little-known desert interior of Lower California. After having lived all my early years in the high Rockies of Colorado, I was unprepared for the vast sweep of sunstruck desert with its flat wastes, clumps of cacti, and barren parched-rock ranges. Its emotional impact was so profound, I was impelled to give voice to it with pencil and paper. (vii)

It is not surprising, then, that landscape plays such a central role in *The Lizard Woman*. In this same preface, Waters notes that he began with a description of the remote and utterly barren valley of the Lizard Woman, a goddess based loosely on American Indian mythology (Blackburn 28). With the description of the desert valley in hand, Waters next needed characters and a plot. In the preface he freely admits that, "I found myself using the desert and the Lizard Woman herself as the main character. This, after all, was my reason for writing. So I did not hesitate to indulge in long descriptions" (viii). Emily Plec, in her essay "Frank Waters' Ecofeminist Sensibility," builds on Waters' observation and rightly claims that, "Indeed, the story is as much landscape as plot — the landscape *becomes* plot" (169). So, while Waters claims in his preface to have grabbed an "adventure story" from "common pulp-paper Westerns" (viii), a more accurate explanation is that he found a narrative hook that allowed him to portray his own profound reactions to the Sonoran Desert.

Waters composes *The Lizard Woman* in Conradian fashion. A group of men sit on the porch of La Casa Blanca, a border cantina, listening to Eric Dane tell the story of his friend Lee Marston, who sits on the other side of the porch in the shadows, oblivious to the narrative unfolding nearby in the arid night. Marston is a civil engineer who surveys railroad lines between the lower reaches of the Colorado River to the Gulf of California. For Marston, the job's attraction was the land itself: "The desert, the land. That was what held him. Like the sea, its illimitable expanse had gripped his imagination" (4).

So when Arvilla, a half-Indian, half-Mexican percentage girl and prostitute, seduces Marston with a fantastic tale of the far-off valley of the Lizard Woman, where the gold is so rich it runs in "great flakes," he is ready to follow the lure of her story literally anywhere. Arvilla shares her tale because in that far off, impossibly remote valley of the Lizard Woman, another man, Jim Horne, is patiently waiting for Arvilla to return with someone who can assay metals, and thereby determine which minerals are truly gold, which are silver, which are copper, and which are worthless. For Arvilla, Marston is that man.

Arvilla, therefore, becomes Marston's guide to the unknown realms, a place of hot sand and rock with names like "Los Llanos de Los Perdidos" (8). Arvilla is a potent mixture of contradictory forces. Her Euro-Mexican blood gives her an obsession for gold, and a willingness to ruthlessly use her body to gain it, particularly through Marston and Horne. In her essay "Passion, Obsession, and Enlightenment in the Desert," Denise Chávez, author of *Loving Pedro Infante*, explains Arvilla's character and motivations:

> Arvilla's desperate greed drives her to talk Lee Marston into taking her to the mountains of the Lizard Woman to find gold. She has been promised gold by her lover Jim Horne, el hombre conejo, who is waiting for her return. Without guilt or any tinge of remorse Arvilla uses both men for her own purposes, pitting one against the other. There are few such selfish, dark-hearted, grasping villains in American literature as Arvilla. (146)

However, Arvilla's Cocopah Indian blood grants her a superb knowledge of the desert and a profound humility before its dangers. Without Arvilla's knowledge, the pair of adventurers would never survive the barren wastes they must cross to reach the valley of the Lizard Woman, and throughout the novel, it is Arvilla's wisdom that saves them from certain death. As Thomas Lyon states in his book *Frank Waters*:

> Arvilla knows how to get water, knows how to shade herself in the sun, and remorselessly and purposefully drives the ill-suited horses to their death. In contrast, Marston is a sun-blistered greenhorn through most of the action; and he resents the cool competence of the mestiza girl, as well as the way she has assumed leadership [...] Marston's white alienation from the land is deep. (71)

Perhaps the most powerful example of this resentment and alienation may be when the pair spend the second night of their journey in the wickiup of an old Cocopah woman, the last human being they will encounter until they reach the valley. Ancient and shriveled, with hair like "matted strands of dirty rope" (28), she is clearly the story's crone, the wise old goddess who warns them of their peril. "She say, Señor," explains Arvilla, "that we should not go to the land of the Lizard Woman. That it is a land not for God, not for us, or for any living thing" (30). But rather than feel gratitude for elder's sage advice and hospitality, Marston, who wants to make love to Arvilla, only feels resentment for her presence and fears her strangeness. In a case of Jungian projection, Marston sees her as "an old witch mixing an infernal brew of the desert" (29).

Novelist and critic Alexander Blackburn recognizes Marston's resentments towards Arvilla and the old Cocopah woman as classic masculine hostility towards the dual image of the goddess. Inspired by Erich Neumann's studies on Jungian archetypes, Blackburn, in *A Sunrise Brighter Still*, his insightful study of Waters' fiction, discusses Marston's failure to recognize "the old crone" as the "alter ego of Arvilla." Blackburn believes this failure results from the European tendency to embrace the "Good Mother" and reject the "Terrible Mother." This produces in European culture "a loss of contact with the unconscious." In *The Lizard Woman*, this loss explains Marston's final "eruption into violence" (32).

Thus, it is understandable why Marston projects the image of witchcraft onto the old Cocopah woman, for he has crossed the border into dark world of the "terrible mother" — in terms of race, nation, and consciousness. It is the shadowy realm that Jung names the "deep" or "collective unconscious," the origin place of archetypes (34). For Marston, as for many Anglos, to cross the Mexican border is to slide into a landscape that constitutes for America its own deep unconscious, and the unknowns found there often stir up nightmarish fears. As Waters states in *Pumpkin Seed Point*, "The course of witchcraft whether practiced by witches or witch hunters is first the possession of them by the dark shadow side of their dual nature they have repressed, and then their projection of it upon another individual, race, or nation" (125).

So, when Marston leaves the Casa Blanca and follows Arvilla into the heart of the Sonoran Dessert, he has entered this shadow realm of the collective unconscious. His crossing of the border takes him to strange lands forsaken by God and humanity, according to the Cocopah legend, since creation — a parallel to repressed psychic imagery that has not yet surfaced to consciousness. Thus, Arvilla's promise of gold and romance plunges Marston beyond the maps and the safe routes he has always encountered:

> From the Colorado to the Gulf, Marston in his work had followed a well-beaten path. That the path was in reality only a matter of red dots on the maps of the company surveys made no difference. He knew the next one, after a day or so of traveling over flat stretches of desert, through hills of brown parched rock, or between immense thickets of chaparral, manzanitas, and scrub oak, would be sure to appear [. . .] . He felt that to drop on either side was to be plunged into the immensity of the land which stretched interminably beyond the eyes. (14)

Waters himself notes the Conradian influences on *The Lizard Woman* (viii), and he may well have found the inspiration for this image of Marston falling off the map from Joseph Conrad's short-story "The Secret Sharer." In this story, Leggatt, the First Mate of the *Sephora*, kills a sailor during a storm in order to save the ship from the seaman's inaction. Leggatt is imprisoned onboard the *Sephora* awaiting trial, but he escapes and swims to the narrator's ship. The narrator, a newly appointed captain, feels sympathy for Leggatt and hides him in his cabin. Leggatt becomes the secret double of the narrator and is essentially an unconscious projection of the narrator's fears over his first captaincy. Just before jumping overboard to escape certain discovery, Leggatt ponders some maps of his destination: "He looked thoughtfully at the chart as if surveying chances and distances from a lofty height — and following with his eyes his own figure wandering on the blank land of Cochin-China, and then passing off that piece of paper clean out of sight into uncharted regions" (691).

But in *The Lizard Woman*, Marston goes with his secret sharer off the map's edge, and disembarks with Arvilla into the "uncharted regions" upon "the immensity of the land." At first, this is a great and exciting adventure, and Marston has all the excitement of an Anglo on a lark in exotic lands: "Having once made up his mind, he began preparations for the trip with all the joyous abandon of a school boy on a vacation" (17). Waters experienced the same rapture upon encountering the magic border country between Mexico and the United States, for he too was caught up in the exoticism of wide-open, wild towns filled with Mexicans, Americans, Chinese, Hindus, Indians, and all manner of mixed bloods. Waters describes how his young soul stirred upon his arrival to El Centro and Mexicali in a biographical note he wrote for his friend John Manchester in the early 70s: "For a boy in his early twenties such a spot has an inexorable, fatal fascination [. . .] . And as he lurches drunkenly along a new hushed and fetid lane at midnight under a wan desert moon, all that he had just known and seen and smelled and sensed seems to him more rich and powerful and naked and vibrantly alive than anything he has ever known and loved" (78).

But soon this rapture, this romanticism of the new and strange, disintegrates from the desert's grim realities. As Marston and Arvilla cross the sun-scorched earth, their skin becomes raw from burns, their horses die, their water runs out, and their senses addle in the solar blaze. As noted, it is Arvilla who has the knowledge to survive this crucible. Marston soon realizes this, and while he resents it, he must bow to her wisdom.

Still, it is Marston who has the transcendent experience upon their arrival at the valley of the Lizard Woman. Geologically, the valley is an ancient seabed, and now that it is totally devoid of water, it is awash in white crystals of salt, borax, and mica: "All the shimmering, incandescent softness and sterile whiteness of a sea within a sea, deeper than the level of the desert floor without" (75). As the old Cocopah woman explained, this is the realm where the Lizard Woman, who created the earth for God and under God's direction, lay down to rest, refusing to transform it. "[She] begged God to grant her for her own this little spot of mountains and sand which was left over from making the world." And God grants her wish: "He warned all the animals and all the birds, saying that never should they enter the horrible land of the Lizard Woman, for it was hers and not theirs, or even His" (70).

Marston's reaction to this place beyond the reach of God is ultimately Emersonian and blissful:

> He could have cried aloud and his words would have followed too closely to be recognized and their context would have at once defied and admitted all religions. He threw out his arms and felt that should a brush have been placed in his fingers he could have painted the form of that transient heart of all beauty for which men have sought in vain. He was in accord with the music of the Infinite. And with that unlocking of all boundaries, all limitations, all the empty forms of that beauty which is known to man, he saw it as it was, the bare, untouched depth of all humility. (75)

Marston is seeing the world's center, and it has produced a profound transfiguration in him. As Thomas Lyon states, "He is being granted a vision of primal nature, a look into the White Heart of Creation . . ." (74). Alexander Blackburn finds parallels between the white valley of the Lizard Woman to the white horse of the Bible, the albatross of Coleridge's *The Ancient Mariner*, the mysterious Antarctic lands at the conclusion of Poe's *The Narrative of Arthur Gordon Pym*, and the white whale of Melville's *Moby-Dick* (28), to which one could add the white horse that gallops past the sleeping Dean Moriarty in the night-enshrouded Mexican jungle of Kerouac's *On the Road*.

Still, it is both surprising and disturbing that Marston's ultimate reaction to this "White Heart" revelation is violence. Marston and Arvilla finally reach Horne at the far end of the valley of the Lizard Woman, and Marston proves with his assay kit that Horne has indeed found gold and silver in almost unimaginable quantities. But after several days of watching Horne fondle Arvilla in an assertion of his earlier claim to the percentage girl, Marston, who became Arvilla's lover during the voyage, confronts Horne. Believing Horne is holding a knife, Marston kills him in an act he believes is self-defense. Too late, Marston realizes the "knife" was one of his own test tubes, but in a kind of trance, he mounts the burro and rides off toward Casa Blanca, leaving Arvilla to die in the desert.

There are many ways of interpreting this moment of violence. Chávez believes it is the culmination of "Marston's obsession with Arvilla, which is poignant, stupid, fantastic, and surreal, all at the same time" (147). Lyon proposes that the violence results from the problem of "how to reconcile the cosmic order and the human, or how to adjust the mystical insight (without perverting it) to the ordinary size of human affairs" (76). Blackburn's answer is rooted in his Jungian perspective: "Although Marston recognizes Arvilla/desert/Lizard Woman as part of himself, that is, assimilates unconscious elements into consciousness, his ego, being predisposed to give value to the Good Mother and to exclude the Terrible Mother, loses touch with the unconscious and resorts to violence" (32).

This may well characterize the reaction of many Anglos who delve into the disturbing dualism of the Mexican-American border experience. Unprepared to fully accept the shadow side, an Anglo may find the border both attractive and repellent. He or she may find the exoticism appealing, but there is a shadow to this appeal, and even the severity of the landscape itself may forcefully confront the voyager. "To live in the desert is to live with struggle," Chávez states. "We are reminded in the desert of the impermanence of all life, in its shifting from darkness to light, light to darkness, water to desert, life to death . . ." (147).

But with maturity, the Anglo voyager may find an inner truth, a harmony with his or her shadow-self, by crossing the border. After all, in Waters' novel, the valley of the Lizard Woman forms a uroboros — a serpent biting its own tail — and as Waters describes in the novel's preface, the uroboros symbolizes "the universe embracing all heaven and earth [. . . the] primordial unity enclosing the infinitude of all space and time [. . .] the fullness of divine Creation" (ix). So, the border experience and an encounter with the vastly "alien" landscape of the Sonoran Desert may hold out the potential for the integration of light and shadow, a unification of opposites, of consciousness and unconsciousness, what Jung called the transcendent function (279). Or, as Plec asserts, "[Like] Arvilla, we can converge symbolically with much of the world, forcing recognition of our implication in the larger, planetary life . . ." (175).

This border-inspired convergence occurs in a later novel by Frank Waters set partly in Mexico, *The Dust Within the Rock*. In it, March Cable, a young man torn between his Anglo and American Indian heritages, becomes a mine engineer in Mexico's Sierra Madres. There, in a moment possessing Edenic imagery, he meets Conchita, a beautiful young woman, swimming nude in the mango-lined river behind his house. They become lovers, and her goddess energies begin to heal the rift in March's soul. After only a few months, she receives an assignment to teach high school elsewhere and the affair ends, but not before she has prepared March's soul to accept Mexico's tranformational alchemy.

After Conchita's departure, March makes a pilgrimage through the Sierra Madres, which climaxes in a Tarahumara peyote ceremony. During this rite, he has a vision of "all humanity streaming out from its common womb of the unconscious, beginning its slow climb into light and freedom of consciousness" (236). This realization becomes Cable's transcendent function, healing the rift between his consciousness and unconsciousness, and his Euro-American and Indian-American selves. "Mexico! The motherland of America," Waters writes, "whose remote sierras and faint trails had led [March Cable] from space to depth, the only answer to the flow of time. Mother Mexico which had settled forever the spirit of his tormenting unrest and given him the answer to himself" (245).

When Waters wrote *The Lizard Woman*, he was a young man newly arrived to the borderlands of the southern California desert. Apparently, he sensed in it the potential for transfiguration and inner completion. Thus, he placed at the heart of his imaginary adventure for gold in a land beyond God, the uroboros of the Lizard Woman — the symbol of unity, wholeness, and psychic fulfillment. However, in 1925-1926, when he wrote *The Lizard Woman*, he was perhaps, like Marston, a young Euro-American male caught up in the border's exotic sensuality and romance. But in his life journey, he transcended this surface understanding and learned to see the essential nature of the Sonoran Desert's transcendent "White Heart," and therefore replaced Marston's violence with Cable's inner healing. As Denise Chávez writes, "It was with wonderful surprise that I came to read about this lizard spirit in the works of Frank Waters and to appreciate how he has bridged the gaps of the sacred and the profane, myth and reality, and gone before us so willingly with courage to point the way for his fellow travelers. His writings leave us a road map to the familiar unfamiliar and the unfamiliar familiar" (147).

Denise Chávez
Passion, Obsession, and Enlightenment in the Desert: Frank Waters' *The Yogi of Cockroach Court* and *The Lizard Woman*

(Dedicated to All Fellow Pilgrims, Friends on the Path,
and most especially Brother Frank Waters)

The invitation to present this talk is a great honor. I would like to thank Barbara Waters and the Frank Waters Foundation for the gift of their belief in me and for allowing me to channel through this work the spirit of Frank Waters, a man of great spirituality and soul.

When I was asked to join the centennial celebration, I knew immediately it would be a stellar event and that it would have a lasting impact on many. Having been awarded the dubious distinction by one of my graduate school professors at the University of New Mexico of possessing what he called "appalling scholarship," it's not hard to understand the fear and trepidation with which I began my inquiry into the work of Frank Waters for this presentation at the centennial.

I have been a professional writer for many years, but always within me there has been nervousness about seeing myself as a bonafide "critic," someone with an "authentic and clear critical voice." I have no doubt this anxiety began when Sister Caritas, a nun at Madonna High School, an all girls Catholic school I attended in Las Cruces, asked me not to sing out loud but just to "mouth the words" as I stood at the front row of the choral group. In no uncertain terms Sister Caritas let me know that she didn't think I had a good voice.

I admit I am not a scholar, a singer, or a critic. Yet I like to think that this has helped me to understand the work of fellow writer and life teacher Frank Waters on a deeply emotional and intuitive level. And this is why the two works I have chosen to address appeal to me so profoundly.

I met Frank Waters only once, at a writers' conference at New Mexico State University. He was the keynote speaker for the event. It was my good fortune to attend his talk and then to meet him personally. He was gracious and kind, very warm to everyone there. I was left with a long and lasting impression that I had indeed met a great writer, a wonderful man.

Throughout the years I have come to know Frank Waters best through his writings, and most recently through my deep inquiry into his powerful and universal novels *The Yogi of Cockroach Court* and *The Lizard Woman*.

It was hard to absorb the incredible range and scope of Frank Waters' work when I set about planning my talk. Initially I thought in the course of one year I would read all twenty-seven of his books, rereading some, catching up on those I hadn't yet read. I can report that this goal was not achieved. After a time I realized I needed to focus on a single aspect of Waters' work, to absorb this, and to connect with it as deeply as I could. But what work? And where to begin? With resolve, I turned to the source, Frank Waters himself.

One day I spread out on a large table all the books by Waters that I had, waiting to hear from him about which ones I should concentrate on. After a while I felt myself increasingly pulled to *The Yogi of Cockroach Court* and later, in the same manner, to *The Lizard Woman*. What a relief it was to realize these were "my books," books whose themes I felt I could approach with freshness and passion.

These two books are spiritual, psychic, emotional, and cosmic bookends to each other. They connect profoundly with both Frank Waters' and my own study of the nature of humankind with its cycle of *duhka*, or suffering. In that regard, Sri Ramana Maharshi's statement that Frank Waters quotes in *Mountain Dialogues* — "What is in the world is in the body, and what is in the body is in the world, also"[1] — exactly corresponds to the intrinsic and underlying themes of both books. Their bedrock is the study of this yin and yang of essential being, the balance of the sacred, the profane, the base and the spiritual, as well as the struggle of the characters in these two books to find true and lasting happiness.

The denizens of Cockroach Court and the hot dusty border cantina world play out their human drama in the midst of their own deceptions and illusions. Waters' alternately fascinating and excruciatingly terrible manifestations of *duhka* are profoundly explored in *The Yogi of Cockroach Court* and *The Lizard Woman*.

In his essay "Ley Lines" from *Mountain Dialogues*, he paraphrased the primary belief of R. A. Schwaller de Lubicz, author of *The Temple of Man*: "The one goal of human existence is to attain this higher universal consciousness, to return to its original wholeness. Each mineral, vegetable, animal and human species also represents a stage in the evolution of this higher consciousness."[2]

This progression of evolution, this striving for consciousness, is at the heart of *The Yogi of Cockroach Court*. It seems fitting to begin backwards, so to speak, by discussing this book which took Frank Waters twenty years to write. It is a book he worked on during the Depression and World War II and at various other times. It is a book that I feel was very close to his heart and spirit.

The Yogi of Cockroach Court begins with a prologue in which a terrible storm sets the stage for what is to come. We meet violent nature in both its physical and elemental manifestations. As the torrential storm rages, we view the insufferable and brutal *yanqui* El Borracho, father of the boy Barby who later figures so powerfully in the book. There are few beginnings in literature that are more terrible and compelling than this one as the youngster finds his way in the violent storm to the house of an adoptive father, the Chinese merchant Tai Ling, owner of The Lamp Awake.

What a cast of characters this is! We meet the suffering Romeros, the Mexican family who are caretakers of El Borracho's boy child with an unnamed Mexicana. We feel pity for the meek Señora with her kids, and for Jesús Romero, her impotent husband, who is unable to stand up to the Ugly American, El Yanqui. It is sad to see the cycle of abuse continue with El Borracho's illegitimate son, later the brutish young man given the moniker "Barby," short for "bar boy." It is he who sells his wares of peanuts and cashews inside the dark walls of the border cantinas and casinos while he lives with Tai Ling. Barby is a wounded groveling animal, always at the edge of imminent evil like a scurrying cockroach in an unpleasant and consuming darkness. At night he throws himself on his pallet, never finding that respite he truly seeks with his "enlightened" foster father, who meditates on the Four Noble Truths and the Noble Eightfold Path[3]_ as the world crashes in around him in The Lamp Awake.

Waters has a power of naming that has seldom been paralleled in literature. Both the names of his characters and the places he evokes are memorable.

The Yogi of Cockroach Court is set in an unnamed border town, and the power of not naming is the naming in this case. It could be any border town on the American-Mexican border it seems so familiar. We feel the push and pull of "them and us," the "other and the like," the "coming and the going," and above all, the wrenching impermanence that all the characters yearn to lessen as they struggle in their shifting border world. We identify and know the Llano de los Perdidos, the Plains of the Lost, as we come to know Cockroach Court and The Lamp Awake. In the midst of this vague and unsettled border world the characters struggle for moments of passion and happiness that are few and far between.

When Barby encounters Guadalupe, the beautiful but selfish percentage girl in the cantina Las Quince Letras, he thinks he has found a true source of joy in life. While his love is passionate, it is also obsessive and controlling. Over time, Barby attempts to find out everything about Guadalupe's life, interrogating her mercilessly, attempting to possess her as he would a caged animal.

Waters draws a fine portrait of the lost souls in this sultry and teeming border world. I am reminded of my own border towns, El Paso, Texas, and Juárez, Mexico. I grew up only forty-two miles from these parallel cities, and I found in Waters' work a quintessential border portrait, this one set in his particular moment in time.

El Paso Street in El Paso is a history of the immigration of the Chinese who worked the railroads, followed by the waves of Koreans who now are the business leaders in this border city. Today you can see this *mestizaje*, or mixture of cultures, in these Koreans speaking perfect Spanish to their Mexican customers and Mexican workers. The former Mexican movie theater El Colón was built on the site of the former Chinese cemetery, and the nearby restaurant Super Tortas was the place where the corpse of a young Chinese woman was found when the building was remodeled. You can go to Juárez to eat at the Shangri-La Restaurant, formerly owned by Paco Wong, and know that you have crossed into a world that is as unique and special as Waters' world in *The Yogi of Cockroach Court.*

The history of El Paso mirrors in many ways the story of Waters' unnamed border town. There is a ring of authenticity in his finely drawn portraits of the cantinas with their percentage girls and the background "cages of cockroaches," the rooms of the prostitutes who inhabit this world of darkness.

The Lamp Awake lies at the end of the Callejon de los Chinos. It faces the railroad tracks; to its side and rear is La Plaza de Las Cucarachas. "A dimlit maze of lewd patios and shrieking courtyards, Cockroach Court was aptly named for the prostitutes who filled its cribs — the inafortunadas, putas and parjaritas who here were known as cucarachas."[4]

Guadalupe is one such woman. She is both out of place and comfortable in her world. She embodies many of the positive aspects of someone who has overcome the abuses of her world, free of brutal, uncaring men who take advantage of her at every turn. Although she is a prostitute, she still has self-respect and a will to survive. A cunning, headstrong, and willful young woman who believes she has the talent to dance, she sets about making her way in this cruel and merciless world. She is drawn to the loutish Barby because he dotes on her and loves her. She wants and needs this adulation. Though seemingly a simple woman, she is really a schemer and can't be trusted.

The character of Tai Ling is in many ways the most complex and compelling of the book. Certainly he is the most inscrutable.

> . . . So quiet was the old man that his impassivity matched that of his favorite Bodhisattva, seated in the Buddha-posture, on a lotus-throne enhaloed by a rainbow; at his feet a fish immersed like all sentient beings in a sea of illusion, and a human skull symbolizing renunciation of this world of ignorance.[5]

Tai Ling spends much of his time in meditation, but because of this sense of detachment, he *allows*, and this is the crucial word, *allows* the damaging actions of others to run rampant and unimpeded. He so passively watches the world go by that he sets himself up for the terrible and shattering movement of events that inevitably happen at the end of the book: Barby's violent death,

Guadalupe's thoughtless selfishness and egoistic absorption, and his own terrible death in a blazing inferno of bullets and flames.

Even the book's minor characters are crucial to the action and are part of the whole; all are elemental players in the inexorable drama that pulls them forward to destruction. The coyote named Mendoza is a dark and malevolent character, a former pimp who greases the palms of the border patrol and immigration authorities. Chewlee Singkee, the prosperous butcher and old friend, serves as a Greek chorus to Tai Ling's musings. And who can forget the image of Chino Juan counting money heaped on a table, or the tormented Sal locked in her room and running out of time and money.

The themes in *The Yogi of Cockroach Court* and *The Lizard Woman* are universal and enduring. We encounter the play of light and darkness in both books. This is never so evident as in the portrayal of the women protagonists, Guadalupe and Arvilla. Guadalupe in *The Yogi of Cockroach Court* comes alive in the daytime and shrinks during the nighttime.

> What a child of the sun the girl was! Like a lizard, she could not move until the light had penetrated every fiber of her being. And then how suddenly and intensely alive she became and remained throughout the day. It was as though through every pore she absorbed an energy that impelled her every act. Curiously enough it carried her through the evening as if the casino's bright lights and music were a prolongation of her mood. Sunlight! It was her life as she was its symbol.[6]

It is exactly the opposite for Arvilla, the single-minded temptress who reigns in the night world of La Casa Blanca, the dusty cabaret on the edge of that harsh border world. In *The Lizard Woman* she drives Lee Marston insane with passion.

> Arvilla of the night was of his dreams. She held all the alluring essence of the something he had all but reached the night before. Arvilla of the day was another creature. She was of the desert, hard, unfathomable, inhuman, devoid of all feeling . . . .[7]

The dual poles of nature fight for dominance in this world of darkness and light. We never know who is the clear winner. Can there ever be a winner in a world of illusion and impermanence? This is the question we need to ask ourselves. Waters leaves us in both novels with a sense of stinging urgency to live deeply and without illusion. Can we?

We know we don't want to live like Barby, driven to obsession by his fluttering, caged lover, Guadalupe, a woman he knows doesn't love him, can never love him, just as Lee Marston in *The Lizard Woman* knows Arvilla can never love him. And yet these two men are driven insane with desire and forge ahead to their own perdition, knowingly and yes, willingly. Lee Marston moves from passion and obsession into the twilight world of either madness or enlightenment, whatever you choose to call his "awakening" at the end of the book.

We are able through Waters' profound characterizations to see that we don't want to be these men or these women. But is it better to be the detached, dispassionate, and removed Tai Ling, watching from the sidelines? Isn't it he who is the engine that affects the tragic fate of the others through his casual acceptance of evil?

We are all connected. This is what Waters tells us. The death of certain characters, actual and symbolic, affects all the others. Yet at all times, falling down and then picking themselves up, the characters attempt in their own ways to survive and thrive as best they can, given the roll of the dice they have inherited.

The richness of characterization is what holds and delights readers of these two novels. We meet the evil couple: Trinidad, "Señor Thinco Thentavos de Athucar," and his nasty cohort, Peña, who seduces and later enthralls Guadalupe. One of Waters' themes ("Lust, Ill Will and Stupidity, the Three Fires of Desire; by these all their lives were lighted. None of them was free"[8]) is played out by these characters, as well as by the floozy boozy Sal, a wasted and used-up percentage girl. In a horrible and haunting scene at the end of the book, she finds herself in her dingy crib with a lust-driven Barby, who is horrified later to discover that he has made love to his nemesis.

Sal is the perfect type of character for the screen. It is surprising to me that no movie has been made of *The Yogi of Cockroach Court*. Wise, but foolish, a *pendeja*, or fool, with some desperate sense of intuition and native smarts, Sal is a tragic figure who lives long in our memories. Driven by fear, she is the epitome of the type of haunted, grasping character inhabiting this novel of *duhka*.

Fear is a peculiar thing.

Not the sudden fright that stabs out from the dark, the awesome hush that gathers heavy as a pall about Death's departing heels, nor all those momentary terrors with which we are most familiar. For mercifully they are too quick. Their very unexpected swiftness serves but to shock the nerves and numb the mind so that we stand paralyzed.

A really terrible fear is not an affair of the moment. It is a parasitic worm that sucks at every nerve and fattens upon the heart. By night and in the cheerful sun of the day it fastens upon your thoughts, preys unceasingly upon your secret soul. Its coils thicken with monstrous growth until every little window of your mind has been closed to escape. But always the fear grows there, an insidious thing moving and twisting about within the pregnant womb of your mind. Fear of poverty and of slow hunger is like that, and the inevitableness of an approaching end. A fear that cannot be hurried any more than it can be escaped, like a cancerous growth that spreads at its own slow pace.

Thus it was with Sal.[9]

This theme of parasitic and consuming fear threads through all the characters, even the stoic Tai Ling. Waters offers us a sad commentary on humankind who live mired in a paralyzing fear so overwhelming that they are forced to breathe in a shallow and fetid way, giving them not a whole but a half-life of continual anxiety.

In the book's epilogue, Waters notes, "Why is it that those we have abandoned are not always waiting unchanged to welcome us?"[10] How sad and comic it is to see Guadalupe return to her border town with her current lover, Gloria, a red-haired singer, to find that both Tai Ling and Barby are dead. She feels the terrible twinge of impermanence that signals to her "the end" of an era. The people who loved her no longer love her. She must move on to other lovers, continually perpetuating her cycle of yearning in that ceaseless predatory search for "happiness." Guadalupe is a lesbian; and while she prefers sexually to love women, love — any love, or rather any lover's love of her — is important, no matter whose it is. How small her life is. And how sad.

Guadalupe says at the end of the book, "Life is simple if you know exactly what you want."[11] And on some level, she appears to have been successful with this philosophy of life. But has she really? She is getting older. And although she has not been unsuccessful, she still needs to be carried along by someone who desires her, in this case the older American woman La Señorita Burrell, a tourist agent. Guadalupe is a woman who uses people. When she has used them up, she discards them. In this regard, she is a sister spirit to Arvilla in *The Lizard Woman*, who uses Lee Marston to further her own ends.

Arvilla's desperate greed drives her to talk Lee Marston into taking her to the mountains of the Lizard Woman to find gold. She has been promised gold by her lover Jim Horne, el hombre conejo, who is waiting for her return. Without guilt or any tinge of remorse Arvilla uses both men for her own purposes, pitting one against the other. There are few such selfish, dark-hearted, and grasping villains in American literature as Arvilla. One has to wonder why this taut and thrilling book, as well as the other, has never been made into a movie.

In Waters' work the desert is a character as well: ruthless, unbending, merciless, occasionally kind, but more often than not harsh and cruel. We see its great beauty and revel in its majesty, and then curse it for its implacable honesty and unforgiving nature. The desert, for those of us who live in it, reminds us of the ocean. It is true that all of this part of the world — New Mexico, Arizona, and Texas — this harsh dry land was once an ocean. One has only to visit certain nearby areas to find sea shells and the remains of a once flourishing marine life.

To live in the desert is to live with struggle. To live with the darkness and the light, the unknown and the known, the ominous outlines of mountains on the horizon, their cold stone breasts seemingly impersonal and uncaring. We are reminded in the desert of the impermanence of all life, in its shifting from darkness to light, light to darkness, water to desert, life to death, and death to what?

Waters says about writing *The Lizard Woman*:

> I began with a description of a remote desert valley enclosed
> by barren rocky mountains, around whose circular rim lay the
> semblance of a gigantic lizard with a woman's face meeting the
> end of her scaly tail.[12]

This theme of the uroboros embodies Waters' philosophy in *The Lizard Woman*, "the uroboros as the symbol of primordial unity, enclosing the infinitude of space and time . . . the fullness of divine Creation. The serpent itself, linking the beginning and the end, symbolized timeless time."[13]

He goes on to say the Azteca believed that the earth rested on the back of a monster of sorts, "a crocodile, serpent or lizard . . ."[14]

I have personally had dreams of this crocodile/lizard God, or elder, and have spoken to him. It was with wonderful surprise that I came to read about this lizard spirit in the work of Frank Waters and to appreciate how he has bridged the gaps of the sacred and profane, myth and reality, and gone before us so willingly with courage to point the way for his fellow travelers. His writings leave us with a road map to the familiar unfamiliar and the unfamiliar familiar.

As readers and fellow humans, we tragically identify with Lee Marston's obsession with Arvilla, which is poignant, stupid, fantastic, and surreal, all at the same time. Marston can't help but be pulled along by this woman who had "the dancer's legs, the torso of a toreador and the face of a brown Madonna."[15]

As a writer and reader, I have wondered who Guadalupe and Arvilla were modeled after. Last night I saw the name of this woman in a dream, but alongside her name were shadow names of two other women. This leads me to guess that the one true name has other names merged with it. This name is for the writer to know and the reader to know, each in his or her distinct way. The power of Waters' work is that he brings us into the story of our own passions and obsessions and moments of enlightenment.

Guadalupe and Arvilla are separate, but joined in a tragic sisterhood. They are, no doubt, two of the most compelling contemporary women characters that I have ever read about in any literature. Arvilla the percentage girl is like Guadalupe in her "grim forcefulness of character."[16]

Marston's passion for Arvilla is inescapable and this is his tragedy. Anyone who has loved the wrong person will identify with his obsession.

> Lee Marston was in an ecstasy of bewilderment. The throb of his senses left him inarticulate. He heard her boots drop to the ground. She stood up beside his outstretched body, and he heard the faint rustle of her garments as she unbuttoned her shirt and loosened her clothing for sleeping. Lying quiet on

the blankets he saw patches of her outlined in the splotches of moonlight which dropped through the tatters of the roof. A beam, light as a feather, fell on her face, showed her cheeks as a white patch in which her wide brown eyes rippled like a deep sink. Her throat where it met her breast was a pale splotch of snow, light and fluffy, fresh-fallen, as though unsoiled. She dropped beside him and yawned sleepily. "Buenas noches, mi vaquero," came her words, easily, softly in old Spanish.

Marston breathed deeply. He did not answer. As he closed his eyes, he seemed to feel the weight of her glance resting on his face. He wanted to stretch out his hand: he trembled at the thought. He wanted to cry out, to tell her all things which oppressed him, to cry, "Arvilla, you are beautiful! Arvilla, hold me in your brown arms. Never, Arvilla, let me go back to men, to cities." Forever would he go with her across the expanse which lay like the soft moonlight before his eyes.[17]

This heat of passion and obsession is what drives *The Lizard Woman*. The struggle of Marston and Arvilla is interminable and painful. As a reader, the book is hard to put down for all its anguish. In their Garden of the Devil, we always feel a pervasive and heavy sense of ever-present, impending evil. As we know, however, evil can be seductive!

Barby and Lee Marston are drawn to these two women who can't love them. They don't want to be deserted by them, but they know in their hearts and souls they ultimately will be. This is the *duhka* of their lives.

Waters goes on to describe Marston as a sleepwalker, "For all that long trip Lee Marston moved like a man in a dream. For the desert was a dream."[18]

Our business, Waters strongly suggests, is to wake from this dream of suffering.

There is no end to any tale, as in *The Lizard Woman*, for the nature of impermanence is just that: one thing becomes another, endlessly, ceaselessly, and with its own order and without regard to our petty will to break the cycle set for us before time. And for those who live the tales, the stories go on, at least in the minds and hearts of the characters. Again, who knows what awaits after death and that transformation from body to spirit realm?

"What are you?"

"What am I?"

These are the questions the characters of *The Yogi of Cockroach Court* and *The Lizard Woman* ask of themselves and each other. Their answers are dependent upon and related to each other, as the sun is dependent upon and related to the moon.

The Lizard Woman was first published as *Fever Pitch* in 1930 when Waters was twenty-eight years old. He had been "working as a telephone engineer in Imperial Valley, on the California-Baja California border."[19] The power of that time lives in *The Lizard Woman* and continues to grow in *The Yogi of Cockroach Court*, which was begun in 1927 but not published until 1947. Still today, at the celebration of the Frank Waters Centennial, we feel the vibrancy and life of these two novels that have so profoundly touched the very core of our humanity.

As I was drawn to these two tales of passion, obsession, and enlightenment, I felt great pity and sadness for the characters in these similar and desperate worlds. I would offer them peace from desperate illusion and needless suffering.

I thank Don Francisco Waters, fellow pilgrim, compassionate traveler, for entering in and inhabiting this magnificent world of light and darkness, and for illuminating for the rest of us so clearly and with such mercy the world of The Lamp Awake.

Linda Lizut Helstern
Mixedbloods: Stereotypes and Inversions
in *The Yogi of Cockroach Court*

Published in 1947, some twenty years after it was drafted at the height of Prohibition, *The Yogi of Cockroach Court* showcases what Frank Waters described as the border Southwest's "conglomerate cross-breed underworld...– the part Mexican, part Indian, part white, mestizos, creoles, and coyotes."[1] A casual reader might be puzzled by this assertion, for of the four principal characters–the Chinese merchant Tai Ling; his surrogate son, Barby; Guadalupe, the young woman Barby falls in love with; and Guadalupe's friend Sal, the sometime Kansas City prostitute with a heart of gold–only Barby is immediately identifiable as a mixedblood. In the prologue we meet him in the squalor of a Mexican village on the Sea of Cortez where he is left to grow up by his brutal, hard-drinking American father. Following his father's example, however, the very young Barby flees the village and the devastation brought by the much-feared storm that comes predictably each fall. Like so many illegal immigrants, first Chinese and later Mexican, the boy makes his way north hidden in a vehicle, his ultimate destination unknown. His first refuge and home of convenience until he dies smuggling illegal immigrants north from his hometown is Tai Ling's shop in a nameless Mexican border town.

Waters, in fact, gave his manuscript the working title, "Barby."[2] If the title change shifts our focus away from the tragic young mixedblood trapped between two worlds, it also gives us a lens for considering Waters' racial constructions, especially those of Barby and Guadalupe, who are both Indian mixedbloods. In this way we may take our clue from Tai Ling, the Chinese merchant and Buddhist practitioner of the title. Tai Ling has a wonderful eye for the ironies of stereotyped ethnic representation in the American media and at times affects "make-believe pidgin-English" for American tourists.[3] He sometimes uses it on Barby as well, but only to comment ironically on the issues of profit and loss. Barby, who knows that Tai Ling can speak perfectly good English and Spanish, never understands this linguistic appropriation, which is strategically related to the final ironic newspaper accounts of their deaths. According to American reports, Tai Ling is only apparently a reclusive retired shopkeeper; he is presented as the opium dealer and evil genius behind an imagined tong war, the "perfect one-dimensional American movie" stereotype Tai Ling himself eschewed.[4]

If Tai Ling's principal purpose is to represent the ethnic Chinese, Waters also clearly understood the conventions of Indian and mixedblood representation, both using and inverting the stereotypes to create his young lovers. The mixedblood stereotype tends to exaggerate the gendered traits that mark stereotyped Indian representation in its negative manifestation. In men, these traits include savage brutality and an underlying threat to white womanhood, lying, thieving, cowardice, and drunkenness. Women are marked by nubile sexuality and/or an earth mother identity. In both cases, the stereotype incorporates the naiveté of the perpetual child. The very different fates of Barby and Guadalupe, it seems to me, reflect the two traditionally different attitudes toward *mestizaje* demarcated by the Mexican-American border. While a series of racial incidents marks Barby's retreat from the white world, Guadalupe's artistic success in that world is ambiguously tied to her Indianness, to the race that, in this novel of deracination, dares not to speak its name.

Guadalupe's story reminds me of another that Waters told in *Masked Gods*. In a small Mexican village, it seems, the priest took great pride in the devotion of his parishioners, who adorned the altar of the church with flowers in every season. He was startled to discover, when an earthquake displaced the altar, that beneath it lay the stone sculpture of a Native goddess.[5] Beneath Guadalupe's patina of mission school whiteness is the Indian attuned to her visions, "a stubborn little pagan."[6] As Sister Teresa, her only advocate on the reservation, is buried, carrying to the grave the shame of her sexual desire, Guadalupe opens her eyes to a vision of the mountains "with outflung arms… covered with a dark blue mantle and dotted with specks of light like toasted maise grains, by the bright morning sun."[7] In this moment, Waters tells us, "[s]he was free."[8] Here two points, both important to Waters' configuration of race in this novel, remain unspoken. First is the fact that Guadalupe's vision is one of Tonantzin, the indigenous precursor whose identity was subsumed by the Virgin of Guadalupe. Second is the ironic association between Tonantzin and freedom. The Virgin of Guadalupe, perhaps the New World's premier example of cultural hybridity, blending Tonantzin and the Virgin Mary, is traditionally associated with freedom, for she became the patron saint of the Mexican nation when Fr. Miguel Hidalgo proclaimed Mexico's independence from Spain. Truly La Alma de Mexico (a name that Guadalupe will eventually claim for herself), Our Lady is also known to the devoted as Mi Vergen Morena.[9] And devotees of the fictional Guadalupe frequently call her "the little morena."

That Guadalupe's freedom derives exclusively from the indigenous Tonantzin rather than the dark Madonna speaks to the importance of the racial thread in Waters' novel. Ironically enough, the young woman is an American reservation mixedblood, though this seems apparent only to Barby. What Barby remembers after seeing her for the first time are Guadalupe's black hair, black eyes, and "creamy oval face."[10] Her first night as a percentage girl, Barby takes another close look: "She was small and well formed, her skin a light iodine. Only her hair was that of a pure Indian."[11] If these are the only suggestions that Guadalupe is a "breed," it may be due to the fact that this stereotype is gendered, almost exclusively, male. Barby's Indian lineage is obscured almost as carefully as Guadalupe's white lineage. It is explicitly mentioned but once in the novel. Barby is always the son of his American father, never the son of his nameless, unknown mother. Our first glimpse of the adult Barby connects him directly with the American called El Borracho, The Drunk, "for with the broad brutal face of a halfbreed, he stared drunkenly down the street."[12]

There is no small irony in Waters' portrait of Barby, which simultaneously constructs and deconstructs the stereotype of the drunken Indian, a stereotype that Waters otherwise avoids in this novel. The only Indian with a tribal affiliation in *The Yogi of Cockroach Court* is the Cocopah who scavenges for scraps at the celebration that marks the opening of Barby's cantina. If drunkenness and brutality go hand in hand in depictions of the Indian savage, they are the principal legacy of the racially tainted "breed" who can never aspire to the status of nobility. The breed is a liar and a thief as well, another trait Barby demonstrates early. "[C]aught stealing sacramental wine" as a schoolboy, he assaults the priest.[13] Even as he retains the stereotype of the mixedblood in all of its dimensions, however, Waters deconstructs it. That Barby is so obviously his father's son asks readers to interrogate the very construction of the breed stereotype. Our single view of Barby's father reveals not only his penchant for alcohol but his brutality, physical and verbal. El Borracho's scientific disdain for peasant belief marks him very much as a modern American, proof that Indians have no monopoly on drunkenness or brutality.

In the face of his father's brutality, the boy cowers, a stereotypically breed response that ultimately renders Barby incapable of proving his manhood. Having crossed the Line to work as a farm laborer, Barby's industry has won him a promotion and some favors from his white boss. One Saturday night, back in Mexico and fortified with tequila, Barby, who refuses to associate with his fellow workers and now speaks only English, fancies himself the social equal of his employer. Massey happens to be escorting a white woman dressed in white, and Barby's approach is immediately perceived as a threat, emphasizing that the discourse of whiteness is a language he will never speak. Massey's response is first physical and then verbal abuse. Having tripped Barby with a contemptuous laugh, the overseer apologizes to his companion, "'—just one of these cowardly, stinkin' drunk greasers! A white man's got to teach them their place ever so often!...'"[14] A week later when he plans to defend his honor and take his revenge on Massey, Barby cannot wield his knife. He is paralyzed, just as he was as a child when El Borracho hurled the same epithet.

Truly the son of his father, Barby is himself capable of extreme brutality, as when he discovers the truth of Guadalupe's sexuality, the secret of her extended sexual relationship with the old woman Oakie. Barby punches Guadalupe, then kicks her when she falls to the floor, lashes her a dozen times with his belt, and finally rapes her. Waters attributes this brutal outburst, pure and simple, to race. "If [Barby] had been wholly white or Indian," Waters tells us, "he would have killed her coldly and forgotten her. Or being Spanish, done the thing in heat and turning sentimental carried roses to her grave. But being what he was, a half-breed, he merely did the brutal thing..."[15]

Barby's inability to assert his manhood in the face of whiteness also marks him forever as a boy, the identity coded in his name, a contraction of "bar boy." Not even Tai Ling's best efforts to turn him into a responsible adult have a lasting effect. Barby fails as a bookkeeper for The Lamp Awake. When, in the tradition of family patriarch, Tai Ling gives Barby his own bar, a gift intended to make Barby an appropriately patriarchal match for Guadalupe, the new toy occupies him for a while. Eventually, Tai Ling comes to realize that Barby is no more accountable for the cash flow at El Sol de Mayo than he had been at The Lamp Awake. Far from becoming a potential patriarch in his own right, Barby is a perpetual child who needs looking after. In this, he is Guadalupe's match.

As perpetual children with no sense of money, Barby and Guadalupe are visibly and stereotypically Indian, reminiscent of the Osages Waters remembered from his Colorado Springs boyhood. If one day they peeled off a hundred dollar bill to pay for an apple, expecting no change, the next day they might try to purchase an entire bolt of Chinese silk for a dollar, much to the merchant's chagrin.[16] Such examples have shaped the stereotype of Indian fiscal irresponsibility and perpetual childhood used to justify the patriarchal treatment of the tribes by the U.S. government. Waters makes no textual link between race and fiscal naiveté, but the repeated links between fiscal responsibility and whiteness, often not positive, suggest its import. How little money means to Guadalupe becomes obvious in her relationship with Sal. Sal dives to the floor after rolling coins the first night Guadalupe dances at Las Quince Letras. When she tries to give the money to Guadalupe, however, Guadalupe refuses to take it. Sal puts it away to pay their bills. "Somethin' else," she observes, "you don't know much about."[17] Beyond their novelty, the gifts Barby lavishes on her mean nothing to Guadalupe either. Child that she is, she does form an attachment to a favorite toy, the tiny mice crafted by a blind beggar that have no intrinsic value. Throughout most of the novel, Guadalupe is content to let her friends take care of her money, and by extension, Guadalupe herself. Gloria eventually rescues Guadalupe from Trinidad and Peña's fraud but she is less than enchanted with caring for the perpetual child who cannot do her own mending. Guadalupe, she realizes, is a user.

Guadalupe's magnetic sexuality is the trait that marks her most obviously as Indian. So implicated is sexuality in the representation of Indian women, who are often cast as types of the nubile Pocahontas, that Native scholar

Deborah Miranda suggests Native women have been "invisibilized as erotic beings by American mythology."[18] Influenced, perhaps, by the psychiatric term for homosexuality, *inversion*, Waters explicitly uses Guadalupe's lesbianism, her obvious crossover identity, to invert the gendered Indian stereotype. It certainly renders Guadalupe visible and erotic against a background of pervasive, and largely white, commodity sex. The effect is notably double edged, however, to make the sexual Guadalupe ultimately inaccessible is to configure Barby as the breed forever trapped between the white world that rejects him as a social equal and the Indian world that rejects his sexual desire. "The socially ostracized of two races," Mourning Dove called the breed she hoped to deconstruct in her own 1927 novel *Cogwea: The Half Blood: A Depiction of the Great Montana Cattle Range.*[19]

If Barby has idealized Guadalupe of the creamy skin, raw sexual desire is inscribed in darker tones. The boxer Fuera is the first to call Guadalupe "the little morena" the night he hatches the plan for a double date that matches him with Sal and Barby with Guadalupe. "I fix you up to fight and make love," he laughingly assures Barby.[20] It is "the little morena, the little dark one" that first the cantina's customers and then Gonzales, the manager, pick out of the chorus line for her singular eroticism.[21] None of the other Seductive Señoritas— two redheads, two faded blonds, a too-skinny Mexican girl, and a matronly Mexican woman—begin to match Guadalupe's appeal, which, it would seem, given the Mexican presence here, rests not so much in darkness as in Indianness. Watching his customers' response, Gonzalez dispassionately observes, "She couldn't sing or dance worth a damn. Green as grass. But she had something: rampant, shouting, youthful, unconscious sex! A regular little bitch in heat without knowing it."[22]

Like Gonzalez's customers, all of the women who desire Guadalupe, and whom Guadalupe desires, are white. From the beginning, this whiteness is linked with death. Her acceptance of it and desire for it mark the death of the Indian Guadalupe, particularly because eroticized whiteness is also linked to Guadalupe's growing comprehension of the commodity value of her performance. All of her lovers except Peña, the flamenco dancer, are of the lineage of Sister Teresa, the nun with the long, blue-veined hands, "bloodless lips," and face as "cold white as that of a corpse."[23] Peña's very name suggests the transformation she effects, for the change of a single consonant transforms *peña*, shame, into the rocky fastness reminiscent of Guadalupe's mountain vision. If Peña ultimately teaches Guadalupe to accept her sexuality "without fear, shame, or revulsion," Oakie, with her watery gray eyes and missing teeth, beckons with the inevitability of the Grim Reaper.[24] Sal warns her early on that Oakie wants her money, and Guadalupe remembers her "slimy clawing."[25]

Although "Peña's body was so startlingly white and voluptuous [Guadalupe] caught her breath," Gloria's principal erotic attraction is her "transparent, blue-veined, white flesh" so like Sister Teresa's and yet so different.[26] Gloria, in fact, initiates Guadalupe into the mysteries of the money economy, stealing her from Peña's deception. Having made Guadalupe money-conscious, she herself seems destined to become the victim of Guadalupe's new desire for upward mobility. By the time Guadalupe meets tourism director Heloise Burrell, with the premature white streak in her hair, Miss Burrell can see nothing at all Indian in Guadalupe. The Spanish dances Guadalupe performs, she pronounces decisively, are her "cultural background," what she, indeed, "belong[s] to."[27] Miss Burrell's close association with the moon seems ultimately linked with the coldness of death, not the passion of romance.

Guadalupe's career has grown out of her personal passion for dancing, a passion that does not seem idly chosen given the importance of ritual dance in Southwest Native cultures. Dance, not surprisingly, marks important moments in the evolution of the personal relationship between Barby and Guadalupe, even as it does for Martiniano and Flowers Playing in *The Man Who Killed the Deer*. I believe that the parallels are worth investigating as we look at the construction of Indianness in *The Yogi of Cockroach Court*. In both novels, commitment to relationship begins with social dancing. Martiniano honors Flowers Playing for her social dance performance with gifts of extraordinary generosity and an offer of marriage, promptly accepted. Barby and Guadalupe's first dance also captures the essence of the relationship that will evolve. In this case, it is a jazz dance in an after-hours bar, a dance initiated by Guadalupe for pleasure, not pay. As they dance, Guadalupe remains utterly unconscious of her partner, while Barby feels "an overpowering sensuous softness, the flow of intense and consuming vitality."[28] He soon enough discovers that he will never possess its source.

His revelation comes in a public performance, much as Martiniano, anticipating the dance in the pueblo plaza, feels his alienation from the feminine energies of the Deer Mother embodied by his wife. Immediately, Flowers

Playing becomes "a stranger. A woman who seemed no longer his wife, but a symbol of something in all women he could not but resent."[29] The first time he watches her dance with the Seven Sweet Seductive Señoritas, Barby sees the real Guadalupe, "awake as he had never awakened her. She was the soft heavy earth waiting for the plow, and birds screeching over the corn milpas, and the tules bent backward by the wind along the washes."[30] Her "public orgasm" removes Guadalupe utterly from the realm of personal relationship. "The very moon leered down remote and untouchable as she."[31] Barby does not see her perform again until the opening of his own cantina, but the truth is once again obvious to him. Dancing, Guadalupe "moved back into another world to which he did not have the key."[32]

Guadalupe embodies the rhythms of the universe and the second principal stereotype of Indian female representation, the earth mother. In Waters' inversion, however, this cosmic connection is not entirely positive, for to be in harmony with the universe is to lack a will. Much to Sal's early morning chagrin, Guadalupe's vitality is strong when the sun shines; but in the darkest hours of the night she becomes a "sullen, black negation," an emptiness waiting to be filled, nothing more than the acquiescent object of desire.[33] To become a desiring subject, Guadalupe must develop her own will; and her development as an artist, as Trinidad points out, involves nothing less than this. Instinctive talent is not enough, he admonishes, when he gives Guadalupe his grudging assent to travel with his troupe for the first time: "A bull must smell the blood. No more. But understand: you are nothing. Nothing but a dull child who has been dreaming much. To Trinidad a body that is tired already–look at the knees trembling! You must make it one of steel like that of Toledo which can be bent only because it cannot be broken..."[34] The will is of European fabrication, Trinidad reminds us, and is not a constituent of the stereotyped Indian. Certainly it is not characteristic of the "slow and apathetic" Cocopahs, Yumas, and Mojaves, with whom Guadalupe grew up on the reservation.[35]

Only when her will is sufficiently developed can Guadalupe leave Barby–and her Indianness–behind for the life of a professional dancer. She dances flamenco, a highly ritualized, if secular, European dance form, and a sharp contrast to the popular and openly sexualized Mexican hybrid renderings of the costumed charro and chinapoblano, the other two members of Trinidad's troupe. From an ocean away, flamenco, associated with Trinidad's pure Castilian Spanish, carries with it an aura of racial purity (despite its own history of cultural hybridity). With Guadalupe's departure, Barby, who inherited a "foolish will" from his American father, retreats to the world of crime that is the singular habitat of the breed.[36] The first time Guadalupe leaves, El Sol de Mayo replaces The Lamp Awake as the last stop for illegals crossing the border. Only when she leaves for good does Barby discover the nature of his underworld involvement and make the conscious choice to become criminally involved, helping move others across the border that marks his own exclusion from the white mainstream.

Mexico, where mixedblood *mestizaje* is the norm, always represented for Frank Waters the future to which America might aspire. *Pike's Peak* protagonist March Cable, about to leave Mexico, envisions the

> ... gradual amalgamation of races [as] an inevitable necessity.... An amalgamation that would not be a scientific mixture of customs, beliefs, and wills, that would not be an economic trade, but which would gather these in its flow. A fusion that would be the death of each, the white and the Indian, as he was today. A death and a great rebirth. And from them, together, the new American—a new continental soul reborn. ...[37]

To claim American identity, as the young Barby wishes to do, is to come inevitably face to face with the old breed stereotype. To cross the Line north is not to find economic security but to discover a legacy of detestable breed traits—brutality, lying, thieving, cowardice, drunkenness, and fiscal naiveté. Indeed, when *The Yogi of Cockroach Court* was published, thirty states had laws prohibiting miscegenation, and the majority stayed on the books until invalidated by a 1967 U.S. Supreme Court ruling. To cross south, on the other hand, as Guadalupe does, is to discover the possibility of a mixed cultural legacy accorded the respect reserved in the United States, at least until recently, for the racially and culturally pure. Guadalupe finds her true self in the inversion of patriarchal expectation and gendered stereotypes. She is not a perfect human being, but through the co-evolution of her will and her art, she is headed in the right direction.

John R. Milton
Intuition and the Dance of Life:
Frank Waters' *Pike's Peak*

Frank Waters in his trilogy offers long and solid portrayals of late-nine-teenth-century-early-twentieth-century mining in Colorado, with forays into New Mexico and with obvious leanings toward Indian-oriented values. Pike's Peak becomes a symbol in the mining trilogy, both of the spiritual quality of the search and of man's proper relationship to the earth. It is majestic, immense, upthrust, and enduring. Rogier goes into the mountain to unlock its inscrutable will. When the mountain seems to defeat him, he becomes contrite and humble, realizing the insignificance of man and the offensiveness of his folly. This in turn teaches him a lesson which is from the land:

> Like a man dumbfounded by the simplicity of life once ev-erything else has been taken from him, he realized that there might be nothing more sublime than his completest adjust-ment to that earth and its elements, those intangible forces which had molded him unwittingly in their ceaseless flow.

At the end of *The Wild Earth's Nobility*, Rogier feels that the mountains are a barrier shutting off from his sight "the ever inscrutable vision that rose again before him." The vision is still with him at the end of *Below Grass Roots*, and the mountain still seems to be blocking him from it:

> His square stern face assumed for the moment in the light of the flames a look at once profound, timeless and enigmatic as the face of that immutable Peak which had stood before him and will stand for those to follow, an eternal jest of nature at men whose folly and salvation is the blind perpetuation of a quest which has no truth but this — a flashing vision, darkness and eternal rest.

It is not until Rogier's grandson, March, has acquired additional experience and knowledge of the earth in New Mexico that the mountain in Colorado ceases to be a barrier and becomes instead a monument of faith. Before that point is reached, however, Rogier must go through several mystical experiences in which flashes of vision occur to him and spur him on toward his own ultimate vision. At an Indian dance he feels the rhythms of blood and earth in the beating of the drums, and he understands that here is a "place-spirit of the great western aridity that had made and kept him an exile in the land of his adoption." As he tries to overcome the place-spirit, or to succumb to it, the rhythm grows in his own blood until the inner-feeling response to the scene is stronger than the mental recognition of it. Contrary to the arguments of several western writers and critics who have insisted that only rationalism can bring Western literature to maturity, Waters insists upon the validity of the blood, or (better) the intuition which is the link of man to the earth and to the mystery of creation. The difficulty with Rogier is that he wants to combine knowledge of the earth's pulse with the acquisition of gold. Later, in the mine, deep inside the mountain, he wants "to pierce that body of living rock into the warm flesh that hides its secret heart, to drain its veins of golden life, to learn at the last that even a stone may throb to an unseen pulse, may vibrate in unison with all eternal life." The feeling that the mountain is alive persists in him for years, but finally he is defeated in his search for gold, and his son-in-law dies from pneumonia while working in the mine, so that Rogier never quite reconciles himself to the full commitment needed to make his earth-feelings complete.

It is the grandson, March, in *The Dust Within the Rock*, who at last recognizes that everything is of a piece, that a man is his grandfather and his father, and also the leaf that falls as well as the leaf that sprouts, the rock that crumbles in time as well as the dust that is timeless within the rock, and, indeed, everything — "indivisible and intermingled, adobe and granite." Here, at the end of the trilogy, March sees Pike's Peak, higher than all the mountains around it. And "like a religious exile granted the divine concession of a world to be built at his will, he [walks] humbly but resolutely toward that imperishable monument of an enduring faith."

The three novels commonly referred to as the Colorado mining trilogy show some of the flaws caused by enthusiasm over personal discoveries. Allowing for these impurities of style, and recognizing that structural difficulties are not uncommon in a long work (1511 pages in this case), it is possible to say that Frank Waters has written one of the richest and most detailed stories in western literature. A family chronicle, the work is also a discussion of history, a repository of ideas, and a journey through the soul of the West. Underlying these concerns is a personal quest, Waters' own search for meaning as revealed through two characters who share the author's identity. Joseph Rogier, the mainstay of the narrative until very near the end, represents Waters' maternal grandfather. Ona [Rogier's daughter] marries a part-Indian, Jonathon Cable, and their son March is the fictional Waters. Perhaps to keep the biographical elements at a safer distance, Waters places his artistic aspirations within another character — Boné — who composes music. However, as with other fiction of this kind (based on family experiences), the narrative rides along on themes and perceptions which are more important than the parallels between fictional family and factual family.

As a portrait of the West, especially in Colorado and New Mexico in the half-century following the Civil War, the trilogy is both objectively detailed and subjectively motivated. Silver and gold discoveries in the Pike's Peak region form the historical basis of the narrative, and the working of the mines provides the realism from which Waters reaches for the primacy of the land, the timelessness and age of the arena in which man strives for new opportunities. The "wrinkled faces of the mountain peaks" and the "dry skin of the prairies" seem to oppose man's efforts to exploit what to him is a new place, a fresh start, a land of riches. Only Rogier's insight is capable of discerning the durability of the land; it will not be molded at will by the peoples who dwell upon it and try to make it their own. Indeed, it is a severe testing ground for man, whether desert, plains, or a mountain pass:

> For like the sea it was a land that slept in solitude promising nothing and giving all — a vast realm of geology alone, raised high above the earth, close under the inscrutable eyes of a Heaven that attested the heroism of man's labor, his greed, his faithfulness or his unfitness to the futile task of its subjection.

Ever changing but forever fixed, the land harbors a sadness that is repeated in the people, especially those who stay. Waters is not precise when he catalogues the many tribes of Indians and insists that the land has done something to all of them. The effect of his suggestion, however, is that of domination, of the power of the land to touch strongly and lastingly all of its creatures. A change may seem to be in the offing as the country is invaded by new hordes of people, more than ever before, representing races and nationalities from all over the world. "But the land remains." Waters' point is that population does not make a people, that the heterogeneity of the invaders will make fusion into a whole more difficult than it was for the Sioux, the Hopi, the Navajo, the Aztecs, and the other older cultures of the ancient continent. Even if new temples should rise, the cost in human hearts would only confirm the greatness of the land.

In time — friendlier to the earth than to its creatures — the humans who have come from England, Italy, Ireland, Sweden, China, Africa, like birds migrating mindlessly, might call the land their own. Rogier feels that he has crossed half a continent to discover his soul and that there is a chance that he may be able to call at least a part of the land his own. He worries, however, that he and everyone around him will remain homeless, uprooted from their origins and unable to find a new place of peace. Even the Indian, once rooted in the West, possessing the "unity of form and substance motivated by the spirit of his place," has disappeared. How will the new people find their kinship with the land? For the moment, at least, the question evaporates and in its place rise the Rockies with more than a thousand peaks soaring ten thousand feet and higher.

With Cripple Creek as a hub, the spokes of activity shoot far out onto the plains and into the mountains — gold mining, silver mining, construction of new towns, shipping lines, farms and ranches, and oil wells in Wyoming. As though the expansion into the West could indeed overcome the timeless land, men swarm over the wrinkled skin in their search for wealth. Waters repeatedly affirms the truth of earth's yielding up the riches in the form of gold, silver, and oil, but what he sees as the tragedy of the people is that they fail to realize a harmony with the earth. There is no sense of unity, and often no integrity. Speaking of a moment in history, Waters recognizes the chaos and confusion, the "story without plot," the swiftly moving panorama of westward expansion as marks of newness, of unbridled enthusiasm. At some time in the future the people and places notable in the history of western exploration, conflict, and settlement will presumably take on the quality of legend and take their place beside the journeys of Ulysses, the Round Table of King Arthur, and the exploits of Siegfried.

> But today — today their cadence is not yet measured, their tones not yet suave and polished. The veil of time has not yet blurred their sharp outlines. They stand there, close and untouchable, they move truthfully with all their faults and without form.

We might assume that Waters' intention in the trilogy is to provide the form, but what emerges is a long search rather than a satisfactory resolution. Pike's Peak, as the center of Rogier's quest for ultimate meaning, is a point of emphasis; yet the frame is lacking except for horizon lines, and these are at a great distance in the West. The history of the period, then, and the characteristics of the landscape, serve as analogy. Men are tested as ore is tested. Some assay successfully, and some do not. The bones of men are hardened by the same iron that stains the rocks of the mountains, and those who are perceptive enough to see the intimate relationship between man and land will sense at least a little of the secret at the center of the world — the bottom of a mine shaft symbolizing this center.

Until his grandson, March, assumes the search toward the end of the trilogy, it is Rogier who is most troubled over the question of alliance with his land of adoption. He reflects upon the unity of life which had been his on the Carolina plantation before he moved to the West and wonders whether he can regain it from the new earth. "Unity" has two meanings for Waters. The first is the cohesion and common purpose of a people, whether they be members of an Indian tribe, a mining community in the hills, or a growing city such as Colorado Springs. The second meaning is spiritual and primal, its significance lying in an indefinable relationship between man and earth, man and his sources, or man and his God. This union can be accomplished only through intuition. Rogier becomes aware of both meanings, one on the level of social idealism — although it involves insight and the spirit as well — and the other on the higher level of mysticism. What complicates the ultimate understanding of the two levels of unity is that they also should become one in a final and complete unity of all things. This concept, it seems to me, goes far beyond the transcendentalist's notion of oneness. It is more Oriental than American except as it is a major belief of the Indian, that curious mixture of Oriental and First-American.

In his business dealings — primarily in architecture and construction — Rogier subscribes as best he can to the unity of people and place. When he is confronted with the beat of an Indian drum at night, and experiences an intuitive response to the regular and insistent sound, it is not so much a discovery of oneness as it is a recognition of earth power, of timeless dream, of rhythm and mystery — the dance of life. The beating of the drum echoes the elements of the earth and the pounding of the blood stream. Rogier senses that his heart is "trying" to beat in the same time as that of the drums, and as he watches the Indians dance he feels their contact with the earth, as though they are drawing energy directly from the ground upon which their feet stamp. It is a hypnotic scene for Rogier, one which draws him out of himself and makes him aware of the rhythmic connection between man and nature. Believing "with his blood" rather than with his intellect, he has seen intuitively the timeless mystery of creation.

Rogier is not a simple man caught in the normal way by gold fever. As a respected builder in the town, and the patriarch of his family, he is a fairly typical well-to-do member of a growing white society in Colorado Springs. But he experiences, however briefly, the Indians' homage to the mysteries of creation, and Indian blood is introduced into the family line when daughter Ona marries Jonathon Cable. Cable's background is never completely known to the family; some of his behavior suggests that he has been raised within a white society, but his movements and his psychological darkness seem to be those of an Indian. As Rogier develops an obsession for mining — not for the money but to get closer to the secrets of the earth — he resembles a type of man better identified by psychologists in our own time than in Rogier's, the man who has had a successful career but who has not discovered his soul.

Rogier's approach to the second phase of life is drastic. Putting almost everything he owns into a mining venture, he insists that Cable work with him even though Jonathon knows the effort is futile and is eventually killed by the mine. In a curious misunderstanding, Rogier convinces himself that mining is "breaking the thin crust" that separates him and perhaps other men also "from complete harmony with the earth" of which he is a part. Not having learned the more important lesson of the holiness of the earth, he cannot see the breaking of the skin of the earth as destructive of the very place with which he wishes to unify himself. To him the rape of virgin earth is somehow logical, balanced, and rhythmical. Breaking through the grass roots of the surface, he will go down to encounter granite, "sterner stuff," and will find the "heart vibrating in unison with all eternal life." Rogier has, in fact, become a hopeless mystic, ironically removed from the earth just as he goes into it to locate the secret.

In dramatic terms, Rogier is clearly the major character of the trilogy. Yet as part of a family chronicle he is important not for his beliefs and his obsessions but for the impact these have on key members of the family, especially Ona, Jonathon, and their son March. It is March who is left with the task of putting together the strands of his heritage, of finding his identity and purpose, in the concluding events of the trilogy. He has seen his grandfather go mad, his father killed by the mine, and his mother turned into a stoic but tragic figure who perceives what is wrong but is powerless to change anything. His inheritance is one of integrity and mystery, courage and passivity, patience and darkness, love and wonder — the union of two races. Subtle characterizations of the parents point up the boy's peculiar position. As he wanders through the West, he becomes acutely aware of the "mystery and dark beauty of his own soul," and of the fusion of blood streams on a much wider scale, so that he can characterize America (or at least Western America) as half-breed. His recognition of the American soul is of a spiritual nature and is more profound than the sociological theory of the melting pot. At the end of his quest — which, like all the other endings, is a beginning — March sings of his family:

> "I am the flesh of their flesh, and their flesh is of the flesh of
> the earth. We are all one flesh! What man can say it is ever
> dead? Together, undivided and eternal, we echo the pulse which
> throbs through stone . . . we crumble and wash away, and rise
> ever again in eternal palingenesis."

At this point individual identity becomes irrelevant. All are one, and it is the earth which endures and holds all together. Waters combines, here, the Indian's communal spirituality with the normally more personal and private belief in the possibility of rebirth into a higher form of being; a belief which is often looked at with skepticism by the white man who wonders at the case of "rebirth" at frontierlike revival series. It is problems such as this which make it difficult to assess religious experiences and to recognize the true mystic when he appears.

Since the trilogy is autobiographical in part, we may be excused for wondering about the aspirations of Frank Waters as writer. Boné, Martha Rogier's nephew, is a secondary persona who is rarely mentioned in discussions of these novels. He appears early in *The Wild Earth's Nobility*, brought to live with the Rogiers after his father has died. He is slight and dark, with black curly hair, and has exceptionally acute hearing. Obsessed with music, affected by the Indian drums just as Rogier is, he sets high standards for himself as a composer:

> That by thus fulfilling himself complete and without a flaw, he might bridge with ease the unfathomable chasm between mankind's incompleteness and that perfect harmony forever beyond his human reach.

More specifically, the artist's task is to extract meaning from gangue — a word which is important to Waters. In mining, gangue — the nonmetaliferous minerals found in a vein of ore — is considered worthless. Gold itself would seem to represent the unattainable: "Even to the artist the earth remains resistant and enigmatic." Yet one must look toward "that perfect harmony" even though it may be, or seem to be, out of human reach, and even though the materials through which the search is conducted — the materials available to the writer — are impurities. Boné's approach to the problem of communicating his feelings and ideas is not willful but intangible, "an elusive persuasiveness" which describes Waters as a writer quite well. Even more precisely, the problem is to lift out of a racial stream the forms and rhythms that are centuries old and represent or re-create them in the words, structures, and devices of a mechanical form — literary narrative. It is all the artist can do, Waters says, to take one step toward perfection.

Boné senses that Rogier's life was wrong because it did not blend properly with the intangible whole. The failure lay in the attempt to locate the meaning of life through reason, an attempt which could end only in madness (a process similar to that of Curt in Walter Van Tilburg Clark's novel *Track of the Cat*). Creation and understanding come not from reason but from necessity and an opening up to "the inward flow of life." Speaking again in biographical terms, it is apparent that Waters was deeply affected by his grandfather and learned a great deal from his weaknesses as well as his strengths. To remain open, to be "alertly passive," to rely on the unconscious, and to close the mind to whatever is mean and inferior — these are the requirements of the writer, the artist, and the intuitive man who would discover the dance of life.

José R. Martinez
El Abuelo of Hispanic Literary Characters

In our futile and contradictory attempts to label Frank Waters, we call him the "best known unknown author in America." Even though the phrase captures an important facet of the writing career, this memorable label does not reflect the many other sides of Frank Waters. So we call him the "dean of western writing" or we call him the "grandfather of western literature." But again these labels fall far short of the whole.

As good students of Frank Waters we understand the problem, even as we juggle the various labels. The dilemma is that we deal here with life, the life of Frank Waters. We cannot confuse one side with the whole. We learned in *People of the Valley* that "Life is a great white stone. You, a child, stare at it and only see one side: You walk slowly around it. You see other sides, each different in shape and pattern, rough or smooth. You are confused; you forget that it is the same great white stone."[1]

While trying not to forget the whole, let me focus on a foundational side of the writing career and add yet another label: Frank Waters as the grandfather, *el abuelo*, of Hispanic characters in United States literature.

In the creation of Hispanic characters in the twentieth century, Frank Waters arrived early, writing *People of the Valley* in the late 1930s with publication in 1941. This prototypal portrayal of Hispanic life in the Southwest set the gold standard for all other literary coinages of Hispanic experience.

In his enduring novel Frank Waters gave us the primary characters of the Hispanic family and a full foundation of the Hispanic characters who make up an authentic community. Most notably, Frank Waters gave us the best imprint of the Hispanic version of the archetypal wise old woman, Maria del Valle. Moreover, *People of the Valley* established in print a crucial cornerstone of Hispanic life: the grandparent, *la abuela*, Maria del Valle, passing on elementary knowledge to the grandchild, *la nieta*, Piedad. For the first time in twentieth century American literature we had variegated Hispanic families, multiple generations, and a complex spectrum of Hispanic characters–all deeply rooted in the Southwestern landscape. We had American Hispanics at the center of an American novel.

In *People of the Valley* Frank Waters implanted basic paradigms early in the past century. Thus, in subsequent decades, when we read *Bless Me, Ultima* (1972) by Rudolfo Anaya, we measure his Ultima and his Antonio against Maria del Valle and Piedad. When we read *The Rain God* (1984) by Arturo Islas we measure Mama Chona and Miguel Chico against the gold standard set by Waters in *People of the Valley*. We repeat the exercise when we read *Woman Hollering Creek* (1991) by Sandra Cisneros. Future Hispanic novels will be held to the rigid requirements set by *People of the Valley*.

Across the decades *People of the Valley* has emerged as a foundation text, a teaching work, destined to endure in a timeless way. Better than any other work, the novel contains the historical core of Hispanic life in the Southwest. In the novel Maria del Valle personifies timeless endurance. At age seventy she sits on the "weathered cliffs" of the "beautiful blue valley" at the "point of a completed circle." An elder, Maria del Valle has "outlived virtue and vice, having proved invulnerable to both and more powerful than either." Earth mother, founder, teacher, penultimate *abuela*. Waters writes, "She had gone long to the people of the valley; now they came to her."[2]

Like Maria del Valle, like the novel, Frank Waters has emerged as founder, as teacher, as the *abuelo* of Hispanic characters in U.S. literature. Serious readers and writers of Hispanic literature now come to Frank Waters to find and to learn the essences of Hispanic characters, the essences of Hispanic life in the Southwest. We come for guidance, for wisdom, to Frank Waters and his novel, much as the people of the valley came to Maria del Valle when she had attained the stature of elder, *viejita*, honored *abuela*.

At age ninety Maria del Valle, "resembled an ancient Santo," her body "shrunk like seasoned wood." In this final phase of her life she takes on a major aspect of Hispanic life: to pass on her wisdom to a sympathetic grandchild. The two, wise old woman and protégé, embark on a winter of teaching and learning.[3]

> "Mi abuela, my grandmother Doña Maria," she asked, "why is
> it that children call that frightening boogie man whom none
> have [sic] seen 'El Abuelo'– a grandfather? Surely you frighten
> me not at all."
>
> My child," replied Maria. "To youth, age is incom-
> prehensible. To ignorance, wisdom is frightening. So that El
> Abuelo having age represents the learning which the ignorant
> child fears. Now this is wrong. But even grownups have it.
> They possess learning and knowledge, and still fear the wisdom
> which they have not attained. We must all learn to be unafraid
> of the dark, the child of learning, the man of wisdom. hence we
> shall all reach the true maturity which is eternal youth."[4]

All winter *abuela* and *nieta* play out the timeless ritual of philosophy before a fire, the passing down of accumulated knowledge from generation to generation. "Piedad threw on another stick. The flames uncoiled, rose up and shook like snakes."[5] Maria del Valle speaks and the season of instruction continues.

> "It is like this. A child looks at life as a wolf at the trail of his
> quarry. He has no sense of the past, only a hunger to devour
> the future. Thus, to pursue it with success, he soon stops and
> raises his head. He sniffs the wind. He observes the signs—even
> those on goat skulls. He listens to all the world around him.
>
> "Now, you understand, he is at middle age. Having
> memory, he can see part of the trail behind him as well as the
> present he treads. But still the future unwinds unseen before
> him, up toward the cliff top shrouded in mist. He reaches it.
> Pues! That dreaded and hungered for future is no more than
> the present which resembles the past. They are all one. his fears
> were nought, his predictions useless.
>
> "Entiende, muchacha? I will say it again for your simple
> ears."[6]

As these passages illustrate, Frank Waters understood the deep value of passing the culture's wisdom down through the generations. He understood that if this fire ever goes out, if this connection of the generations is ever broken, the Hispanic Southwest captured in *People of the Valley* will turn into ashes. He knew that if we lose our children we lose everything. In short, Frank Waters understood one of the basic fears in the Hispanic mind, as represented by the central myth in the Hispanic Southwest: *La Llorona*, the wailing woman endlessly searching along the waterways for her lost children, one of the great cautionary tales.

Working from this deep understanding, Frank Waters created authentic Hispanic characters by giving us the many sides of their lives, not just the surface gestures, the visible actions, or the rhythms of speech. He gave us the insecurities, the conflicts, the daily struggles, the impairing ignorance, the deeply rooted fears. But he also showed us their survival skills, their honest hearts, the will to endure, their complex wisdom.

Frank Waters was and is a true *abuelo* because he understood the role of fear and the role of cautionary tales. *Abuelos* own cautionary tales. In *People of the Valley*, as in his other works, Frank Waters warned us not only about the loss of cultural wisdom but also about the dangers of imbalanced science, materialism, and the relentless damage to the deep ecological systems of the planet. Frank Waters, being Frank Waters and a true *abuelo*, all his warnings come with the necessary knowledge to address the dangers. Frank Waters is not one of those writers who leaves the reader with questions and dangers and no answers, no guidance, no wisdom. In his works he teaches us how to cut through the "youthful fears" and the "useless predictions" of middle age, even when we labor under the limitations of "simple ears" and "imperfect eyes." In the tradition of wise *abuelos*, the works of Frank Waters always have winter seasons of instruction.

Yet, for some of us, especially serious readers and aspiring writers, a major mystery remains. How does Frank Waters do this? How does he tap the deepest part of a character? How does he get inside a person from a different culture? How does he find the heart of the Hispanic character?

Despite much scholarship and commentary, no one knows how Frank worked the Waters magic, how he could absorb a culture, a people, a village and then—with careful words and cautionary honesty—authentically depict them on paper, avoiding stereotypes, happy natives and noble savages. No one knows how he did this, or as a Waters character might say, or even Frank Waters himself, "*Quién sabe?* I myself have never questioned it."[7]

In any case, working this "magic of words," Frank Waters gave us some of the best Indian characters of the past century and some of the strongest women in literature. And in *People of the Valley* he gave us Maria del Valle, the ultimate wise old woman, *la abuela*, the grandmother, the Hispanic characters of the century. We don't have to understand the magic to appreciate and embrace the majesty of the achievement.

Like his characters and like his view of life, Frank's achievement has many sides. The side of his achievement producing the most telling impact on my life is that he gave us authentic Hispanic characters when we Hispanics needed them most–during the 1940s and 1950s. I came of age in the late 1950s when Hispanic characters in U.S. literature were rare. Whole novels inhabited by Hispanic characters were even more rare, mostly nonexistent.

I remember fruitlessly searching the library shelves for just the right book in those days. I needed a book that spoke to me, a book with Hispanic characters who resembled my uncle, my grandmother, my neighbor. I wanted to see Spanish dialogue on the page. I wanted the landscapes of southern Colorado and northern New Mexico with the Rio Grande running through them. Mostly I failed in this search.

John Steinbeck and Ernest Hemingway were easy to find and the infrequent Hispanic characters in those novels and stories didn't feel right. Stilted in dialogue, a false posture, some of them too simplistic and one-dimensional, many of them too close to stereotype. but it was more than that, something fundamental was wrong with those characters. They were hollow. Reading and rereading, I finally figured it out. These Hispanic characters lacked a deep grounding, a center, thus the voices didn't ring true. These false voices spoke from behind and through Hispanic characters, a form of ventriloquism.

Reading these depictions I felt an absence and a sense of loss. I knew there were novels from Spain and Latin America, but the temporary attraction of those books, in Spanish and in translation, also felt weak and ultimately unsatisfying. I needed something closer to home. I knew Madrid wasn't San Antonio and Buenos Aires wasn't Santa Fe. I needed the valleys along the Rio Grande. I needed Mora. I could settle for Mexico, but I needed New Mexico.

Later in the 1970s and 1980s, I learned that I hadn't been the only one on this kind of quest. Tomás Rivera, who wrote *Y No Se Lo Trago la Tierra* in

1971, tells the same story in an essay. He describes his search, in Texas in the 1940s and 1950s, looking for just the right book with Hispanic characters. In another part of Texas at the same time Rolando Hinojosa, who wrote *Estampas del Valle* in 1973, was conducting the same search in the library in the 1940s and 1950s. Rivera and Hinojosa both describe how one day, by chance, by magic, they did find the right book. For both of them it was *With His Pistol in His Hand* by Américo Parades, a book that spoke to their Hispanic hearts. They describe reading and rereading the book, amazed that such a book, though rare, did exist.

For me, in southern Colorado, it was a red book with white lettering, an image imprinted on my brain to this day. Near the floor at the end of the shelf I saw the title: *People of the Valley*. Days later, I realized that this magnetic title could have referred to numerous places in the world–Scotland, Russia, and Italy, for instance. After all, people inhabit most of the world's valleys. But in that fevered moment, in that dusky library on my knees, as I reached for the red book, I knew with deep certainty that this was my book, my people, my valley. And it was.

I remember opening the book in the middle and reading a page. Maria del Valle lived on that page, and two paragraphs later I realized I knew her. She was mostly Grandma Miguela, with equal parts from my Aunt Rachael and Mana Christina, my next door neighbor. I read most of the book in the library that day and finished it at home that night. I reread the whole book that weekend and have read it dozens of times since then. The magic of words never works better than when the words feed the hungry heart, healing as they do.

I'm never surprised when I hear yet another version of this same story from members of my generation. How they found *People of the Valley*. A couple of years ago I was teaching *People of the Valley*, as I have most semesters for many years, and I stopped by the bookstore a few days before the start of classes to make sure the books for my classes had arrived. I found that the copies of *People of the Valley* weren't on the shelf so I tracked down an assistant manager. Looking at his records, he said, "There's something wrong; the books should be here."

Finally he tracked the books down; they were in the section for the sociology department. A person there also was teaching *People of the Valley*, but her books hadn't arrived yet. Needless to say, I was quite interested in this and I made sure I met and had coffee with this person. Margarita was a graduate student from California teaching her first class in Colorado; and she told me how, a few years earlier as a new graduate student, she had been tracking down books with authentic Hispanic experiences and having some difficulty. She was telling one of her professors about this and he asked, "Have you read *People of the Valley* by Frank Waters?" She'd never heard of Frank Waters, and he gave her a copy. She read it in one sitting that night and reread it that weekend, and the next semester she started teaching it in a sociology class.

I still play a role in this never-ending story, for I've introduced hundreds and hundreds of students to Frank Waters; and they, in turn, go out and introduce him to hundreds of others. We're out here asking the key question: Have you read *People of the Valley* by Frank Waters? Since he is the best known unknown author in America, many people haven't; but when they do read him, they often complete the book in one sitting, and they never forget the experience.

Today the Hispanic population in U.S. literature has increased and we have many books full of authentic Hispanic characters. We should note that many of those characters are the children and grandchildren of Maria del Valle, with Frank Waters as enduring *abuelo*.

But–even as we acknowledge the fundamental contributions of Frank Waters to the depiction of Hispanic characters and even as we record the crucial comfort he gave Hispanic readers during our period of famine–let us remember that the Hispanic side of Frank Waters is not the only side. Let us remember the great white stone. Let us walk around it,

> … stare at all of it at once from the hillside above. Verdad!
> Then you see it: how it has many different sides and shapes
> and patterns, some smooth, some rough, but still the one great
> white stone: how all these sides merge into one another, in-
> distinguishable: the past into the present, the present into the
> future, the future again into the past. Hola! They are still the
> same. With wisdom who knows one from the other? There is
> no time, which is but an illusion for imperfect eyes. There is
> only the complete, rounded moment, which contains all.[8]

As we look at the life of Frank Waters, let's make sure that we look at "all of it at once from the hillside above." Let's make sure that we see all the sides, rough and smooth. Let's make sure that we see the great white stone of the career and the life of Frank Waters.

Inés Dölz-Blackburn
Imagery and Motifs in Frank Waters'
People of the Valley: An Introduction

A close reading of the text of *People of the Valley*[1] reveals Waters'
preoccupation with ancient humanistic dilemmas such as eternity,
timelessness, and dualities. Recurrent images and motifs express the intensity
of this preoccupation in a way in which beauty and truth constantly lift the
spirit and the soul. Among these images and motifs I would like to emphasize
constants such as Mother Earth, collective characters ("they," "the people"),
sounding silence, remoteness, the world of nature (mainly in the form of a
blue valley), kaleidoscopic pines, water, snow, mountains — and the enigmas
of a brown-orange blanket and mysterious goats' skulls. This delicate and subtle interweaving of images contributes to intensify the splendid final message
which I perceive mainly as the belief in the harmonious unity of dualities and
the power of strong androgenous spirits — symbolized in Maria del Valle —
to defeat through wise and humane leadership the uncertainty brought by
Progress and Technology.

The apparent simplicity of the text is denied by a careful rereading.[2] The
complex and skillful balance of imagery and motifs, the constant leading to
fundamental incognitos,[3] the poetic expression of the Hispanic soul and beliefs — whose nuances are hard for many to accept or understand — [4]contrib-
ute to make the reading a joyful but difficult journey for the mind.

Because, as Tanner's bibliography shows, critical attention to *People* has been sporadic and scant, I believe that approaches to the book are almost unlimited. After reading the comprehensive and illuminating study of Waters by Thomas J. Lyon in his *Frank Waters*, I almost feel inclined to affirm that the essence of Waters' thought, as Lyon presents it, is contained in *People of the Valley*.

The pastoral symphonic tone of the first couple of pages sketches in the reader's mind — among murmurs of thunderous and bursting clouds, rushing snow, peaceful trout streams that with rains can break into a flooding fury — the timelessness not only of the majestic "blue valley" in which the narration will take place but also of the people, the collective character of the story "with a wild remoteness in their eyes" (3). We encounter also in this beginning the mystery of the eternal, but also we face reality — "the politicos for whom we made crosses on our votes, as instructed" (4) — and death — the tiny river no longer meanders . . . "dead chickens are cast upon the beaches of flooded corrals" (4). Also in the first few paragraphs there is presented the reality of the dam, the technological savior that will defeat death across the valley, saving people from the fury of floods. As I perceive it, this kaleidoscopic initial presentation establishes the poetical and pastoral tone of the book and announces the fundamental imagery, motifs, and themes which will be even more masterfully displayed to convey effectively the final messages of hope given to the people — Hispanic in origin — by their local leader, Maria del Valle, one with the earth, wise and simple, who has the androgenous spirit able to defeat the uncertainty of Progress through faith, rebirth, and creation.

Imagery:

Nature imagery is recurrent even for descriptions of the main character, Maria del Valle: her cheeks are "piñon knots," and she is "straight as a pine" (12), has the "eyes of a hawk" (9), features "cut out of rock" (9), "beak of a nose" (9), and again the cheeks "enduring as the red brown earth" (10)[5].

There is a constant sprinkling of varied colors which strike the mind synesthetically. The predominant colors are the ones of the rainbow or the natural ones which Maria knows how to obtain from nature: blue-green, blue, yellow, green, purple, Indian red, and orange.

> Natural colors for spun wool she knew how to obtain. . . .
> Chamise for yellow and lichens for light orange; peach leaves

and cedar bark for green; oak bark for wine; walnut hulls for
brown; chokecherry roots and berries for purple; urine with
cedar twigs for Indian red (76).

> A rainbow brilliantly colored as a Chihuahua serape
> hangs over the shoulder of the sky (77).

Blue, which in the Hispanic tradition points to poetry and spirituality, appears
repeatedly as a leit motif associated with the valley inhabited by Maria and her
people. The result is the enhancement of its ethereal and mystical quality:

> It was the beautiful blue valley's three faces fusing in their short
> and transient hour (34).
>
> In Spring too the valley is beautiful and blue, but the
> beauty is muted and the blue is diminished by the intense
> white light of the steadily rising sun (57).
>
> The mill still ground grain for the people of the beautiful
> blue valley . . . (94).

These three instances, isolated from among numerous samples, combine two
polarities: the static constant of the blue valley and the dynamic one of races,
springs, and the mills which sustain the people.

There are other blues which stop the moment, associated with nature:

> A blue jay screamed from a pine outside (23), clay blue from
> Cañonato and Chacon (33), the valley a long crescent lake of
> blue between the steep black hills (51), blue hour between yel-
> low sunset and black night (7), blue mountain peak (59), the
> morada . . . slate blue (64).

We also have negative images as blue, which are disruptive, not harmonious.

> . . . men with eyes colder and bluer than the valley (20), blue
> veins stuck out (22), staring blue eyes (39).

And one last important reference points toward the immutability of the blue
associated with Maria's spirit:

> But the beautiful blue valley and Maria do not change. They
> are like time itself, the one impregnable constant (102).

Red is mainly linked to earth or the simple man and at times to a rooster (which, I am convinced, carries a symbolic meaning worth investigating):

> Red clay banks (33), red sandstone cliffs (37), red brown earth (10, 19, 58), blood and mud (81), the mud itself was red slimy (89) or red marks on Onésimos' back (63), like clotted red paint (63), red brown flesh (6), cheeks enduring as "red banner" (12) or "a rooster of red cedar" (52), a red rooster flees squawking (11), a red rooster . . . deaf to honking cars (161), the rusty rooster (77-78).

But we also have:

> red flair of the sinking sun (188).

In general, red seems to instill energy and life in all the images. The color *brown* is blended with earth and the skin of a timeless race.

> Brown faces tinged red from Indian Picuris (5), men rolling cigarettes in paper less brown than their stubby fingers (8), brown bare backs (63).

There is the same kind of blending with *yellow* — "dry yellow skin" (8), or the "yellow tierra" (33), or "corn husks" (190-92), "the yellowy sunlight" (41) — and *orange* — faces are "muddy orange" (23).

One recurrent image is of an old burnt orange blanket (21, 120, 134, 138, 176, 181, 200) stolen by Maria (27) when she was a young woman from two simple Hispanic-Indians, country philosophers (28-29). It accompanies her until she dies. At one point, full of holes, it is taken momentarily away from her by an art dealer who vaguely apprehends its magic:

> His mouth watered when he saw it glowing in the sunlight, felt its weave and wonderful softness (120).

In times of decisive crisis, Maria looks to it in her quest for strength and wisdom:

> . . . wrapping herself in the soft burnt-orange blanket (176), the suspicion never entered her head that she was philosophizing (134).

Finally, at death, after having accomplished the resettling of her people, she gets ready to rest in peace in a dark corner and "covered herself with the faded burnt-orange blanket" (200).

For me, the burnt-orange blanket stands as a symbol of authority transmitted from the high priesthood of knowledge, which is believed to be exclusively male in the Hispanic culture of the "people" — in this case the two old philosophers who had befriended Maria. And perhaps it also takes us with its orange stripes to the regenerating image of the sun, also male in mythology. Because of these associations, by wrapping herself with the blanket in a ceremonial way, Maria might acquire and feel a kind of androgynous nature that she thinks she ought to have to lead wisely and with authority.[6]

Green is "the green of oats, wheat and corn, of pine and spruce and piñons," green which "has lost its yellow component, but still retains its blue" (7).

Purples are seen through mixtures of roots and berries (76).

Black and *white* are closer to death than life throughout the book. For black, we have images of "black rebozos" (12), Maria's eyes as "two black caves that no one entered" (73), "the black shawl" on her face (73), "huge black crosses" (63), "rusty black cloth" (64). White takes us to "white washed wall," "dirty white cloth" (63), or Death as a "pale white head" (64), or a priest with a "pale white face" (71), and "his trembling white hands" (70). The animal in man is reflected in "his teeth gleamed white, like a wolf's" (80) and his evilness in a "cruel face . . . carved from a cold white icicle" (36). Finally, there are "washed white walls" (63). Apparently white, purity, is often to be associated with decay and death in Waters' book, with the exception of the snow, a strong image given in so many nuances that it deserves more pondering than I can give it in this essay.

Here and there are also some references to gray, of lime rocks or "gray scrub oak" (21), and dancing images of light and darkness alternately converge and dissipate in harmony (9, 34, 63, 65, 177).

> The pale white effulgence, without source, made a well of light in the dark forest (65).

. . . or death

> . . . a cold white light filtered through the pines upon patches of snow. The cañon was a dark mouth that swallowed a narrow trail. It held death and silence (64).

Images of pines are also as numerous as the ones of snow, the valley, and the mountains, and, in my opinion, their artful and delicate design also heightens the timeless and ethereal setting of the narration. At one point, they can even be shown in a splendid unity:

> The night was clear and cold, the valley a long crescent lake of blue between the steep black hills. There were patches of snow on the lower pine slopes. The peak cut sharp and white into the sky (51).

These images, along with the ones of water, deserve more analysis than I can give them here. Their expression can be complex. Water can be life and death:

> Water is like life. It is life. It permeates everything. . . . It trickles down the snowy peaks, the little streams . . . (177). The creek brings down not only wreckage and willows, but fresh pine tips. . . . Behind them splashed twenty head of loose stock. . . . The valley was no longer beautiful and blue. It was gray and slimy. It smelled sour (110).

Besides the burnt-orange blanket, another unconventional image is that of skulls of goats, which point to wisdom and tradition. We see them in Maria's hut as "rows of pale skulls" (76, 82). In them she reads life's mysteries, especially on "winter nights" (9). Part of her wisdom derives from their study (76):

> For she never abandoned her goats and the wisdom derived from reading their skulls. . . . The skulls came back to sit with others. . . . They were pages of a book she bound together year by year. They were a chronological record of the span of life that flowed past her. And sometimes she caught glimpses of its course ahead (76).

Like the burnt-orange blanket, the skulls symbolize fundamental and essential knowledge. They are linked to the cosmic forces of the universe and to "the seasonal patterns of moons and stars on the skull of the heaven above. . . .

By goat skulls they read the record of floods and droughts . . . measured the movement of stars" (28). They are transmitted to Maria along with a unique perception of time in which one cannot distinguish past from present and future. When Maria speaks, we encounter her perception of it:

> There is no time, which is but an illusion for imperfect eyes — there is only the complete rounded moment, which contains all (159).[7]

Motifs:

Remoteness and silence are conveyed with rare intensity infusing the novel with a mystery that intensifies its lyrical quality.

We encounter a wild remoteness in the eyes of the men of the valley (3), in the frequent use of shadows (e.g., a wagon "dips down into the shadows of the pines" [91]), in the sounds of the bell of the village church striking "with a *faint* silvery chime" (7, italics added), or a barking dog "choked by the silence" (9). We even see in Maria's eyes a "repellent remoteness" (75) or "queer remoteness" (117).

The silence thickens but it is heard "when earth is still" (62) or when "the stream rippled noisily at the silence" (40).

Remoteness and silence may blend in unison, as happens with some images previously discussed (snow, pines, and mountains):

> The silence is thick and heavy, a little lush and holding the wild remoteness of the dark, narrow cañon (9).

Mother Earth and the collective character of the people, almost a chorus at times, are, however, the predominant motifs. "The land is our Mother," says a voice. "What would we do without land?" (7) Mother Earth is shown in eternal recurrence. As a Hispanic traditional poem conveys it through the miracle of cyclical rebirth:

> I am dust/and I will become dust/but in between/the dust sustained me (52-53). Death of the earth . . . not accepted lightly . . . eternal resurrection which is a struggle worse than death (66). The earth cries for renewal (74).

It is shown as eternal and immutable and sometimes as paradoxical:

> The earth, timeless and immense, had not changed. It was all as
> before . . . (57) . . . cruel and unresistant, so gentle and yet so
> enduring (68).

Slowly, Maria becomes one with the earth; she becomes the valley (75), a
Ceres associated with seeds, fruits and herbs (75). Her features are timeless
with "sorrow and fecundity," "savage and enduring as if cut out of rock, a rock
beaten, mashed and worn by waves" (9).

Also, she is the people:

> I am a simple, old and nameless woman, my power is that of
> the people who do not think but feel . . . the power of the sim-
> ple, the customs, of the earth and the seasons, the power of the
> blood that rests in me (90).

Being people and Mother Earth, she can passionately and genuinely advocate
unity, rejecting differences in a eulogy of brotherhood:

> There are no tribes, no races, no people separated by the color
> of their eyes, their hair and skin. There is only mankind. All
> men are brothers. Each has the same passions, thirsts and hun-
> gers. . . . Now what is a man but his earth? (127)

The motif of the cross (9, 179, 180) leads us to beliefs — the beliefs of the
simple Hispanic people that appear blended with superstitions. It is a matter
to be extensively explored in further studies, and I can only anticipate that
Waters knows extremely well the thoughts, way of being, customs and beliefs
and philosophy of life of the Hispanic people of the earth.[8]

In conclusion, Progress and Technology — symbolized in the building
of the dam — may attempt to destroy the timelessness and beauty of Nature,
and thereby impair the physical and spiritual freedom of Man. However, there
is hope in defining, searching out, and lifting to positions of leadership "the
chosen ones" who are able to lead from decay to new territories in which the
blue, the heights, the pines are still intact, making possible a cyclical resurrection and continuous rebirth through faith and deep humanity. This last

belief is asserted through the presentation of dualities — black vs. white, light vs. darkness, simple wisdom vs. sophisticated abstraction, pastoral setting vs. technology and progress. One might observe that in this presentation of opposites there is always a disposition to balance and resolve the conflict through harmony or to present the concepts with an unconventional connotation — "white is decay" — not only to challenge the mind of the reader but to convince him of the relativity of Truth, and therefore direct him to a less rigid approach to life.

Finally, I must add that we have been dealing here with a work of art in which we find "la difícil simplicidad" (difficult simplicity). Apparently we are encountering a candid pastoral folk tale, but as we reread, our pondering and reflecting show the book to have a difficult and impressive structure which slowly emerges to convey those intangibles for which man must live. Images and motifs have all been carefully woven in an immense tapestry, or rather a huge Indian serape, which works Faith, Acceptance and Optimism[9] into its final image, the image of the eyes of a dead woman:

> Steadily gleaming eyes that burned through time with faith
> which could not be dammed, and with a gaze which saw nei-
> ther the darkness of the day nor the brightness of the morrow,
> but behind these illusions the enduring reality that makes of
> one sunset a prelude to a sunrise brighter still (201).[10]

The music at the beginning and at the end of the novel combines the music of nature and that of reflective man: once again harmony and unity of apparent opposites. The symphony closes in the harmony emblematic of Waters' art of "la difícil simplicidad":

> Life moved in a sustained adagio. The night breeze awoke in
> the pines. The little stream played its arpeggio on the rocks. A
> deer bounded over a string of logs, its quick hoofs striking a
> pizzicato (199).

Thomas J. Lyon
on *The Man Who Killed the Deer*

L *yon*: There are so many ways by which we could approach *The Man Who Killed the Deer*. We could look at it historically or psychologically, or from the point of view of myth study, ways that are really applicable, and yet I feel, whenever I discuss the book from any one angle, that it's somehow not quite the whole thing. My strongest sense about *The Man Who Killed the Deer* is that it is the product of a total vision. The book was written by a man with a vision of earth, of what life is all about, what life could be about. Moreover, I don't see this book in the major tradition of the novel since about 1740, let's say. It is not a manners-and-morals novel at all, not a novel in the classic European, or maybe Eastern American sense in which we rely for a lot of the meaning of the interpersonal relations on the existence of a traditional hierarchic society. Rather than being in the European and Eastern American novel tradition at all, *Deer* is a complete book, its range something like the range of our whole lives. So that whenever you start criticizing this book, say from the point of view of characterization, you are missing the point somehow, or you are not quite getting out as big a territory as this book covers or suggests. I see *The Man Who Killed the Deer* as a major work, as a very important work of vision, a complete embodiment of this writer's view of life, and so I'm impatient with the purely historical interpretation which could go back and, say, start with 1551, when Charles the Fifth of Spain made sure that the Indians had their title to their lands in New Spain, and go back to 1687, when a Royal Council confirmed it, and then come up with the treaty at Guadalupe Hidalgo in 1848, when the Americans, victors in the Mexican War, confirmed the title of the Indians to their land. You could do that and come on down to 1970, when President Nixon signed the bill which gave the Taos Pueblo the simple title to 48,000 acres of land. You can trace all that out, and it is all true, and it's relevant to the book, but it does not quite say what needs to be said.

The approach that I'm going to take is to suggest the *total nature* of this novel, the *unconventional*, the *untraditional* nature of what I think Waters has attempted. I think you can look at the novel as constructed on concentric rings of influence and interaction. He talks about a pebble dropped in a pool and how the rings go out and come back. All these different levels of relationship, you might say, act upon one another. There is the protagonist, and his interior of character, his personality in mind. Start there with Martiniano and the problem that Martiniano has, especially as pronounced in the early stages of the book, the problem that he has with the fragmentation of being human, and you can see the effects of that problem immediately in the relationship with his wife and in what's wrong with the marriage, the fragmentation, discord and disharmony in the marriage. You can see the problem as part and parcel — I think this is the genius of Waters here — you can see it as part and parcel of discord and fragmentation and discontinuity within Martiniano himself and then, to come out another level, you have a man, a man and wife, or family, let's say, then you have the local tribe, the society, the discord between Martiniano and the tribe as obviously a manifestation of the same kind of fragmentation. I think what Waters has done here just with these first few levels of meaning is dramatize how it is that it is so hard for us to get along with one another. Quite apart from the Indianness of this story, he's got something there, he's touched on something there that is quite universal, not in this strict historical situation.

And then in the relationship between the tribe and the surrounding white society, the American society, the United States of America, the same fragmentation is writ large, the same kind of discord is going on. Now we are out to a pretty big level, because we are involving millions of people. Here we see we are repeating, in our historical mistakes and misdirections and conflicts, the same thing as is seen in this Martiniano. And I think this is just wonderful, what Waters has done. To show these microcosm and macrocosm relationships in such a lively fashion that it doesn't really seem like he is constructing a model such as I'm talking about. You don't get this feeling when you read this novel, because everything seems natural and right; it doesn't have to be mapped out. And then you've got — I could go on with this model, maybe it's a bit artificial — the whole human race in nature and the discords and the discontinuities, the mistakes that we make again. We're doing what we do because what's in us is what's in Martiniano. You don't have to be an Indian to identify with Martiniano. When you look at *Deer* in this fashion, the book means all of our history, all of our presence, you might say, in this universe. Now I'm way out "cosmic," but I think it's legitimate to do this, for Waters has suggested this kind of interrelationship all the way out, so, to go back to that business of 1551, 1687, 1848, and 1970, history is definitely part of the book, but it leads us into the bigger picture.

I'm looking at this book as something as major and as complex and as hard to get a handle on as our life. The greatness of this book, the reason it lasts, is when you read it you don't have this feeling you are getting a big philosophical abstraction. You might occasionally have the feeling that you are getting a lecture — I think you have to say this about his book — but I think what Waters has definitely tried to do is keep it off the level of pure theory, tried to give us the grip on the actual personhood involved in the issues. He deflates all of this big stuff. Waters will get out to that range and then suddenly you'll be back to some particular image, some really homely image, practical detail that saves you or returns you to a focus on where you are. It saves you from becoming too cosmic. He does this, in *The Woman at Otowi Crossing* almost comically, humorous at least in that novel, and actually right from the beginning, in 1930, in his first book Waters keeps things on the ground, keeps things more or less validated, in his common experience, keeps things more or less particular.

One of the first criticisms about *Deer* was in an article written in 1949 which said basically this is a philosophical treatise masquerading as a novel, not really a novel, the characters are mouthpieces for Frank

Waters' philosophy. I think that is a criticism we ought to take seriously, because what it says is that the characterization is sub-standard, and, if you know rule number one, I suppose, of literary criticism of fiction, characterization is prime. You have to have real, subtle, complex, believable, contradictory, paradoxical human beings as we all are. You can't have a fiction that is just a novelist speaking or an idea. That was the criticism of *The Man Who Killed the Deer*, and of Waters' other fiction too. The writer of this article may have hit upon something. From the territory that this critic was coming from, there is a legitimacy to the criticism. What he says is that Waters is following in this masquerade a kind of "regional imperative," and he says that a lot of Southwestern writers, overpowered by the mysticism of landscape, have followed this line, and so what you are getting in the regional imperative is not the kind of subtlety, not the kind of complexity, depth, and realism of characterization that you should expect in a novel, but something like fables, in which you get italicized portions of the text which are supposed to deliver to you immediately the interior thoughts of one character, or many characters, the elders of the Pueblo, for example, sitting in the kiva, portions which are carrying in essay fashion the complex dramatization, interpersonal relations, and all of the other things that a novel should have done. So this critic said, as a traditional novel, *Deer* is not so hot. And what I'd like to say is, from this perspective of the traditional novel in which social interactions, manners, morals, all of the nuances of interpersonal relationship are so primary, in that respect he may have something.

But what Waters is trying to do in his work is from a different perspective. He is trying to create a different whole way of looking at character, a different whole way of looking at what a person is, and what motivates a person to do what he or she does. I think we could even argue that Waters' sense of what a person is could be *more subtle*, could be *more complex*, have a *greater range* to it, than what we have taken as traditional in our culture and what we have reflected in our novels as traditional. It may be that *The Man Who Killed the Deer* challenges the typical idea of motivation and will of a person, what we mean when we say of a novel whether its characters are realistic or not.

So let's talk about characterization. That's one of the great questions that is always asked about American regional literature and art. Is the

Western novel weak in characterization, dominated by landscape? Is it a lesser kind of fiction than what we are seeing out of the East?

So there is that whole thing and then, another thing I'd like to discuss, the philosophy in the novel. Particularly, I think, one of the most important parts in the book is when Martiniano takes, early on, the Peyote Road, takes the road toward transcendence, you might say. Because, it seems to me, one of Waters' great preoccupations in his whole career as a writer is the *difference between transcendence on the one hand and emergence on the other.* It's a different kind of philosophy, fundamentally different. On the Peyote Road, on that whole episode, Waters was awfully prescient in 1941 and 1942: he was 13 or 14 years ahead of Aldous Huxley in talking about the larger philosophical significance of the psychedelic experience. You may recall that Huxley in 1954 wrote a book about his experiments with a derivative of the peyote cactus. Huxley came to some of the same conclusions as, but at least in my view didn't go as deep as, Waters had done in *The Man Who Killed the Deer* in 1942. I would argue that Waters was way ahead of American society's and maybe Western civilization's estimate of the meaning of drug transcendence. I don't think that is a small issue in our culture, because again it comes right down to transcendence on the one hand versus emergence on the other. To talk about the Peyote Road instance from another angle, too, if Waters is accused of being a mystic, for many critics a convenient category which means lesser, an unclear thinker basically, if you want to call Waters a mystic, you have to look at that peyote section where Martiniano has eaten the little cactus buttons and has flown off somewhere. That section is the *dreamiest* section in the book! Just look at the descriptions — very dream-like — whereas the other kinds of experience, which we'll call emergence for now, are much more sharply seen, much more particular and imagistic, much more natural. I think Waters is definitely *not* dreaming. I think that we should really look at that term mystic closely. Just how subtle is Frank Waters and how subtle is *The Man Who Killed the Deer*? Is it subtle enough to answer to what we feel life is like for us day by day? Are we looking at this book as a kind of projection of an ideal, or does it really *answer*, does the vision really look clearly at this world that we are in, and this life we are leading? To me, the word *mystic* connotes some sort of escapism, some sort of transcendent attempt. My own opinion is, I don't think that is what Frank Waters is about. So if that is the definition of mystic, I wouldn't want to go along with that, I think he is much more concrete, but at the same time you will have Waters making statements again and again, about the one great solidarity of which we are all a part. And you will find him using the word "indivisible" many, many times in his works. And if the classic definition of a mystic is somebody that sees all life, all existence, as one then, I suppose, technically, Waters fits. It's the connotation of escape or transcending, going to a higher sort of realm, that I would not want to go with. Because I don't think that is very subtle, to say, here is this world that we live in which is definitely not what it should be, other than "here," which is something else. And I don't think that is subtle, or what Waters is suggesting.

Another thing, what is regionalism? Is there such a thing as regionalism? Can we really say that Waters is representative of the Southwestern mystique, the Southwestern regionalism? What is the significance of ritual? What role do these dances, these stories, the fables that are told at night in the winter, these ritualized practices of the Indians, play in this book? Is it just anthropological interest or is there something really positive, something mechanically happening in the story, something that is moving this world forward, that is expressed in these rituals? And the sense of ritual. How about this ritual business of asking the tree if you could cut it down, or of asking the deer for his life, which possibly is the essential ritual in this novel, the most important ritual? How meaningful and in what way is it meaningful, that kind of ritual? Is it just superstition?

Audience: This asking a tree whether it may be cut down or not ties into a larger theme throughout the whole book, I think, the perspective of really looking at what a person is doing, looking at the connection of the tree to a person's point of view on life, the thoughtlessness about environment and where you are.

Lyon: The reason we do the ritual is to come awake to where we are.

Audience: Maybe not in that particular way, but I think any one of us is capable of thinking about what we are doing, coming more awake to life.

Lyon: This is the big mistake that Martiniano makes in the beginning of the book. He didn't get "*his*" deer, as they say in Utah, get his deer in the deer season because they wouldn't let him use the thresher. You go up to the mountains, and you go get your deer, and you didn't do the ritual. It is almost secondary that Martiniano broke the white man's law, too, bringing in that other world.

Audience: I'd like to comment on characterization. I think the characterization is really marvelous. I think Waters accomplished a very clear picture of the characters in very few words. He doesn't, as so many present-day writers seem to have to do, go on and on and on about the details of what made the character. The principal characters come through to me very strongly as to what they really are like and to some extent how they got to where they are.

Audience: I think that Waters himself has something to say about that in his art, in a section on Byers. To *perceive, rather than explain,* is important when you are talking about characters, whether or not the characters are fully developed.

Lyon: Byers is really an interesting character in this book. You know he is modeled on a real person, who is a friend of Waters, a trader in Taos named Ralph Meyers. Byers is curious for a Western character type because he is able to get mad at the Indians, and a lot of people have pointed out that this makes his responses quite believable, realistic. He's sort of the "white way" to get a perspective on what happens in this book. If it is hard to identify with Martiniano, because you haven't been pulled from your circumstances and sent away to boarding school, and so forth, and if it is hard to identify with Flowers Playing for the same reasons, the different ethnic circumstances, Byers is there. You could come into this book on Byers, so to speak. In a lot of ways he is the man in the middle like Martiniano, but the anger, the impatience that Byers has goes a long way for me, for realism.

Audience: The fact that Byers reached into the bush with his hand to get the rattlesnake is pretty weird.

Lyon: Why do you think he did that? He felt sick all day, felt like something was really wrong, he felt driven, he felt not himself.

Audience: Then that was the same as with Martiniano confronting the deer and going to get it. We *each* have *our* deer. . . . We have all had our dreams, *we have all killed our deer, and we have to somehow find a way back from that.*

Audience: I find it extremely interesting that Waters deals with the fact that he's essentially a white man writing about the character of the Indian and doing it absolutely beautifully in a way that, no matter how much respect you have for the differences between white and Indian, and how entitled they are, you are not offended by Waters' treatment of his subject. I have been offended by other writers who assume a condition in the Indian character that isn't theirs. Frank Waters never does that. He discloses so much that, as a white reader, you might dismiss about Indians, and he treats with respect the forms of women, for instance, and the power in those forms that white people are likely to look at them with their fashion-model eye as all this garbage and dismiss things about the Indians, that Frank Waters helps you to appreciate.

Lyon: That part of going past ethnicity and getting into the universal, the human level is, I think, very important. Waters has written that, when he finished the manuscript to this novel, he was living in Los Angeles and sent the manuscript back to Taos, back to the Governors, the elders of the pueblo, and asked if they had any objections. He asked if the book was accurate, if they had any objections to anything in it, to things being revealed. He didn't want to do what the anthropologist does in *The Man Who Killed the Deer*. They gave it the OK, and he has said on a number of occasions that's the best criticism he's had on this book.

But you do have that sense that it matters — and it's true, it is a particular fact these are Indians that are being talked about, and it is a historical circumstance — the feeling all the way that Waters penetrated to a level where we really are *all* sharing the same kind of life. Where we really do all have our deer, as you said.

I would say it takes remarkable subtlety and delicacy to do that. You can't just write a realistic book about Indians and get all the designs right on the pots, on the blankets and the food. Who cares really? It is not a historical novel in that sense. And you could on the other side go all the way to some sort of cosmic depiction of lost wisdom and so forth. He didn't do that either. He got both realms as they really do intermingle. That's what I refer to as emergence. I think it is showing in the particular world, in this life that we are leading, daily life. Look at all in that book, all the minor details that you get, and Waters is constantly doing things, constantly doing action. I think that he is showing, there *isn't* any other world. In fact he says as much about six times in the novel. He just says *this one world.*

So much of the interest, I dare say, of the traditional manners and morals novel, let's say of Henry James or John Updike, is a kind of gossip; you want to know what happens to the character, you might even voyeuristically want to find out about people and what they do, but there isn't that inner or deeper sense. Fans of James and Updike will argue, I'm sure. But I think there is another dimension, another whole dimension in Waters, I'd say, some justification for what you hear sometimes, that this is America's greatest *un*known writer and novelist.

Audience: What is the significance of the continued failure to climb the pole to retrieve the deer, both by the group that was supposed to and by Martiniano volunteering?

Lyon: Well, what Waters says, some of the old Indians think that they have lost their tribal power, or medicine. He describes this situation in *Masked Gods*, of seeing a young Indian fail to climb the pole at a pueblo ritual. That's a blend in from real history. The other thing is that, when Martiniano slid down the pole, down came the last walls of his pride, of his whole egoistic, separate sense of self. He is seeing himself in this incident, he is starting to see himself as The Man Who Killed the Deer, and starting to see himself as some kind of tribal person, a hero. I think Waters really wants to cut that out from under him right away. Martiniano has got to be humbled, got to be humiliated, even though in the beginning of the book, he *thinks* he is terribly humiliated. But he isn't, not in the Frank Waters' sense. He has just been *socially* humiliated, not yet humbled in his *whole relationship with the universe.*

Audience: Martiniano did get up higher than the other climbers, but, as you say, he had to be humbled, to find that balance.

Lyon: Yes, I think that is a good observation. You know, it struck me reading this book again a couple of weeks ago, that the title of the book is a little bit ironic. *The Man Who Killed the Deer* is a title that suggests our classic, traditional Western civilization sense of self. And I don't think that is where this book is going. There's a real irony in the title. The sense of individuality, a sense of separate individuality, is undermined by the whole book.

Audience: Maybe this is why when I read the novel, I had a struggle with

Martiniano's giving up his individuality. I wanted him to get to the top of the pole! It took me a long time to realize what was really happening.

Lyon: I think that is a really important point. When you look at the classic Western, I mean the capital-W or grade-B Western, there is an incredible emphasis on *the hero*, a very solid individual. I think of the first sentence of Jack Schaefer's novel, *Shane*, as being the archetype of this: "He rode into our valley in the summer of '89." It's got everything. The first word there is *he*. An identity. But that is not what Frank Waters is talking about. So my question really is, if Waters has got a whole different conception of what human nature is, if he doesn't believe along with most of us, refuses to go along with most of us that a human being is something quite separate and alone, then how can we hold him to the standards of the traditional novel that have been built on this whole idea of personality? I don't think we can, obviously.

I think this book ends beautifully, in the sense that you don't get any sense of rest, or closure or complete resolution. This is a process, this whole thing is *process*. The world is changing. Byers says this, that there is not going to be a nice little oasis of primitive life in this big world, no ivory towers of thought. That's Waters talking. It's not going to happen that way. So you do not get big fanfares at the end for Martiniano. He's begun an emergence, which is a continuing process, not a transcendence. You don't know really about Martiniano. That's another interesting thing, that his character is based on a real person in the pueblo whom Frank knew for many years, a man to whom an incident of deer killing had happened, almost exactly as in the novel. Frank built this novel on that man's occurrence, and that man came and worked for Frank Waters for a number of years, and Waters says that they never talked about the book. He never asked him if he read the book. And this Indian man never asked Waters about the book. And that kind of reticence, again, is a really good demonstration of Waters' care, his *respect* for things. He's not a very manipulative author either, despite the criticism that he uses characters as mouthpieces. I really don't see Waters as manipulating. And his sense about *The Man Who Killed the Deer*, he says that it wrote itself. He says he always had this very powerful feeling that this book *just came*. He says, I don't mean this in the sense of automatic writing, quote, whatever that is, but it just came, it seemed to make its own way. And so he was able to talk about the novel pretty dispassionately, and, at the same time, he's not a promoter, not a self-promoter, literally speaking. I see that respect for process as part and parcel of his attitude, a whole way of dealing with the world.

Audience: Thinking of *The Man Who Killed the Deer* and the collective society represented there, and also of what Frank writes in *Mountain Dialogues* about his visit to China, I wonder, do you think Frank has ever, to his own satisfaction, resolved the conflict between individuality and the collective? There is a tension there that is important to *The Man Who Killed the Deer.* Do you think there is a continuing question in his mind as to where we could find a resolution between these two usually opposed ideas of human life? I think it is unanswerable.

Lyon: I think it is unanswerable in a good way. I think it is really a question of a constant, continuing process, because what you said I can go along with exactly. What I see is the subtlety of Waters' characterization, its realism, the way he gives full respect to both those elements or what he would call polar energies in our character. We all do have this sense of individual self or ego, and, at the same time, we have this other kind of sense of things, too, of the whole, or whatever. You've got the two sides, if you will; it's the kind of magnetism or polarity or balance, or the tipping of, the back-tipping of the balance, it is the whole relationship, which is a continuing process, and not really ever going to be a kind of final plateau. But it's that tipping balancing relationship where in one second we are rather aware, we are rather sensitive, we are rather knowing of our part in the indivisible whole, to use a phrase of Waters, and in the next instant we could be an unconscious fool. It's this kind of game or whatever that I think Waters pays a lot of respect to, I don't think he is going to *show* you a character. *The Woman at Otowi Crossing* comes close in Helen's high moments, but I don't think he is going to show you a character who finally goes all one way. He is looking at the wholeness, which is made up of the continuing polarity of the parts. He says in *Mountain Dialogues* that those mountains have their dialogue; the mountain behind his house north of Taos represents a silence within him, and he uses the present tense. He says every morning he tries to go out and stand there in the sagebrush and just have a moment of quietness and not asserting, not wanting particularly any certain thing to happen, and not wanting to extract anything from this world of nature but just to be there. You could call that a certain meditative presence. In doing that all the time, he shows me what is going on. But just to recognize that one needs to do that, one needs to go out there and listen and be quiet, I think that's a help we could respect. But to be able to embody or dramatize that kind of vision, that kind of wholeness of vision, I think that is a high skill, a very high order of skill. I want to give Waters full credit. I want to say this is an American writer of *perhaps the highest order.* We should really be looking at this man. We should not be saying, well, he doesn't have the subtle nuances of interpersonal realistic relationship like some authors. What he really has, though, are subtle nuances of tipping the balance which happens within character, way in, the inside realm. I think that is where subtlety *really* is.

The first sentence in Chapter Nine in *Deer* is a wonderful sentence to show Waters' point of view on character. He says, "So little by little the richness and the wonder and the mystery of life stole in upon him." If you look at the sentence grammatically — what's doing the acting and what is the subject of that sentence and what's the object of the prepositional phrase — you get Waters' point of view. That's a wonderful sentence. I really think there aren't too many American authors who have or could have written from that sort of perspective. Our interest is in the workings of the will. *This* is a different ball game.

Audience: The woman that wrote the abstract in the book about the pueblo: was that based on historical fact and how does Waters rationalize doing the same thing?

Lyon: Waters wrote in 1972 in the *New Mexico Magazine* an interesting article about *The Man Who Killed the Deer.* He finished the manuscript, and due to Stephen Vincent Benét's insistence, not one word was changed in the manuscript. Only one thing worried him, Waters says, Elsie Parsons whom he had met in New York and who had published some time before a short anthropological report on the Taos Pueblo, which outraged the Indians. There's your historical bit: several of the informants were called on the carpet and interviewed for punishment. During Waters' own writing, he had used those informants but then feared when the book would appear that his Indian friends would also be accused of having given him "classified" information. He mailed the advance copy back to the pueblo and got the OK. So there is the historical background, but the dates are telescoped. I think it was 1920 when the peyote religion and what later became called the Native American Church first came to the Taos Pueblo. So that event would have been earlier, as I read the book, than most events in the book. It was 1934 when John Collier became the head of the Bureau of Indian Affairs and put the stamp of approval on the Native American Church. Maybe I'm reading *Deer* wrong, but I seem to see 13 years telescoped there. Still, fundamentally, the events, the inner meanings, are apparently as Waters says.

Audience: How in the world could the Bureau of Indian Affairs give support or credence to the peyote religion?

Lyon: Well, it was an ancient Indian practice which, as Waters says in *The Man Who Killed the Deer*, had come up through Mexico and into the Southern Plain tribes and then went back westward to Taos. About the last tribe in America to get the peyote religion was the Navajo, in 1930. It had a kind of movement like this, and he describes that, and so apparently that background gave it a certain credibility. It is still widely practiced, of course. Every tribe in North America now has members of the Native American Church. One anthropologist views peyotism almost exactly as Waters depicts it fictionally, that is, as a kind of metaphysical or philosophical compromise between the other-worldly or transcendental deity-type religion of Christianity, which the white man is bringing in, and the old way, looking at it as an accommodation, which in their desperation and their historical circumstance the Indians have had to make.

The Elders who talk about peyotism in *The Man Who Killed the Deer* reject it on philosophical grounds almost completely, and I see their rejection as a rejection of transcendence, a rejection of going to some other realm. They repeatedly say there is only *one* world — I think this is Waters' theme song, almost, through most of this book.

Audience: To me one of the big things about this peyote cult in the pueblo is the assumption of the younger people that tried and did not find the meaning of the ritual of the old tribes, and therefore looked for the meaning of life through peyote, I guess much in the same way as my generation has gone to drugs in trying to find themselves. I think this is one of the points that the Elders of the tribe make — they see the falseness of it. What it generates instead is not doing something and not looking at oneself in a realistic way.

Lyon: I think all that you say is right there with Waters. I think it is rejected in the end. I think that is very clear. But you could say, too, that it is by virtue of going to the peyote dreams that Martiniano is at least shaken in his, you might say, "white" view. Peyote may have performed some little function, some "good" toward opening him up, but that definitely is not a solution. You come back in the narrative to the world where the deer is still bothering him.

Notice the language when Waters is giving the description of what is going on in Martiniano's mind, after he has eaten the cactus. The descriptions are really dreamy, highly colored; the rhythms in the prose become dreamy. There is not the precision, the sense of concreteness that you have in the rest of the book, that you have for example in the very first scene, when Palemon has left his apartment and is responding to something, which in our rational point of view we would call very mystic, the heartbeat of the earth. But the details, the aspen, the stars, the light coming, and so forth, are very precise. You recognize this as real world.

Huxley spoke naively in 1954 in a little book, *The Doors of Perception*, in which he describes his psychedelic experiments or trips on the peyote road. In that book he talks about the primitive's reality as this beautiful, one, indivisible world, and he felt that he had been keyed in to it by his experiences. I would say if you hold up Huxley's *The Doors of Perception* against *The Man Who Killed the Deer*, my opinion would be Huxley gets only a little ways off the ground, whereas Waters shows his character going on this psychedelic venture and then having to realize a *different* sort of world, having to come to terms with emergence, not instant transcendence. I think there's a really important difference in depth here between the two books, that shows me Waters in the early 1940s way ahead of his times. Because in '54, Huxley, perhaps at least by some, was regarded as being ahead of *his* time, presaging a new era in the consciousness of the Western world which through psychedelic experience would let people become aware of the limitations of the rational outlook. But *Deer* has lasted and now nobody has heard of *The Doors of Perception*.

Audience: I would be interested in hearing a little expansion on the character, Palemon. He is the most ambiguous character in the book, yet Waters started the book with that character. I could see a "left-brain" reader picking the book up and putting it down.

Lyon: It's almost as if in the first few pages, Waters is saying to your "left-brain" reader — here it is. I mean, we are talking about the Pleiades, we are talking about the deer, Wind Old Woman is blowing, it's not just the wind come down from the mountain. It's almost a dare, almost as if he is saying, this is a different world.

Audience: What about the end? The complete circle of life is right there. Beautifully done.

Lyon: That circular way, it's almost too neat if you could stop there, but I don't think that Waters does. I think of this nice little thing where right at the end of the book Martiniano's wife is saying when you go to town bring me some canned tomatoes or something like that. Waters does that. It's very prosaic, it's very much *this* world, and that shows me that their real life, this life that they lead, is moving on, *the whole world is in an emergence.* Waters says this about forty times in different books, I'm sure. It's the whole thing that's moving, not just individual human beings who are realizing kind of a wonderful world which belongs to them. All of this is in the process. In *Mexico Mystique*, maybe Waters' most far-out book, he is talking about a kind of strange historical verge where the polarity, rationalism, the "left-brain" on the one side, and the other side are possibly going to meet, and some sort of synthesis not too far in the future. Maybe what we are seeing now is like what the Hopis and some of the Central American Indian civilizations call a world, a frame of reference, a way of being conscious of the world. In the latter stages, you begin to get more extreme statements. It's almost as in the deer dance toward the end of *Deer* where Flowers Playing plays the role of the Deer Mother and the Deer Mothers in the center are representing the earth, the earth sense. The other part players or "Masked Gods" are representing the individual sense, say the "left-brain" or egoistic sense of identity, and they dance *out* from the Deer Mother center and, inevitably, sort of magnetically, come back, and you get this great pulse, polarity working itself out in the dance. Waters says Martiniano is watching this dance with a sort of hypnotic horror, and it is because obviously Martiniano recognizes his own life is being enacted there. Maybe what we are seeing in history now is as the polarity, as the elements of our world move more toward possible synthesis, a "coming sixth world of consciousness," as Waters sub-titled *Mexico Mystique*. I suppose that is one way of looking at all the travail and violence we see in the world today.

Can you name another American writer who attempts this broad a vision of man on earth? I would really like to say, I think Waters is in a small company of people who have at least attempted a major vision. He says of *Deer*, it was earth, his own earth, and *Deer*, almost as if it were experimental and we have been talking about it as an achieved body of a vision, was a process going on, and there will be other things. There *were* other things after the *Deer*.

How about the characterization of women in *Deer*? It is not just Western writers here that have been attacked on the basis of characterization, but, as some of you may know, American fiction in general is attacked as being either superficial or stereotyped in depiction of women characters and relationship between sexes.

Audience: My own view, I can't think of any male American author who can create women characters for a male reader as convincingly as Frank Waters does. Of course there is Hester Prynne in *Scarlet Letter*, but, though she took over Hawthorne's kinder imagination, she actually is not the central character, given the structure of that novel. I mention Hester as something of a triumph and an exception. Some of Henry James' portraits have to be considered, but Frank has to be in a small class, again, for this capacity to create great female characters.

Lyon: I have always been impressed with how he depicted the character that is essentially his mother in the autobiographical trilogy, *Pike's Peak*. I dare say, not too many male authors have done very much with their mothers as fictional characters, that is, as real and compassionate. This is a wonderful thing that Waters does in *Pike's Peak*.

Audience: There is a paragraph about men inevitably falling back, when assailed by the invincibility of their women. What a neat paragraph!

Lyon: There has been a lot of talk the last five or ten years about so-called androgeny in writers. There is a school of criticism looking at writers in terms of how well they feel into the other gender's experience. Critics of that type should really look into Waters' *The Woman at Otowi Crossing* and *People of the Valley.* . . . Does somebody want to make a final kind of ringing statement?

Audience: . . . I am always interested in the reaction of my students to this book. Essentially I think they see it as a fairy tale. Everything that Frank Waters suggests in the book is absolutely contradictory to the realities of their lives, what they in fact have to do. I find them reacting positively toward the book as only young people can with an ideal vision. But, on the other hand, they never really take it seriously. They say Martiniano is after all going where we came from in the Middle Ages, and we are on a different level of consciousness now. Interestingly enough in that same vogue, Scott Momaday's *House Made of Dawn* they think a wonderful book, even though in *Deer* and *Dawn* the movement is essentially the same, the movement toward tribal relationships and the center of the community. They think that is valid in Momaday's novel, because Indians do have a culture and a tribe, a central place to which they return. But they see Frank Waters' book as really about Anglos and for Anglos, and we just don't have that place of return. Everything their society says to them is that you leave family and friends, keep moving out constantly. And *The Man Who Killed the Deer* is a moving *in*. It's a strange reaction. They enjoy the book but. . . .

Alexander Blackburn
The Allegory of Emergence in
The Man Who Killed the Deer

The Man Who Killed the Deer is a remarkable example of Waters' archetypal imagination at work. Thirty years after the novel's publication he still
vividly recalled how it all began:

> From the day I wrote the first page–in ink on a manuscript
> that was later destroyed–the novel seemed not of my doing.
> I remember that fall morning in Taos, sitting in front of the
> fireplace in the big room above the garage in back of Tony
> Lujan's house just inside the reservation. The story did not
> have to be contrived; it unfolded, like a flower, its own inher-
> ent pattern. The words came easily, unbidden, as the flow of
> ink from my old, red Parker. I don't mean to imply that it was
> anything like "automatic writing," whatever that is. Simply that
> it seemed impelled by the unconscious rather than by rational
> consciousness.
>
> There seems to be some validity for this statement. The
> novel has been used as a subject for a master's thesis at the
> Colorado State University, interpreted from the viewpoint of
> Jungian depth-psychology. A similar approach has been taken

in a *Tesi di Laures* prepared for the University of Genoa, Italy.
At the time I wrote the novel, however, I had not read Jung.

What seemed to touch off the book were two incidents.
I had strayed into the county courthouse where a hearing was
being given an Indian for killing a deer out of season in the
Carson National Forest. A few mornings later, when I was
bending over the washbowl to shave, I envisioned reflected in
the water three figures evidently discussing the incident and
who bore striking resemblances to the old, blanketed governor
of Taos Pueblo, Pascual Martinez in his Forest Service boots
and whipcord, and Ralph Myers, the Indian trader. Right then
the idea of the novel presented itself, and after washing the
breakfast dishes I sat down to write it.[1]

If, as I surmise, the idea of the novel is implied in its title, Waters had begun
by striking into a Paleolithic stratum of world mythology, that of a covenant
between men and animals, suggesting a sacramental relationship of hunter
and hunted beast, an experience in the psychological dimension of their being
one and the same. In the words of Joseph Campbell, "The beast to be slaugh-
tered is interpreted as a willing victim, or rather, as a knowing participant
in a covenanted sacred act wherein the mystery of life, which lives on life, is
comprehended in its celebration."[2] The mythology of the covenant, which
includes a powerful taboo against the taking of life without ritual expression
of reverence for it, was taught for a human season of some 20,000 years, and
memories of the animal envoys of an Unseen Power still must sleep, somehow,
within us. *The Man Who Killed the Deer*, a novel about an Indian who ignores
the covenant and is subsequently haunted by the deer he has killed, is part of
the evidence.

Although the narrative unfolded its pattern easily, the formal perfection
of structure—beginning with a first chapter which is technically one of the
most adroit in modern prose fiction—and the beauty of style signaled the
appearance of a classic. After reading the manuscript for its first publishers,
Farrar and Rinehart of New York, Stephen Vincent Benét was so enthusiastic that he insisted that not one word be changed.[3] Burton Rascoe, one of
the most respected reviewers of the period, stated in his full-page review in
the *Saturday Review of Literature*, "This is by far the finest novel of American

Indian life I have ever read,"[4] and noted its superiority to Oliver La Farge's Pulitzer Prize-winning sentimental romance about Navajo Indians, *Laughing Boy* (1929). Yet the novel was a flop commercially. In the mobilization for World War II following the Japanese attack on Pearl Harbor on 7 December 1941, no one seemed to be interested in a book whose background was the life and religion of a remote Indian pueblo in Taos, New Mexico. Soon the publishers contributed the metal plates to the war effort and remaindered the stock for whatever price they could get. Still, some word about the classic novel had spread, and in 1950 Alan Swallow of Denver decided to bring out a new edition. In 1971 Pocket Books published a paperback edition. Numerous reprintings of these editions have followed, and foreign translations have appeared in German (1960), French (1964), and Dutch (1974). Although it is impossible to estimate with any accuracy the number of copies of *Deer* that have been sold in its first seventy-five years, the figure may possibly be more than three-quarters of a million. At any rate, sales continue steadily. The latest—and best designed—paperback reprint appeared under the Swallow Press and Ohio University Press imprint in 1989.

One reason for the novel's popularity is its subject matter, Pueblo Indian life. As a Southwestern "lifestyle" currently sweeps the country, anything "Indian" attracts attention, and tourists in New Mexico may well be including *Deer* along with their haul of squash-blossom necklaces and reproductions by R.C. Gorman. And here, although I am speculating, lies a critical problem: *Deer's* background materials may obscure its universality and the art that reveals it. Pueblo Indian life is the novel's background, the vehicle for another kind of story and not the story itself. Fascinated by materials with which we have little or no familiarity, we may confine our experience of *Deer* to expository data, to cultural anthropology, and ignore the novel's figurative meanings, its allegoricalness. If we recall that the greatness of *Moby-Dick* can be attributed to what Melville called "the part-&-parcel allegoricalness of the whole,"[5] rather than to the exposition of whaling on which that allegory expands, we may be prepared for an analogous attribution in our reading of *Deer*. The Indian data are controlled throughout the novel by an allegorical meaning which is not in any necessary sense "Indian" at all.

Because the allegoricalness of the novel depends on its total organization, an exposition of plot and background is necessary to show the foundation on which the fable builds. Background materials with which many readers may be unfamiliar I have highlighted in capital letters that they may be discussed later, and, once familiarity with these is increased, the hidden allegory may seem to rise naturally, like a photograph emerging from solution. An allegorical mode aims at both clarity and obscurity together, each effect depending on the other.[6] Although the numinous meaning of a symbolic or iconographic deer can be only enigmatically suggested by the words *mystery* and *wonder*, the deer assembles various accretions of figurative significance which form a clear patterning.

Synopsis:

The events of the novel take place in or near an Indian PUEBLO in northern New Mexico over a two-year period in the 1930s. Before the action unfolds, Martiniano[7] is already a pueblo outcast born of an Apache mother and a Pueblo father. When, about twelve years old, he comes of age for tradition-al religious education in the KIVA, he attracts the attention of the Indian Service, which is looking for "smart" boys, and sent for six years to a white man's school ("AWAY SCHOOL"), the council of elders having offered little resistance and forced the father, under threat of a public whipping, to agree to the removal. Martiniano is trained as a carpenter and acculturated to the ways of whites. When he returns to the pueblo, he has a young white man's outlook: rationalistic, individualistic, willful. His parents are dead, and his "uncles" have appropriated part of his inheritance, leaving him only two small farms outside pueblo walls. Resentful and rebellious, Martiniano refuses to conform to what seems a petty dress code (knocking the heels off his shoes, cutting the seat out of his trousers, and covering his middle with a blanket) and to join in the ceremonial dances, for the meaning of which he has never been prepared. These refusals earn him fines and a public whipping from the council of elders. He scorns them for their injustice and pridefully seeks out-side the pueblo's ceremonial life a spiritual meaning to his existence. When he meets Flowers Playing, a "mountain" Indian (part Arapahoe, part White River and Uncompahgre Ute) as opposed to a "city-dwelling" Indian (or Pueblo), herself a product of "away school," he does not ask permission from her family for a marriage or request from the pueblo that she be adopted into the tribe. He woos and wins her in a white man's way, without regard for such relation-ships. Although his nascent intuitive powers have attracted him to Flowers Playing and prompt him to place his faith in the marriage ritual, he is bitterly aware that she must share in his poverty and disgrace. She does so willingly, even though, in addition to everything else, her exceptional gifts as a dancer are ignored by the pueblo. Only Palemon, who belongs to the old ways but believes in their substance, not their outer form, befriends the couple inside the pueblo; outside it, only Byers, the white trader for whom Martiniano does odd jobs, befriends him.

And now, on a mountain trail leading to the pueblo's sacred DAWN LAKE, Martiniano has killed a deer. He has assaulted a ranger who seeks to arrest him because the killing is out of season, and the ranger, retaliating, has left Martiniano for dead. Palemon, he who is gifted with extraordinary intuitive powers, "knows" something is wrong, finds and rescues his friend, and brings him and the slain deer back to the pueblo. Here Martiniano is censured by the council, not for the assault, but for having failed to perform rituals that amount to asking the deer's consent to the killing. Brought to the white man's court, he is sentenced to three months or $150, but Byers advances money for the fine. The case seems closed. The pueblo governor, however, wonders why rangers should be present on land historically the pueblo's. Reluctantly, an Indian Service attorney promises to get in touch with officials in Washington. And thus from the killing of the deer there unfolds a connected train of events: the pueblo has been moved to action over land seized by the federal government, and Martiniano is afflicted with a sense of guilt.

As conscience plagues him, Martiniano feels estranged from Flowers Playing. Seeking faith elsewhere he tries the PEYOTE ROAD, the "church" that the federal government is pushing as a substitute for traditional religion. The council will have none of this. Martiniano, too, rejects use of peyote but must endure fifteen lashes for having participated in a ceremony requiring the outside stimulus of a drug. Moreover, the punishment is administered by Palemon, who has tried to shield his friend from discovery, and so Martiniano feels especially ashamed for having involved another person in his fate. Influenced by the power of a relationship, he accepts his responsibility and for the first time, instead of being haunted by the spirit-deer, senses its guardianship. Martiniano is reunited with Flowers Playing, she becomes pregnant, and there is contentment in their lives—but Martiniano's acculturation in the ways of the white man continues. Admirably enough, he refrains from killing deer who take shelter on his farm, and he works his land in order to pay off the debt to Byers, but he still thinks that *he* makes the land fruitful, that *he* truly possesses it. Accordingly, he violently ejects from the land a Mexican sheepherder. This act once again brings the pueblo's land claim to the attention of the authorities. Because the council begins to regard Martiniano with a measure of respect, he believes that he has bridged the gap between himself and the pueblo and become its legendary hero. Thus, on San Geronimo Day he attempts to "save" the pueblo from disgrace—the ceremony of the POLE CLIMB has been botched—but he, too, fails to climb the pole and bring triumph out of defeat. Humiliated at last, he begins to perceive the power of the deer as one of necessary relationships to life instead of an adversary.

Meanwhile, Flowers Playing has been invited by the pueblo to enact the role of a Deer Mother in the DEER DANCE. As Martiniano observes her performance, there are illuminated for him the primal forces with which pueblo ceremonialism has always been concerned. In the sequence of events that end the novel, the slain deer ceases to haunt him. Flowers Playing gives birth to a son, and Martiniano repays the debt to Byers and takes part in the pueblo's ceremonial foot races. Above all, he is in touch with his own intuitive powers, and these lead him to rescue Palemon's son from a death in the mountains, in a scene somewhat parallel to that in which Palemon had rescued Martiniano in the novel's first chapter. Because the pueblo has brought the Dawn Lake controversy to a victorious conclusion, Martiniano can take legitimate satisfaction in watching the pilgrims depart for their annual Dawn Lake ceremony. Lacking the religious training to join in it, he nevertheless understands its necessity and vows that his own son will be educated in the traditional manner. He wraps himself in a traditional blanket and is content.

Background:

"[Waters] is concerned primarily with the inner drama that lies beneath the surface of ethnological documentation." So wrote Harvard anthropologist Clyde Kluckhohn in his foreword to *Masked Gods: Navaho and Pueblo Ceremonialism.* The inner drama of *The Man Who Killed the Deer* is also of primary concern, but the ethnological surface or background material plays its part. To describe it, I shall draw summaries almost verbatim from *Masked Gods.* Neither it nor *Deer* has, to the best of my knowledge, ever been seriously challenged on the grounds of authenticity. On the contrary, *Deer* has found acceptance in the Taos Pueblo itself. Fearful lest his Indian friends think his novel a violation of traditional secrecy and religion, Waters mailed the first advance copy to the interpreter for the Taos Pueblo council, but there were no repercussions. In fact, Waters has often been approached by a man or a woman in the pueblo who tells him how glad they are he wrote "that book," for from it their children can understand the "old ways." Moreover, when the Blue Lake (fictionalized as Dawn Lake) controversy came to a head, *Deer* was sent to members of Congress and supporting committees and organizations, as background material, and proved at least partially instrumental when, on 15 December 1970, President Nixon signed into law the bill providing that 48,000 acres of sacred land be kept in wilderness status under Taos Pueblo ownership with the national government acting as trustee.[8]

As mentioned earlier, the rituals whereby an animal consents to be sacrificed have their origin in the Paleolithic Age, an archaeological period which forms a general background for the North American Indians. If Campbell is right, the system of rites actually brought together two mythologies, that of animals and that of female humans, so that there are two contexts, moral and regenerative, to be associated with ritual and taboo.[9] This joint context helps to explain why the male deer killed by Martiniano is nevertheless viewed symbolically as a feminine power.

The story of the PUEBLO Indians begins about 2,000 years ago, according to the earliest dates of Southwestern Indians established by dendrochronology. About this time the Indians were dressing themselves in animal skins, weaving baskets, planting corn, and storing surplus grain. When many families at a time gathered in larger caves and expanded the storage pits into stone pit houses built in the shelter of overhanging cliffs, settlements began and, with them, society, as from caves the people climbed up the faces of cliffs to create cities wherever a horizontal ledge provided support. Great communal houses were built on top of the cliffs, and kivas—round, subterranean structures used for religious ceremonies—were built in open terraces in front of the house groups. Then about 1,000 years ago the people descended from cliffs to establish the great pueblos on the plain, city-states such as Pueblo Bonito in Chaco Canyon that may have rivaled those of ancient Greece. From what we presently know about this civilization of what *Deer* calls the "Old Ones" (called *Anasazi* by the Navajo, nomadic Indians who are late arrivals in the Southwest), its social structure was matrilineal, polarized to the intuitive and feminine in that "man, unguided by reason, maintained a direct intuitional relationship with the primal forces of a living universe" (*Masked Gods*, 30). Although this civilization vanished about A.D. 1300, some people remained and built up pueblos in the desert Southwest and along the Rio Grande. In fact, the oldest occupied towns in the United States are said to be Oraibi and Acoma, both dating from around A.D. 1200, and the Tiwa-speaking pueblo of Taos has probably been occupied for more than 700 years.

Taos Pueblo is located in the mountains about seventy miles north of Santa Fe. Three successive nations—Spain, Mexico, and the United States— legally confirmed the pueblo's ancient rights to its land, and President Lincoln presented the governor of the pueblo with a silver mounted cane in token of the people's right to govern themselves by their own laws. Such confirmations notwithstanding, Spanish, Mexican, and Anglo settlers usurped pueblo lands and water rights. Much of the surrounding area, including Blue Lake near Mount Wheeler, was constituted as Carson National Forest. Not until 31 May 1933 did Congress pass an act giving Taos Pueblo a fifty-year tenure of their lands surrounding Blue Lake.

Pueblo ceremonialism "is concerned with the fact that the deeds of individuals are not confined to their own spheres of social action; they vitally affect the earth, the waters, the mountains–the whole web of life" (*Masked Gods*, 246). It is, therefore, essential to the maintenance of tribal culture that boys between the ages of twelve and fourteen be separated from their families and given religions instruction in the KIVA. A prolonged ritual initiation breaks the "cord" to a boy's mother and to the earth, and the child is born again into a consciousness of the greater life of the spirit, learning that "gods are the invisible cosmic forces of the universe" residing in man "who, if he wills, can evoke them for the common good… a prophecy and a promise of that time when man shall return to and be synonymous with the source power of all creation" (*Masked Gods*, 212). According to Waters, the Emergence myth is introduced to children at this time in the kiva, whose members develop a conscience with respect to all forms of life.

Beginning in the 1880s, the American government set about the task of educating Indian children in "AWAY SCHOOL." Nonreservation schools were established in Carlisle, Pa.; Lawrence, Kans.; Riverside, Calif.; Phoenix, Ariz.; and Albuquerque and Santa Fe, N. Mex. Once captured and sent to "away school," the Pueblo children suffered everything possible that could be done to erase all vestiges of their racial culture and identity. Their hair was cut; they were forbidden to speak their own language, to wear their own clothes, to keep their traditional customs, even their own names. Dismissed from school, they were untrained for anything but manual or menial labor. When finally they did straggle back to the pueblos, they did not know how to adapt themselves. And yet, in spite of their lack of kiva training, many returnees went "back to the blanket," the government schools having given them little more than a thin patina.

On their way back to the blanket, young men returning from government schools often found the PEOYTE ROAD attractive. Pharmacological experience of the ineffable (in various Indian languages *Manitou, wakan, orenda,* and the like) has in some regions always been sought by young men in a "vision quest" and everywhere at least by shamans. Certain substances such as peyote, introduced to Native American tribes from Mexico about 1880, were and are alleged to inhibit metabolically the "restraint" of symbols, languages, and cognitive maps enculturated into people by society and thus to produce a "heightened" perception of ineffable truth Although Aldous Huxley popularized the drug in *The Doors of Perception* (1954), an authority on the peyote cult, Western La Barre, finds it hard to believe that an impaired brain functioning somehow becomes its physiological opposite: heightened perception may in fact be a lowered critical faculty, as in drunkenness and dreams.[10] Perhaps because the Taos Pueblo Council suspected that drugs were no substitute for their religion, the use of peyote had a stormy history there. In 1921 a peyote meeting was raided, and the blankets and shawls of all participants were confiscated. In 1923 two adherents of the cult were whipped and three men given large fines. Nevertheless, the cult has been accepted by various Indian tribes and officially recognized by the Bureau of Indian Affairs as the Native American Church.

The POLE CLIMB, DEER DANCE, and DAWN (i.e., Blue) LAKE episodes or references in *Deer* are obviously of religious significance. According to Waters in *Mexico Mystique,* the pole climb may have originated in ancient Mesoamerica when a great feast was celebrated in honor of Tlaloc, a god of rain and hence of regeneration. A tree was cut down, its consent having been asked, brought to the temple of Tlaloc with songs and dancing, and ceremonially planted. There are modern parallels to this ceremony in Mexico and the Southwest, and the climbing of a pole is a feature of the end-of-September, San Geronimo fiesta in Taos Pueblo. There, a tall, straight pine of considerable circumference (about 48 inches at the base, according to my rough measurement of the pine used in 1989) is planted in the Taos plaza, the fruits of harvest suspended from its top—a deer or sheep carcass, squash and corn, a bundle of groceries. An accomplished climber shinnies up the pole, lets down the treasure to the shouts of the crowd below, and then balances on top of the pole, singing his eagle song of triumph. Although athletic skill is required for successful climbing, a climber's triumph, as I understand it, is not a claim of excellence. It is, rather, a kind of sacred reciprocation between the people and nature, which made the harvest possible, and so it is believed that any break in this interaction, such as a failure to climb the pole, might result in disease or calamity.

As for the Deer Dance, which is prominent as a winter ceremony at Taos Pueblo, its religious significance is translated by Waters into a psychological allegory, as we shall see presently. But the Indian concept of harmony among all things may seem so alien to non-Indian readers that we don't conceive of a spiritual conviction that is communicated through dance, a unique expressive act in which there is immediacy and a perfect unity of thought and feeling. As Jamake Highwater argues in *The Primal Mind*, "The idea that spirituality can be associated with the body is extremely remote from the white man's belief in the dichotomy of mind and body, spirit and flesh."[11] Be that as it may, primal people regard movement as the embodiment of a mysterious force, so that they may imitate an animal in movements (but also in costume) in order to influence the circumstances of nature.

Just exactly why a mountain lake is considered as a sacred place of tribal origin seems to be a question related to Emergence, or the process of evolution considered in mythological terms. One interesting theory, presented by Waters in *Mountain Dialogues* (61-62) is that in the Mesoamerican number system the founding concept of zero represented the ocean, or endless space and time; hence the "foundation" of pyramids in Teotihuacán was water, the first "lifting up" or step or world (the second being fire, the third earth, the fourth air, and so forth). Perhaps an analogous idea is expressed by the sacrality of Dawn Lake, water being the first in the progression of life forms. In the psychology of symbols, water represents the unconscious, and it is this meaning which seems best suited to the allegory of Emergence in *The Man Who Killed the Deer*.

Allegory traditionally presents a gradual evolvement of correspondences between a narrative and a cluster of pieties or religious formulae familiar to the reader. But there is the use of analogy which places most of the weight of a narrative's meaning on correspondences evolved within the story itself, depending hardly at all on borrowings familiar to the reader. Melville, Conrad, Franz Kafka, and D.H. Lawrence tend to effect allegoricalness in this manner, and the same is true of Frank Waters. In *Deer* the various analogies that can be drawn between Indian religion and modern psychology simply point to the oldest idea about allegory, defined by Angus Fletcher as "a reconstitution of divinely inspired messages, a revealed transcendental language which tries to preserve the remoteness of a properly veiled godhead."[12] No one, I think, can read *Deer* without sensing this remoteness, even though revelation may be imputed to Indian sources with which one is unfamiliar rather than to the creative mythology of Waters, a non-Indian with some Indian heritage. But the mythic tenor of *Deer* must be distinguished from the anthropological vehicle, and the distinction, often productive of a powerful dramatic irony, becomes the mark of the work's allegoricalness, the whole work becoming what Edwin Honig calls "the allegorical unit." The whole work partakes of the allegorical unit and also fulfills it, the allegorical unit then resounding with "inherent meanings... built up on all levels of connotation" until "the expository data serve the theme in a way parallel to the way Christian analogy served for the medieval writer." Honig develops his insights further:

> It must seem that the meanings grow naturally out of each action in the narrative. The more complex a writer's grasp of psychophysical relationships, the richer the work is likely to be. For the meanings of allegory depend, as in poetry, upon the accretion of certain tropes. These tropes make evident a consonance between objective facts and their moral or psychological counterparts, so that the reality–the hypothetical nature of the literal–is ultimately transcended by the total organization of meanings, which is the fiction itself. And so we may say the language of allegory makes relationships significant by extending the original identities of which they are composed with as many clusters of meaning as the traffic of the dominant idea will bear.[13]

Honig's statements about "psychophysical relationships" explain why Moby-Dick is more than a whale, Pike's Peak more than a mountain, and the deer in *Deer* more than a deer. Expository data are transcended by the accretion of symbolic meanings driven by a "dominant idea."

As I interpret *The Man Who Killed the Deer*, its dominant idea is Emergence. In the Waters canon, Emergence represents a stage of human consciousness that reconciles the duality of reason and intuition and supersedes these on a numinous plane of increased awareness. This plane is, moreover, an effulgence of an immanent power which relates the inner world of man to the living universe, itself composed of expanding psychic as well as physical energies. From this perspective, which is above all evolutionary, the long journey of mankind has been through successive states of ever-expanding consciousness. From complete polarization to the instinctive or unconscious mentation, man has emerged to his present state of rational consciousness and must not surrender this advantage over the lower forms of life or sink back into the unconscious, a condition mythologically associated with the Cosmic Mother of Creation. Modern man, however–and "modern" here largely refers to Euro-American peoples since the advent of scientific and materialistic civilization in the seventeenth century, with its attendant cult of individualism–has become excessively rationalistic and consequently alienated from the source of life, suffering a loss of relationship to nature and reaching an ethical dead end. Consequently, there must be a redressing of the balance, human survival being at stake, and the reconciliation of reason and intuition will once more enable people to live in harmonious relationship with the emergent life forces of Creation.

Waters' idea of Emergence resembles the Jungian psychology of "individuation" but was developed, at least through 1941, without Jungian influence.[14] Emergence has been influenced both by oriental and by Amerindian mythologies inasmuch as these lay stress on a Way or Road of self-fulfillment. In particular, the Pueblo and Navajo myths of Emergence are a component of Waters' idea or myth of Emergence; he has simply translated or interpreted them in the light of his own moral and religious philosophy. According to Waters himself, the "worlds" in Indian myths of Emergence are "allegories" (*Mountain Dialogues*, 159) of a process of evolution. There have been four successive "worlds," all embodied within the Cosmic Mother of creation, from which man has been born: the fire element of the first world gave him his life heat; the air element of the second world gave him breath of life; from the third world of water man derived his blood and other bodily constituents; and the earth element of this present world gave man his flesh. The Road of Life is thus participated in by every organ and faculty, and the process is cumulative, affirming another "world" or "worlds" to come, identified as a new world of consciousness, this being the lone human faculty left with room to expand. Given that man is intimately related to all forms of life, there is an ethical basis to evolutionary enlargements, and man has, whether he recognizes it or not, an indebtedness to those forms and a responsibility to them. It follows that human conscience, though it may be local and tribal in orientation and enforcement, serves all humanity in a world culture, because conscience pulls individuals back from ego-centeredness into harmonic relationship at all levels—family, tribe, society, all peoples, all living things, the universe itself-and thus pulls individuals forward on the path of Emergence. In fact, conscience in all of Waters' novels but especially in *Deer*—and the point needs emphasis because conscience in American literature (e.g., *Huckleberry Finn*) usually means moral indoctrination—is regarded as the voice of Absolute Consciousness speaking within us to our limited conscious selves.[15] Self-fulfillment is not an achievement of an individual; outstandingness has nothing to do with it. On the contrary, participation in the macrocosmic universe requires "complete obliteration of self that merges at last into one flowing, living whole… that has been, that will be, fused in the ever-living, indestructible now" (*Masked Gods*, 336). And that is why Emergence checks the ego-centered individual's wild lunges for freedom and obligates him "to the dictates of the unconscious which embodies all his primordial past," necessitating "those thaumaturgical rites which acknowledge his arising from the one great origin of all life and which keep him whole"—so that "there can be no Emergence to a higher consciousness without a Return to the fathomless deeps within us" (*Pumpkin*, 64, 153). A return to the Cosmic Mother is the prerequisite for emergence to a new world of the mind.

Emergence is the dominant idea or creative myth that is allegorized in *The Man Who Killed the Deer*. The allegorical hero's actions and thoughts resemble those of a man possessed by a primary illusion that he is in control of his fate. Specifically, he is "cursed" by the egocentric, Euro-American individualism in his outlook. Then the powers of conscience and intuition—the two are envisioned as synonymous—appear in the form of a spirit-deer. The hero loses his illusion by recognizing his obligation to the dictates of the unconscious and emerges to a state of increased awareness. There is a culminating character to this allegory: the hero experiences final moments of illumination, and love and creation triumph following the destructive battle with evil.

Yet it is characteristic of figurative images that their allegorical status is not recognized. "Only a mind which can apprehend *both* a literal and a 'poetic' formulation of an idea," Susanne Langer claims in *Philosophy in a New Key* (published the same year as *Deer*), "is in a position to distinguish the figure from its meaning."[16] Transposed into Waters' terminology, this statement asserts that the form or shell of spiritual endeavor is not to be confused with its substance. Although there are critics of *Deer* who either praise it as a precursor of Native American novels or condemn it as a fictional impersonation of Native American consciousness, Waters not only never pretended to write an "Indian" novel but also took precautions in the novel itself to distinguish between the form and the substance of Indian life.[17]

While *Deer* was still in manuscript, Waters wrote Mabel Dodge Luhan on 14 February 1941, justifying his fictional approach to Indian life as a direct one without intervention of a non-Indian point of view yet nevertheless an outside viewpoint:

> I think a completely true all-Indian novel will never be written. Not by a white for it would stem, as you say, from his own white psyche. And not by an Indian for the very reason that his own psyche is given to an instinctive, intuitive, non-reasoning and non-evaluating approach, too deeply rooted to emerge into a foreign word-form. His own natural forms exist only as great myth and dance-dramas, ceremonials and sand painting, etc., whose meanings are intelligible to most whites only by translation of their values–and which are gradually becoming less intelligible and lost to the Indians themselves.
>
> So that I feel the truest writing possible of Indian substance is from an outside viewpoint, an honest and direct attempt at translation, rather than the fictional method of working out from within....
>
> Now this, in your sense and mine, is not an Indian novel. To consider it such is to accuse me as a man of sentimentality, and as a writer of real hokum or self-illusions about what I am trying to do.
>
> To write at it in sketch form or essay–coldly; to look at it fictionally through a white participant, as THE WOMAN

WHO RODE AWAY [novella by D. H. Lawrence]; or to project the Indian only as a shadow against a white background, as
the SAD INDIAN;–these are the easiest methods. And they are
all indirect and depend upon contrast. What this is, is an outside viewpoint with the looker merely eliminated from within
the Indian envelope. [Tanner, 57]

Waters' decorum does seem justified. If we accept his premise that the Indian
is polarized to intuition and to a nonverbal epistemology and the white is
polarized to reason and to a verbal epistemology, "a completely true all-Indi-
an novel" is unavailable to the psyche of either Indian or white; and even an
Indian novelist writing from within Native American consciousness about
the nonverbalized substance of spiritual power would be basing his or her
attempt, as the white novelist's, on rational modes of expression. The Native
American novel has not been ruled out–D'Arcy McNickle's *Surrounded* (1936)
had already appeared, and the novels of N. Scott Momaday, James Welch, and
Leslie Marmon Silko would appear in the period from 1968 to the present time—but it is Waters' contention that the substance of Indian life will
remain ineluctably bound up in myth and ceremony, for which language can
but produce translation. The category "Indian novel" makes no absolute sense,
but an approach to Indian values through fiction can be attempted by means
of translation of the "natural forms"–myth, dance, ceremony and the like.
The approach in *Deer* is direct and honest, but the translation of substance
into word form must be an approximation and an interpretation, never the
substance itself.

The human substance of Indian life is another matter, for Waters presupposes a common humanity. The difficulty of interpreting, still more of
intuiting, the thoughts and intentions of persons from an ancient culture is
perhaps insuperable and would display itself awkwardly, as if Montezuma
II were being interviewed on television. In a technical sense Waters meets
this difficulty by translating what is essentially Indian silence into italicized
passages. Philosophically he meets it by assuming the presence of constants
among persons of different races. This is standard procedure for novelists and
historians. As Martin D'Arcy declares in *The Sense of History*, "We are aware
that individuals differ and that freedom makes human action unpredictable;
nevertheless we presuppose without an hesitation that certain instincts remain constant, that there is a broad way and a narrow way, that the struggle

between mind and heart, selfishness and generosity is unabating, that communities form naturally and exhibit common characteristics, and that these and other traits of men can be discerned."[18] Water's letter to Luhan justifies his procedure in *Deer* on a similar humanistic basis:

> I believe, differently from you, that [Indians], like a Fiji islander and an Eskimo, like people everywhere of all races and conditions, are yet human entities bound by the same human ties of human passion. From deep within us all well up old, dark, racial blood-forces. Around us, whether in jungle, mountain or city, exist the same problems of existence and environment. And above us, the same spiritual plane to which we all some day will converge. We are all middle-men, all human, Indian, negro and white. Whatever you say of tribal feeling, there does exist in an Indian the simple emotional ties between man and wife, mother and son, regardless of whether he acknowledges it under the name of love, and despite the fact that the individual feeling is quickly submerged in the tribal. In the Indian this is not the important part of life; it is how this is deepened, enhanced, by the wonderful, unspeakable essence flowing up into it from deep within.
>
> Now this exists, in some measure, in all men. And the problem has forever been how to admit it in a clearer stream, a more unimpeded flow. And so the great religious systems have arisen, age upon age, throughout the world. And as man has striven upward, he has spiritually, as temporally, gone through the same evolutionary changes. The core of Indian esotericism is the belief that he holds, unsullied because unspoken (i.e., not allowed to become dead through crystallization), the dark flower of primeval truth and power. The Lhasas of Tibet believe, likewise, that in their hands they hold alive against time the same spark of the one timeless flame. Nor do they give it up to all to become a dead, crystallized concept. Only to initiates, to initiates who win to it through many reincarnations if necessary. But toward it grope, and have always groped, all men. The Taoist Way, the Buddhist patterns, remain their shells of endeavor. Now I don't know the Lhasa secret doctrine, nor do

I know the Indian belief. But within the Indian form of life, which is as valid as any other, I can suggest briefly the gropings of all men in the groping of Martiniano. For he, like all Indians, is human, fed by the dark irrational flow yet unilluminated for him, and by the need for resolving his faith consistent with the pattern which forms his outward life.... He may be Indian, but he is human. [Tanner, 57-59]

Regarded in this way, the substance of Indian life and religion partakes of universality, and "the gropings of all men," unlike esoteric "belief," are known to us. It is therefore justifiable to present an Indian protagonist who is in quest of the wordless ineffable: this is the allegorical aspect of the novel's figurative images. The fact that the protagonist resolves his faith "consistent with the pattern which forms his outward life" is no warrant for denying the universality of his quest. It is true that he has returned to the blanket (that is to say, departed from white culture and rejoined Indian culture), and readers with a preference for literal meanings alight here. In fact, it is quite easy to read *Deer* as if it were only the story of an "individual" who eventually submerges himself in the "collective," and in our noncollective society that is a negative outcome, because the protagonist seems to have given up his freedom (in our usual sense of the word as a lack of requirement), and capitulated to his persecutors, the Indian councilors. Of course, students of the culture of Pueblo Indians attest that the highest personal autonomy is often found in the most intricately developed social structure; that the individual who learns to walk safely through life by observing a large number of taboos and procedures is not being inhibited by the structure but guided by it in the acquisition of an essential skill, the freedom to act and to be, and hence is not being required to surrender spontaneity; and that, as the individual develops his inner potential by enhancing his participation in the ceremonies of the unit, which in the last case is no less than the entire universe, so does the entire universe become invigorated, and one's unique being is made significant in this way.[19]

Deer, however, is not a treatise in cultural anthropology, and so these nuances about the meaning of freedom in Indian life will do little to affect an impression of retrogression: the protagonist has returned to the blanket, and that is somehow a resolution foreclosed to the rest of us. On the other hand, once we recognize the allegorical status of *Deer*, the protagonist's return to the blanket is but figuratively a return to the Cosmic Mother, to the feminine power of the unconscious, and his groping for a faith eventuates in a vision which is not culture-specific but universal—in short, a myth. The protagonist, far from abandoning the modern world, has become the type of the truly free, nonalienated *modern* individual who has recovered the richness and wonder and mystery of life. Thus *Deer* remains faithful to the form of Indian life and religion while revealing to our noncollective society a substance that is at the forefront of contemporary ethics: in psychic integration only is there freedom, the ethic of fullness demanding an organic relationship whereby an individual is dependent on the existence of all other persons and of all living things, "*breathing mountains, the living stones, each blade of grass, the clouds, the rain, each star, the beasts, the birds and the invisible spirits of the air*" (18),[20] for all of which the metonymical figure is a deer.

Now, I live in an area of the country where the slaughter of *tame* deer is an event authorized by the United States government. Every year, hunters are invited into the forested premises of the United States Air Force Academy for the alleged purpose of thinning out the herds of these half-domesticated animals. So it wouldn't surprise me if there are readers of *Deer* who write off the symbolism of the deer as yet another "mystical" expression of Indian life, and certainly from the Euro-American perspective the idea of a deer as a "spirit" must seem at the very least extraordinary. And it is true that the Native American grasp of the solidarity of life is often expressed as a kinship with animals, who are not addressed as underlings in the world of nature but as representative of the abiding power of the cosmos, a power with which to seek communion.[21] Yet I do not think that conscience and intuition are confined to the sensibilities of Native Americans, nor does Waters think so, as revealed in his letter to Luhan:

> We all break away. We look outward, and inward, and finally see in ourselves the macrocosmic universe, and the world outside as a microcosmic replica of ourselves. And what prompts us, and ever keeps us on the track of self-fulfillment, is that peculiar thing we call conscience which turns us back, or the intuition which illumines the forward step. It might just as well be called a deer. [Tanner, 58]

Even though the fundamental life force may appear to the Indian in the form of an animal, people everywhere depend on intuition for their life-affirming discoveries and imaginings and on conscience for the preservation of life. We all, so to speak, have our deer.

There is one character in *Deer* whose primary narrative function is to keep us alert to the distinction between the form and substance of Indian life: Rodolfo Byers, the white trader who lives on the boundary of the reservation. Long experience has brought this old man, like the sage Dansker in Melville's *Billy Budd*, to a kind of bitter prudence and to representative authority, for he has "something of all men, and of the wilderness around him" (26). Having studied books about Indian history, ethnology, and anthropology, he finds them lacking in "the substance of life he loved" (29), which he identifies as the Indians' "living awareness" (31). He asserts that their "premises of life were based not on the rational, the reasoning, the evaluating approach, but wholly on the instinctive and intuitive," and it is this power of intuition which is "the very core of the life and the wonder and the mystery which had ever held him" (32). Intuitive himself, a man with "two natures, two lives" (28), he can approach understanding of Indians, but the living awareness itself is something that "could never be put into words, even by an Indian" (31). In these respects, Byers serves as Waters' spokesman, and Waters echoes his character's language at the critical moment when the protagonist himself is losing ego-identity and becoming receptive to substance: "So little by little the richness and the wonder and the mystery of life stole in upon him" (134). Byers puts us on guard against expectation of an inside viewpoint and in effect can do no more by way of interpreting Indian life than to isolate one factor, intuition, which he himself possesses even though he is polarized to the rational. At the same time, he effectually warns us against a too-literal reading of a novel with a psychological theme.

To liberate his allegorical hero into the substance of Indian life, Waters shows that a strong sense of tribal unity has been achieved and at the same time articulates feelings productive of a complex, permanent attitude which governs all individual lives once it is recognized. In the light of the mystery of life, we may perceive our own role in the cosmic plan and return to psychic balance and right attitudes. *The Man Who Killed the Deer* is not an "Indian novel" in the usual senses but an "Everyman novel," in which salvation is at stake.

The consonance between objective facts and their moral or psychological counterparts provides the basis for an allegory. As correspondences evolve within the story, the dominant idea begins to be revealed through accretion of meanings. Thus the deer that Martiniano kills is a figurative one and is increasingly amplified to "become" any deer, the constellation of the Pleiades, the Deer Mother in the Deer Dance, the Cosmic Mother, conscience, intuition, the unconscious, the ineffable, and so on. As Martiniano progresses through successive states of mind, so his capacity for relationship to the symbolic deer grows until he lives in harmony with it. When he is not in harmony with it, an ironic discrepancy between symbol and state of mind invalidates authenticity. Like as not, he will seek to accept substitutes for the reality as yet unilluminated for him. This is a pattern cherished by allegorists. For example, because Christendom in the Middle Ages was fond of listening to homilies on people's futile efforts to find a substitute for salvation, *Everyman* presents an allegory of a person who accepts all the substitutes society offers but finds himself suddenly confronted with the reality of death. Martiniano defies the pueblo, seeks legal redress for his grievances, looks for a faith in marriage and then in peyote, wants, like Captain Ahab, vengeance against an animal, and works up a savior complex, only to be haunted and "defeated" by the spirit-deer, with which he must finally learn to live, in order to be "saved," to be authentic, to emerge. I do not of course intend to imply that *Deer* is homiletic. Its moral sense is consistent with the familiar aesthetic enunciated by Henry James in *The Art of the Novel*, namely, "the perfect dependence of the 'moral' sense of a work of art on the amount of felt life concerned in producing it."[22] Martiniano's gropings are indeed *felt*, and if we were not engrossed in the fable, were not persuaded of its human truth, were not warmly allied with a proud social outcast who is, after all, behaving in a manner that few of us would question as irregular, let alone futile, we might wonder whether morality is even an issue. Only the total organization of meanings, in other words the allegory of Emergence, places events in a moral perspective from which we perceive a rightness in the outcome and a wrongness in the hero's lunges for freedom. This moral perception arrives, not as a comforting affirmation of received ideas and accepted norms but as a reconstitution of these in a new key of harmonic unity.

Actually, the "new" worldview is very old indeed and differs from modern styles of thinking chiefly in the extent to which it is analogical. To antiquity, as to the Middle Ages and the Renaissance, analogy was a natural method of perceiving truth. Because "this" happens in one sphere, so "that" happens in another sphere. There is a plague in Thebes because Oedipus is a patricide who married his mother. There is madness, political disorder, and a raging storm because Lear has broken up his realm and renounced his daughter. It is not that Sophocles and Shakespeare imagined in any naive literal way that whenever a king violated a taboo or lost his mind the world of nature obliged with disease and thunder. In analogical thinking, these are symbols of disorder in that all life depends on observance of the natural order. If, for example, a farmer spreads a chemical pesticide over a given area, the disappearance of the insect disrupts the food chain, leads various species to prey on one another, pollutes the drinking water hundreds of miles away, and generally causes trouble in unforeseen ways. So the idea of order is by no means obsolete, even though we may describe this order in terms widely different from those of Sophocles and Shakespeare. Frank Waters speaks of the reconciliation of reason and intuition, only going beyond this idea of order to postulate, on the basis of various philosophical and scientific systems, a new and higher world of consciousness to come. But always, what is being desiderated is an idea of order that makes for balance, health, and peace. And yet it is symptomatic of modern times that representation of an idea of order–by a Waters or, for that matter, by an Einstein–is brushed aside as "mystical," unless, of course, the idea is attributable to a religious system considered nonobsolete (such as Christianity) or to a materialistic Utopia (such as that put forward under the banner of Karl Marx).[23]

The point I am trying to make is that *Deer* has an inherent pattern based on analogical thinking. As soon as Martiniano kills the deer, a disruption in the natural order occurs, and Palemon, whose intuitive powers are fully alive to the world, picks up the vibrations and rescues a friend not even "known" to be missing. The cause of disorder is then traced to the breaking of a taboo: Martiniano has ignored the covenant between men and animals, itself in ever-widening circles of implication a sacred bond between microcosm and macrocosm. On further inspection, the moral and religious nature of the disorder is traced to its source in the mind, for the reasoning, analyzing, evaluating mind of Martiniano is but half a mind, the all-but-forgotten hemisphere of intuition, instinct, or the "feminine" unconscious not having been called into play. In analogical thinking, the natural order is symbolized by the deer, and so it is the "deer"-ness of life, which is everywhere manifested and which is but dormant in Martiniano himself, that is gradually recognized as the ego-fog clears. The restoration of order is then symbolized by fertility (Flowers Playing gives birth to a son, and Martiniano's fields yield enough produce to pay off his debt), by atonement (Martiniano participates in ceremonies), and by Emergence (he rescues Palemon's son because reason and intuition are reconciled, and he is aligned in the direction of Dawn Lake, to the origin of life forms).

In working out his idea of order, Waters uses the imagery provided by Indian culture, even though the order he envisions is largely independent of it. Thus at the turning point of the novel, after Martiniano has been humiliated by his failure to climb the pole and while he is watching Flowers Playing befriend two does on his farm, his own analogical perception of truth comes to him in a flash of intuition about his people:

> A snake wriggled up Martiniano's backbone; his knees trembled. A vision clutched him by the throat. He had cut his corn stalks and stacked them in little, upright conical piles to shed rain. In the dusk they looked like a far, vast village of tepees standing on the plain. Striding between them, distorted and fantastically enlarged by perspective, came the deer–giant, ghostly figures looming above the highest tips of protruding lodge poles. For an instant, as the old myth-wonder and atavistic fear rose up and flooded him, he saw them as his people had long seen them, one of the greatest animalistic symbols of his race: the deer which had populated forest and plain in uncounted myriads on the earth, and gave their name to the Pleiades in the sky; whose hoofs as ceremonial rattles were necessary for every dance; who complemented at once the eagle above and the snake below; gave rise to Deer Clan and Antelope Priests; and lent the mystery of their wildness, swiftness and gentleness to all men. In a flash of intuition it all leapt out before him. And in its brief glimmer stood out a strange woman with the same wildness and gentleness which had first drawn his eyes to her as she danced–a woman no longer his wife, but as a deer clothed in human form and thus possessing

> the power to draw and control the great shapes that moved
> toward her. [162]

This mythological deer is a power to be accepted and lived with—quite literally, for Flowers Playing has the power—and Martiniano is properly filled with fear and trembling. Like Lee Marston in *Lizard Woman*, he has seen both the luminous and the fierce and terrible aspects of God.[24] Formulated as if through a Native American consciousness, the idea is a realization of profound religious import, well known to us in the Western tradition from the Book of Job to the Book of Revelation: *God can be loved but must be feared.*[25] And that this *is* a moment of illumination and self-fulfillment is conveyed by the imagery of a snake uncoiling from some instinctive realm and wriggling up the backbone into the visionary region of mind, for this is the serpent power of yogic wisdom, as well as of Indian mythology, and its release signifies the beginning of the hero's emergence into higher consciousness.

The culminating point in Martiniano's quest is reached when he observes the Deer Dance, in which Flowers Playing plays the role of a Deer Mother, *the* Cosmic Mother of all Creation. Significantly, Waters translates the movements of the dance into a psychological allegory about the bipolar tensions of conscious and unconscious forces and about the dangers of allowing a dominating rationality, or the light, male principle, to break free from the dark, feminine principle with its emotions and instincts reaching back into the depths of time and rooting us to our past and to relationship with all the living universe. As the Deer Mothers dance softly before the male dancers, who represent deer in bondage, we are given this description:

> They gave way before her as the male ever gives way to the female imperative. They tried to break free of the circle only to be irresistibly pulled back as man in his wild lunges for freedom is ever drawn back by the perpetual, feminine blood-power from which he can never quite break free. And all the time they uttered their strange, low cries, the deep, universal male horror at their submission. Out of them it welled in shuddering sobs of disgust, of loathing and despair, as still they answered the call. On all fours, as the undomesticated, untamed, archaic, wild forces they represented, impelled to follow her in obedience to

that spiritual cosmic principle which must exist to preserve and
perpetuate even their resentment. [174]

Martiniano watches this performance with "a hypnotic horror" and recognizes
his own fate:

> He felt himself cringing before that manifestation of the blind
> force which had pulled him back from his own strivings toward
> a new and resplendent faith–back into that warm flow of hu-
> man life of which he was still a part. His own revolt, his anger
> and his fear; it all came out of him anew and was echoed by the
> sobbing, tortured cries of the deer before him. [175]

As the dance redefines the bondage that each person (not just the male) owes
to the cosmic principle of origin and unity, Martiniano comes to grips with
the meaning of his life, its misdirected attitude transformed by perception of
its limitations:

> Now, for the first time, he sensed something both of the
> conscience which turns us back, and the intuition which illu-
> mines the forward step, and so holds us on the upward road
> of self-fulfillment. Sensed dimly, as one only can, the invisible,
> undefined and irrational force that has no meaning outside its
> living truth. It stood before him, silent, inscrutable, clothed
> in loose white buckskin–in the anonymous shape of a woman
> who had been his wife, and was now the commanding mother
> of all men. [175]

Thematically secured, much like Dante's Beatrice, as an earthly woman, incar-
nate creative force, and judicial principle, Flowers Playing has the most significant role in Martiniano's quest for redemption, albeit that the terminology
for divine grace in the Christian allegory has been shifted into transpersonal
psychology. Martiniano's consciousness still resents and fears the numinous
power of the unconscious, but recognition of the reality of the natural order
has still transformed his personality into a higher consciousness of his total
goal on "the upward road of self-fulfillment." Irrespective of the wishes and
fears of his conscious mind, the goal of life has been spontaneously produced

by the unconscious, and his conscious realization of what he is living out and his acceptance of responsibility for what he has done or proposes to do make all the difference before the bar of nature and fate. He can no longer regard himself as a victim of the natural order because the meaning of the numina has manifested itself before his very eyes.

The ambivalence in attitude toward the irrational is typically suited to the method and purpose of allegory. Among modern critics Edwin Honig, for one, asserts that in allegory the irrational is "given an authentic, undiminished force which otherwise–according to law, custom, dogma–would be distorted or obscured."[26] The constant layering of meaning in allegory proves to be decisive in creating the whole effect a literary work can have upon us. The irrational becomes viable, and thereby marvelous and forbidding insights assume a form which, if taken literally, might be destructive of social codes. Certainly in a society such as our own, one that favors the patriarchal principle and harnesses the idea of freedom to rational consciousness and the idea of God to a one-sided power of goodness and love—even as the threat of world destruction hangs over us like the sword of Damocles—an archetypal vision on the order of *The Man Who Killed the Deer* looks to allegory's quality of elusiveness to conceal seriousness of intent. Perhaps that is why Martiniano's emergence is not expressed in the language of ecstasy but in that of resentment. Like Job or an Oedipus, he resents the limitations imposed on him by the horrible and irrational. Nevertheless, the allegory of Emergence, formulated in *Deer* as the redeeming necessity to return to the unconscious, creates a new sense of wonder out of the mystery that lies buried, apparently, in us all.

Benjamin S. Lawson
The Men Who Killed the Deer:
Faulkner and Frank Waters

Our writers' search for the essential America, their drive to define a time-less underlying paradigm, has often taken the form of an imagined and frequently ritualistic hunt that of necessity links the human with the natural world. Writers and critics have also interrogated the truth of these natural and national mythic patterns by positing limitations. Are the images arbitrary and nostalgic, evocations of appealing simplicity? Mere dream fulfillments prompted by increasing industrialization and modern urban life? Irresponsibly escapist? Androcentric if not sexist? Do they involve falsifications of the realms and realities of Americans themselves, the Native Americans in antiquated literary rhetoric dubbed "the children of nature"? These are old issues. More recently, however, contention over "agendas" has made possible a re-examina-tion of this theme. We have refigured the force of race, ethnicity, and gender; we have since Faulkner's time institutionalized ethnic and women's studies. In addition, scholars re-examine a persistent American regionalism; they theo-rize regionalism as a concept and they redefine supposedly discrete American regions. Only academic naïveté would lead us to believe that what we find is unaffected by what we are looking for.

Yet what we do look for can reveal a great deal about our subjects as well as ourselves. In particular, our foregrounding of race, gender, and region enables germane new perceptions of these phenomena and their figurations in specific authors of specific times. The influence of the Tainian "epoch" sometimes almost seems to suggest itself. In 1942, for example, strikingly similar scenes of the killing of a deer occur in major novels by Faulkner and by Frank Waters: *Go Down, Moses* ("The Old People") and *The Man Who Killed the Deer*. The very impossibility of cross-influences indicates overarching predispositions in these writers which help us delimit national if not 1940s themes: the scenes are parallel despite one protagonist being Native American and alone, the other white and tutored by a part-Native American; one tale is set in the Southwest, the other in the South. Martiniano and Isaac McCaslin clearly enact primal and meaningful killings, but Faulkner and Waters have chosen to communicate their visions through these characters: they, too, are the men who killed the deer.

Faulknerians are familiar with Sam Fathers' "initiation" of Ike in "The Old People." (Sam's great-uncle in this account — different from that in "Red Leaves" — is Issetibbeha, whose name means, "he has fought with a deer" [Krefft 33]) marking Ike's face with "the hot smoking blood" (GDM 121) of his first deer signals the twelve-year-old's accepting of and being accepted by the wilderness and the people almost mystically linked with it, the Chickasaws and the Choctaws. Ike thenceforth understands and reveres. He will know "love and pity for all which lived and ran and then ceased to live"; he inherits an experience and a value system from Sam's "vanished and forgotten people" (135). His revelation will underlie his adult attitudes about the arbitrariness of private ownership and misuses of land and the people of the land, his washing his hands of the plantation and the heritage of slavery — however idealistic, irresponsible, and ineffectual these gestures might ultimately be. His cousin McCaslin Edmonds tells him that "there is only one thing worse than not being alive, and that's shame" (138) in the context of a final conversation about the hunt. Ike swears he had seen a large buck ("the buck sprang, forever immortal" [132]) seen by no one else. McCaslin, also a novitiate of Sam Fathers years earlier, philosophizes that "the earth is shallow" and cannot absorb all the living, "even suffering and grieving" (138), but must surrender them as ongoing spectral presences. After the hunting ends, the haunting continues; the spirit of the deer becomes the spirit deer.

Students of Southern literature may be somewhat less familiar with a contemporary novel from the West, Frank Waters' *The Man Who Killed the Deer* (the Swallow Press edition carries on the cover rather than the title page the subtitle, "A Novel of Pueblo Indian Life"). In the novel's opening, Palemon heeds Martiniano's wordless call, following instinct to the site of his fellow Native American's killing of a deer:

> . . . the mare shied round a boulder: the one marked with the strange signs of the Old Ones — a circle enclosing a dot, the imprint of a hand, a strange long-legged animal with a longer neck. The rider felt, as the mare, the lingering vibrations of the life that had never died but only lost its nonessential bodily form. (5)

"Nothing dies," but continues "living with a slow serpent-pulse in a perpetual dream of time" (6). (We recall Fathers' ritual saluting of the "chief, grandfather" snake as well as the deer in *Go Down, Moses* [137, 245].) Palemon transports the bloodied and weak Martiniano along with the carcass of the deer back to the settlement.

Again and again deer or images of deer reappear. Sometimes memory or hallucination, the psychological trace of a spirit deer pursues and troubles Martiniano. The deer often symbolizes a universal organic wholeness violated by Martiniano's slaying of the deer without proper rite and reverence. (He had not, for instance, "dropped drops of his blood and bits of his flesh on the ground for Our Mother Earth" [Waters, *Deer* 24].) Deer are central to the communal festivals of San Geronimo and the Deer Dance. Just as Ike on a memorable occasion does not shoot the bear when opportunity arises, Martiniano later stays his hand because of the deer's "untrammeled freedom and wild gentility" (184). Not only the content but also the style of some passages strike us as Faulknerian: "and suddenly the deer was gone. Without a movement, without a crackling of the brush" (106); "from the darkness a long-legged antlered shape had stepped forth, touching both their lives, and then dissolving into light. It was no longer a deer, but an evanescent glimmer of the truth . . ." (140). Faulkner alludes in "Delta Autumn" to "the last puny marks of man" (GDM 252), and Waters to "man's puny efforts" (252).

For both authors gender becomes an aspect of the symbolic significance of the deer. Both identify the deer with a universal female earth-spirit and with specific women who figure significantly in their plots. In the coded conversations and exposition of "Delta Autumn," Roth Edmonds' paramour becomes a doe "that walks on two legs" (248), and the delta itself becomes "this inverted-apex, this V-shaped section of earth between hills and River until what was left of it seemed now to be gathered and for the time arrested in one tremendous density of brooding and inscrutable impenetrability at the ultimate funneling tip" (253). Ike is not a woman, but his puberty is nevertheless marked by blood. Inscrutable and impenetrable, the fecund wilderness world of the deer and bear nonetheless dwindles, and its destruction is coterminous with the killing of game and as much a betrayal of the beloved as Roth's rejection of his part-black lover. McCaslin Edmonds' "explanation" of why Ike did not shoot the bear is to quote John Keats' "Ode on a Grecian Urn": "She cannot fade, though thou hast not thy bliss," and Ike responds, "He's talking about a girl" (220). Ike's embracing of an unviolated wilderness, his rejection of "the tamed land" (187-88) cursed by ruinous agricultural practices and the labor system of slavery, entails the loss of a wife, the would-be plantation belle whose materialistic and social values dissociate her from nature. Endings in "The Bear" take the form of Ike's being childless, the deaths of Old Ben and Sam Fathers (and their being childless), and the lumber company's encroachments.

As a Native American, Martiniano, on the other hand, discovers his destiny in accepting his wife on her own terms. Flowers Playing serves as a deer symbol par excellence. The husband's alienation is defused and defined by his increasing appreciation of his wife and traditional community values; his mode of killing the deer was less initiation than transgression. The mystique of associating the very soil of America with Native Americans is common enough among elitist as well as popular white (and many nonwhite) novelists as seemingly disparate as Zane Grey and Willa Cather. (The windows of cliff-dwellings in Riders of the Purple Sage seem to be ancient eyes, watching the intruding white protagonist [107]; in The Professor's House "the city of stone" looks "down into the canyon with the calmness of eternity" [201].) Poets like Hart Crane, for one example, fantasize a bridge connecting European-Americans to the American land by an anthropomorphized and gendered identification: "Who is the woman with us in the dawn? . . . whose is the flesh our feet have moved upon?" Pocahontas is "the mythological nature-symbol chosen to represent the physical body of the continent" (57, 248). The steeple and cross of imported Christianity in *The Man Who Killed the Deer*, "the phallic symbol of the male lustful to conquer," contrasts with the kiva of traditional belief, "the female symbol of fertility imbedded in Our Mother Earth" (Waters 67). Several critics describe this "feminine-dominated culture" (Hoy, "Archetypal Transformation," 44; Lyon, 26); Blackburn concludes that the buck killed by Martiniano is "nevertheless viewed symbolically as a feminine power" (95). Clearly, this manipulation of gender-counters merges with stagings of ethnic discriminations. Native American emergence myths of creation contrast with white (male) myths of western movement and conquest. The initiation rites of young men include their emerging from the womb-like kiva.

After Wolf Red Belly Woman recounts the legend of a young woman transformed into a deer, Flowers Playing responds that she will one day tell the story to her and Martiniano's son. Before that birth, Flowers Playing herself feeds and tames two deer, thereby estranging her husband: "It was evident she preferred the companionship of the two deer to his" (Waters, *Deer*, 205). During their brief courtship she herself had seemed possessed "with all the grace, timidity, power and wildness of a deer" (209). He feels he has been rejected and defeated, as he had been by the deer he killed and by the deer skin he could not reach atop the ceremonial pole employed in the Mexican/Anglo/Pueblo festival of San Geronimo. When Flowers Playing decides to become a Deer Mother in the ritual dance, he concludes that the deer he killed is striking him "at last through my wife, herself" (210). The masked dancers represent "forces made visible to portray this great blood-drama of their common heritage" (211). Martiniano enters into the spirit of the dance, which enacts an eventual triumph of "perpetual, feminine blood-power" (213) — as against the temporary illusions furnished by "Our Father Peyote" (107). Since he is fated to rejoin "the anonymous collective" (Hoy, "The Conflict," 56), "The Deer Dance is a restitution ceremony for Martiniano" (Hoy, "Archetypal Transformation," 52). In the novel's denouement he himself again participates in community rituals; again he wears Pueblo garb; again he embraces Flowers Playing. The birth of their son, Juan de Bautista, during spring planting season, marks beginnings and a contrast to Ike McCaslin's childlessness. Reconciliation with his culture coincides with his exorcising the deer he killed: "It no longer troubled him. It no longer existed to give him a sign" (254).

Clearly there are differences between Faulkner's and Waters' scenes, and just as clearly these differences, too, create contexts which are revelatory. Martiniano is a young married man; his hunt is therefore not in the same sense an initiation, and, in any case, his being mixed Pueblo and Apache invests him with a supposedly inherited intimacy with the natural world. Ike McCaslin has heeded valued imperatives whereas Martiniano's act violates not one but two "laws." Whereas Ike is a somewhat deracinated white man affected by Native American life, one whose project by definition cannot be the rediscovery of his true Indianness, Martiniano is a Native American caught in the cultural and identity crisis resulting from having spent six years at an assimilationist white "away-school." There can be for him no redemptive but escapist "American" individualism which, even for Ike McCaslin and Huckleberry Finn, may finally "represent nostalgic and negative reinforcements of American pastoralism" (Blackburn, 126-27). He must answer not only to his people for improperly killing the deer, but must also be judged by the government officials for killing the deer out of season and for resisting arrest. His injuries had been inflicted by game authorities on patrol. Martiniano pleads privilege and necessity: "I am an Indian. I am hungry. Why should I hurry for Government men?" (Waters, *Deer*, 16). (The obvious intertext in American literature here is the cultural "half-breed" Natty Bumppo's shooting a deer out of season in *The Pioneers*.) Martiniano is found guilty, his fine paid by the shopkeeper Rodolfo Byers.

Individual ethics, natural law, Indian law, and white law are played off against one another as the story unfolds. Martiniano gains notoriety as "*the man who killed the deer*," and as he rediscovers his ethnic heritage becomes involved with related issues about the uses of nature. He becomes both "trouble maker" and "savior" because "he had roused all the people to desire back their land" (Waters, *Deer*, 181), particularly the "sacred tribal lake," "the little blue eye of faith" (6-7) near where he had killed the deer and ousted a Mexican shepherd from land seasonally used by the Pueblo. As some critics might say of Faulkner's themes, Waters' central concern is "the spiritual relationship of people to land" (Lyon, 70). Identity, including gender and race, not only affects events in Faulkner's and Waters' scenes, but it also dictates impact and larger contextual meanings. Just as Ike's decisions affect his people and his land, Waters often refers to seemingly insignificant deeds as stones tossed into water, sending out ripples.

In these novels deeds have consequences. The texts themselves also and inevitably possess a reality partly determined by the cultural and temporal identity of readers. Rippling effects inspire us to our own responses, responses neither consciously anticipated by the authors nor fully available in 1942 (actually, much of *Go Down, Moses* had been written during the 1930s). As structuralists we might assume that in any text "Indian," "female," or "Southwestern" are and logically can only be textual tropes which enable presentation and apprehension in a fictive world. But the growth of Native American Studies as an instance of an essentialized ethnic critical approach, along with controversies like that about the authorship and therefore authenticity of the "Indian" autobiography *The Education of Little Tree*, suggests that our readings are often inspired by — and inspire — an academic politics of identity. Although as students of literature we pretend that our subject is texts, suddenly *The Education of Little Tree* became inauthentic and objectionable — yet the words on the page did not change. [*The Education of Little Tree*, a bestselling "true story," was a hoax perpetrated by Asa Carter, an ex-Klansman whose racist speeches helped George Wallace secure the governorship of Alabama — Editor's note] Waters himself mentions the self-reflexive Catch-22 of self-defeated cultural appropriations in the discourse of outsiders: to the Pueblos, "spoken words robbed a thought of power, and printed words destroyed it entirely" (170). However formerly conflated, accuracy and authenticity have become separate issues. The privileged Other cannot apprehend and present without falsifying, condescending, and exploiting. James Harvey Krefft claims accuracy, not authenticity, when he writes that his "research (coupled with Dabney's) indicates that Faulkner has used a good deal more factual material about Indians than has previously been supposed" (5). Howard O. Horsford challenges both accuracy and authenticity, validating Faulkner's "imaginative achievements" and his mythic uses of Indian materials. However, his "concern for authenticity" — not Faulkner's — leads him to condemn Faulkner's "unreal Indians" (311) as instances of his lack of familiarity with early Mississippi history.

Frank Waters presents a special and perhaps a test case on this front. Unlike Faulkner's, his identity and self-identity are somewhat confused. We might ask exactly what one of his Pueblo judges asks about Martiniano's Native American ethnicity: "This young man was an Indian, born in the Pueblo, belonging to our tribe. Or was he, properly speaking?" (Waters, *Deer*,

22). Nurture and environment figure in the definition. Faulkner's race is not in question, and he was speaking through a white protagonist vicariously "willing to commit himself to his totem" (Krefft, 135) and accompanied by Sam Fathers, but is it "permissible" for Waters to speak through and for a Pueblo/Apache and thereby destroy the incommunicable culturally-specific totemistic significance of the deer? Among Waters' later non-fictional books are *Masked Gods: Navaho and Pueblo Ceremonialism* and *Book of the Hopi*. Can Waters be merely ethnologist but never truly "ethnic"? Neither *Go Down, Moses* nor *The Man Who Killed the Deer* is written in the first person, but Waters does present not only Indian words and actions, but also communal interior monologues. Emily Plec even concludes that Pueblo Indian ideas about time and ritual influence Waters' narrative structure (24). Some Native American commentators, like Stephen Wall, join white and Hispanic critics in the expected privileging of Waters' addressing "something higher and enlightened, far beyond the racism and tensions created by the expectations flowing from the two worlds within which I was struggling" (102). Vine Deloria, Jr., credits Waters with communicating a trans-racial and necessary "unity of purpose" while working "within the context of the American Indian tradition" (172). Waters "brought the cultural groups of the west together," writes Rudolfo Anaya (35). (The "third" group in Waters' novel is Mexican-American rather than African American as in Faulkner.) White Western writer William Eastlake similarly praises Waters' treatments of "the humanity in the Indian which is universal in all men" (5).

Thomas J. Lyon (17), Father Peter J. Powell, and others describe Waters as part Cheyenne: "the term 'Anglo' is used because he is not formally enrolled in any American Indian tribe" (Powell, 174). But Eastlake identifies him as an insightful non-Indian writer (5). When Win Blevins writes that Waters expresses an Indian point of view, he is not suggesting that Waters is Indian (149). Lyon and Alexander Blackburn report that *The Man Who Killed the Deer* is read and considered a "memorable depiction" by the people of Taos Pueblo (105, 95), but Wall mentions that many communities protest against the revealing of tribal secrets, or inaccurate representations of them, and believe that Waters "doesn't know what he is talking about" (103). Popular detective novelist Tony Hillerman has met this same criticism. As early as 1968 Leslie Fiedler thought he could spot the phoniness in writers like Waters and Oliver La Farge: "the pretense of writing from within the consciousness of Indians intrinsic to such fiction leaves me always with the sense of having confronted an act of impersonation rather than one of identification, a suspicion of having been deceived" (170). Waters, who maintained that he had lived among Indians all his life (Davis and Davis, 33), defines one version of himself as he spoke of his purposes in *The Man Who Killed the Deer*:

> [W]e excessively rational white Anglo-Americans by our force of will really can't break free from the forces of the unconscious, from the realm of instinct embodied within us. We've got to reconcile the two. . . . We white people, we Anglo-European white people are not yet wholly attuned, as the indigenous Indians are to their mother earth (qtd. in Milton, 66)

In addition to admitting the ineffable nature of experience Waters employs specific narrative strategies that deflate what now would be considered essentialist objections. Like Faulkner, he sometimes mediates and distances scenes through a white character's consciousness. In this novel Rodolfo Byers serves as Waters' "surrogate and spokesman" (Fiedler, 170), framing and distancing scenes by his commentary and reactions. Byers is a book-learned Anglo but identifies with Pueblo life and is married to a Latina. "Like a Faulkner character watching the wilderness of the South being eaten away, Byers fatalistically observes the encroachments on the Indian life" (Lyon, 111). At the same time, Byers is made to seem an empathetic insider through contrast with insensitive tourists and the successful painter of Indian subjects, Benson, who understands only "paint and feathers" (224). Pueblo reality is particularly distorted by "official" texts, like the written Reports of Superintendents of Indians which Waters satirizes in exactly the same spirit that Chinua Achebe attacks government documents at the end of *Things Fall Apart*: "As long as they are permitted to live a communal life, and exercise their ancient form of government, just so long will there be ignorant and wild Indians to civilize . . ." (Waters, *Deer*, 204).

To what degree should we as modern and sophisticated readers be troubled by these essentialist issues in any case? It goes without saying that informed and sensitive readings should disclose the inadequacies of any literary construct, including its lack of insight and sympathy related to gender, place, race, and ethnicity. Faulkner's alleged failings in portraying the Other can all too frequently be reduced to the unspoken assumption that he is answerable for not being African American, Native American, or female. Exactly how is literary culpability being defined in this criticism? Are writers answerable for their words not really because of the words themselves but because of who they are? After all, to think that only a Native American can speak for other Native Americans implies the otherwise rejected conclusion that all Indians are alike, and implies, too, that a sense of self does not stem from an inextricably mixed compound of heredity and experience. If being a particular sex or ethnicity is not an experience, then it is not represented in fiction. So often, critics conflate identity issues with culturally-specific experiences consequent upon those identities. Leslie Silko can no more speak for all Native Americans than Frank Waters can — consideration of his "race" to one side.

The very fact of Waters' ambiguous racial identity should remind us of the arbitrariness and pettiness of our preoccupations. The Pueblos in *The Man Who Killed the Deer* are affected by a web of Native American, Hispanic, and Anglo influences, all of which are reflected in Waters' distinctive experience if not his ethnicity. Wide cultural differences among Native American peoples are also stressed in the novel. In fact, many Pueblo consider it a disgrace to their people for Martiniano, already half Apache, to have married Flowers Playing, a Ute (Waters, *Deer*, 61). As we have seen, Waters also uses his artistic freedom sometimes to universalize. Commiserating with Martiniano, Byers admits, "I too have had my deer" (140). Flowers Playing is not merely the mother of Juan de Bautista: as Deer Mother, she is the mother of all. Waters also feels free to communicate opposing images and ideas. Byers, for example, is sometimes labeled "the white man," unrepresented in Martiniano's final reverie as he gazes at the deer transfigured into a constellation, as he hears the "one song, the song of night and summer and Dawn Lake and his people who did not forget" (265). Byers is not permitted the annual pilgrimage to Dawn Lake (262). In "fustian, Faulknerian prose," Waters suggests that "Anglo Americans have yet to discover spiritual America, lodged as it is within the mystic consciousness of Native transcendentalism" (Davis and Davis, 37). "Our" American Transcendentalism is Emersonian and European. If Byers is indeed a mediating authorial narrative voice in a book about "the difficulties inherent in cultural fusion" (Davis and Davis, 35), it is altogether artistically appropriate that ambivalence should predominate: "'This strange white trader!' thought Martiniano. 'No wonder the old men trust him. No wonder I like him.

He understands. He knows much, thinks well and says little. That is the mark of a good man.' But there was nothing to say to him" (Waters, *Deer*, 241).

Only Alexander Blackburn (4-10) has drawn many — and those quite general — parallels between Faulkner and Frank Waters, "our most profound chronicler, both in fiction and nonfiction, of the American Southwest" (Davis and Davis, 43), and whose mother's father was a Southerner (Lyon, 16). Perhaps our academic specializing in the Southwest or the Old Southwest blinds us to their shared regionalism. Although evidently not mutual influences, both were influenced by the ideas of Jung (Barbara Waters, 64). The most pertinent link between Faulkner and modern Southwestern regionalism is through Oliver La Farge, author of the 1930 Pulitzer Prize-winning *Laughing Boy*. Faulkner knew La Farge in New Orleans, owned a copy of La Farge's popular novel, and names a horse Laughing Boy in *Pylon*. Faulkner sent his first "Indian story," "Red Leaves," to the *Saturday Evening Post* just months after the publication of *Laughing Boy* (Krefft, 66). Krefft also mentions that La Farge's Navajos call themselves "the People," and past generations "the Old People" (67). Both writers' Native American characters discuss change and the old times and possess character traits and modes of speech in common (Krefft, 67-69).

Robert H. Brinkmeyer, Jr. begins *Remapping Southern Literature: Contemporary Southern Writers and the West* (2000) by mentioning both "the recent resurgence of interest in the American West" (1) and the fact that a number of Southern writers have been writing about the West as well as their own region. Brinkmeyer believes that region becomes and remains as much a part of writers as race, class, and gender. If nothing else, contrasts with other places remind one of the uniqueness of one's own place. Some "Southern" novels, like James Dickey's *Deliverance* and Larry Brown's *Joe* (described as *Shane* set in Mississippi [Brinkmeyer, 34]) depict a West in the South. Insofar as Faulkner's big woods represents the wilderness and frontier, *Go Down, Moses* and other works are also set in "a microcosmic imaginative West" (11). Without referring to Frank Waters, Brinkmeyer's critique of Ike McCaslin's ersatz-Indian and misguided "Western" (in both senses of the word) individualism expresses some of Waters' themes: "A solitary figure breaking free from the community would, in the fiction of most Southern writers, be less a hero than a potential psychopath, a person tragically alone and isolated, cut off from the nourishing bonds of family and community" (4). Southern conceptions of community sometimes improbably link, say, the conservative Euro-centric Agrarians with Native Americans. For John Crowe Ransom and others, the South and the West had suffered from colonization and exploitation by the pioneering spirit of Northern and Eastern finance capitalism. Writing about the West continues to furnish Southern writers not an escape but rather a vocabulary with which to question American frontier myths and interrogate Southern values, even when (as in the novels of Barbara Kingsolver) the nature of community has been radically reconfigured.

Brinkmeyer's work reminds us that readers are free to consider the West and the South together, not separately, as they formulate their own visions of American culture. National literature has any number of germane and definitive cultural and historical contexts. Perhaps *Go Down, Moses* and *The Man Who Killed the Deer* in their time gained a pointed suggestiveness as explorations of primitive America in the face of a modern, technological, European and Asian World War II. But rather than using the hunt as an analogue for war, as in the film *The Deer Hunter* (1978), Faulkner and Waters employ the hunt as a dramatic device which evokes responses about nationalism and regionalism, gender and ethnicity. And what evokes in 1942 will not necessarily be what evokes now. We bring our own contexts and agencies to what we read. Those contexts, our own values and knowledge, predispose us to interpret texts in specific ways and to perceive parallels. Faulknerians cannot help but be reminded of the Nobel Prize acceptance speech as they read another interview of Frank Waters:

> The regional "tag" merely identifies the locale of most of their work. Lesser writers are limited by their geographical settings. The good ones, like Herman Melville, Joseph Conrad, and William Faulkner, create art that transcends its subject matter. The writer is not different from the painter. To neither of them are the subject and its background primarily important. If the creator is successful, they serve only as the idiom in which he speaks the universal language of the heart, of all mankind. (Taylor, 27)

John Nizalowski
Journey to the World Mountain:
Frank Waters' *The Woman at Otowi Crossing*
and Terry Tempest Williams' *Refuge*

Vine Deloria once observed that Frank Waters was both explorer and prophet,[1] for Waters anticipated by half a century many of the major movements in contemporary literature, including American Indian, Chicano, and Jungian subjects. Ecofeminism is yet another contemporary literary movement that Waters explored well before its full flowering. In 1941, with Maria del Valle of *People of the Valley*, Waters established a connection between a matriarchal world view and a consciousness of earth-centered mysticism. He continued to explore the vital spiritual link between the feminine and the land with *The Woman at Otowi Crossing*. *Otowi Crossing*, with its tale of Helen Chalmers, a woman who leaps across the spiritual barrier into enlightenment through a cancer-inspired crisis, is in the words of Alexander Blackburn, "a masterpiece."[2]

Twenty-five years later, another major work with ecofeminist themes appeared — *Refuge* by Terry Tempest Williams. Like *Otowi Crossing*, *Refuge* explores a woman's mystical metamorphosis brought about by cancer. Both books also examine the western landscape's connection to feminine spiritual consciousness, the development of atomic weaponry, American Indian culture, mother-daughter relationships, and the dawning of a new world consciousness. Indeed, the parallels are so strong that one could argue that Frank Waters, the literary prophet, created in *Otowi* a remarkable forerunner to *Refuge*, a central text of late twentieth century ecofeminism.

Of course, there are key differences between these works. Most importantly, *Refuge* is creative nonfiction and *Otowi Crossing* is fiction. Helen Chalmers, loner and East Coast refugee, is a far cry from *Refuge*'s Diane Tempest, a conservative Mormon with Utah roots stretching back to the 1856 handcart migration. Also, Chalmers has a significant interaction with the Manhattan Project, while Tempest simply has the misfortune of living downwind from the Nevada atomic testing range. Terry Williams has an enduring connection with her mother, Diane, and her husband, Brooke — in sharp contrast to Emily, Helen's daughter, who fails in her corresponding relationships. Nor am I implying that Waters had a direct influence on Williams in the writing of *Refuge*, a book deeply rooted in her own experience and vision. Still, the imagistic and thematic parallels between the texts are remarkable, and reveal the endurance of Waters' literary concepts of human transformation, even within an ecofeminist context.

A major theme in *Refuge* is the tension between the landscape's feminine identity and the masculine attempt to control and utilize it. Williams views the atomic testing in Nevada as the most heinous example of this attempt and blames the testing for the cancer deaths of every matriarch in her family. Williams does not directly state this causal blame until the book's epilogue, when she describes the very tests that in *Otowi* Helen and Facundo flee by entering a St. George motel, but throughout *Refuge* she plants images which hint at the ultimate blame for her mother's cancer. One such passage describes an eighty-three foot high statue entitled "Metaphor" by Karl Momen: "This was the work of a European architect who saw the West Desert as 'a large white canvas with nothing on it.' This was his attempt 'to put something out there to break up the monotony.'"[3] Momen's masculine attitude towards filling feminine space returns in the Atomic Energy Commission official involved with A-bomb testing who describes the Nevada desert as "a good place to throw used razor blades."[4] Williams links Momen's statue to atomic testing by describing its shadow as "a mushroom cloud." She then gives voice to the landscape's disdain for this attempted "rape": "In the rearview mirror, the man-made tree rose from the salt flats like a small phallus dwarfed by the open space that surrounded it."[5] In *Otowi*, Waters also uses a patriarchal tower to express the tension between the feminine energy of the Southwestern desert and the masculine atomic enterprise. This one stands at Trinity site, and it holds the first fission weapon: "A fragile slender steel tower one hundred feet high, it thrust into the brassy sky like a spire of a medieval church, the phallic symbol of man's challenging dominance of the flat, mute, and unresisting earth below."[6]

Along with their feminine vision of land, Waters and Williams use similar images in *Otowi* and *Refuge* to examine linear and circular time. For Waters, the end of the Chile Line represents the Euro-American view of time as a linear, historical flow: "She stood in the doorway, watching the last sparks fly into the darkness from the blur of the receding train. There was a single last whistle — the voice of one of America's last baby railroads confiding its history to memory."[7] Williams' symbol for time's linear passage is another impermanent Euro-American artifact: Saltair, the dance pavilion where the great swing bands of the 1930s performed for Salt Lake City couples, including Williams' maternal grandparents. "I wish old Saltair was still standing guard over Great Salt Lake. The magnificent Moorish pavilion built on a wooden trestle reigned supreme during the early 1900s. Its image captures the romance of another era for Utah residents. Today, I walked where Saltair once stood. A few charred posts from the pier still stand, looking like ravens."[8]

In contrast, encounters with American Indian cultural artifacts evoke circular time in *Otowi* and *Refuge*. Helen Chalmers picks up an ancient bowl in an Anasazi ruin near Los Alamos. She finds the thumbprint of the potter and has a vision of time's continuity: "Her fingers closed over the splotch of clay on the bowl in her arms just as the Navawi'i woman released her own, without their separation of centuries."[9] Williams experiences a similar moment while holding Fremont Indian artifacts at the Utah Museum of Natural History:

> But sometimes the objects run away with you. They seize your
> imagination and begin to sing songs of another day, when
> bone whistles called blue-winged teals down to the wetlands
> of Bear River. You hear them. You turn around. You are alone.
> Suddenly, the single mitten made of deer hide moves and you
> see a cold hand shivering inside Promontory Cave. It waves
> from the distance of a thousand years.[10]

Along with these imagistic parallels, there are similarities between the characters of the two books. The central one is between Jack Turner, Helen's lover, and John Tempest, Diane's husband. Turner, the journalist, and Tempest, the contractor, are both tough, practical western men who have difficulty dealing with their partner's acquiescence to cancer and death. Both men want to take action — to cure the cancer, to defeat the specter of eternity. A parallel also exists between Emily's lover, Edmund Gaylord, and Terry's husband, Brooke. Like Gaylord, who openly embraces Helen's spiritual power, Brooke is a sensitive male who understands the feminine mysticism and love of nature found in his wife and mother-in-law.

Structurally, both books rely significantly on letters and journals, which may grow in part from both authors giving voice to the feminine. In an interview with Mickey Pearlman, Williams evokes feminist linguistic theory to explain the writing in *Refuge*:

> I love Claudia Herrmann's book *The Tongue Snatchers* when she says that [women] literally are a species in translation, that the language as it is defined by the dominant culture today is not the mother tongue. So I am interested, as a writer, in finding what the mother tongue is. . . . I think it has to do with identifying relationships that break through the veneer of what is proper, what is expected. The language that women speak when nobody is there to correct them oftentimes can make people uncomfortable because it threatens to undermine the status quo. It's what we know in our hearts that we don't dare speak, . . . the sense of women and secrets.[11]

Therefore, in *Refuge* Williams uses her own journals, Diane's letters to female friends, and the secret non-traditional blessings given by Mormon women as ways to allow women to speak "when nobody is there to correct them."

In *Otowi*, Helen Chalmers keeps notes for Jack Turner on her spiritual breakthrough, her Emergence. She calls these notes her "Secret Journal." Turner, who never believes in the validity of Helen's spiritual revelations, nearly destroys the journal as "the product of an unbalanced mind."[12] And Helen herself notes that others who may be having similar mystical experiences are keeping quiet about them because "their friends might believe them mentally unbalanced."[13] Like Williams, Waters understood that the patriarchal culture suppresses women's language, driving it to secrecy, especially when it deals with mysticism.

In *Otowi* and *Refuge*, the crisis of cancer forms the basis for these mystical experiences. Helen has her first breakthrough into Emergence when she discovers a lump in her breast. The lump, with its harsh whispers of mortality and a wasted life, throws her into a transcendent revelation:

> A cataclysmic explosion . . . burst asunder the shell of the world
> around her, revealing its inner reality with its brilliant flash.
> In its blinding brightness all mortal appearances dissolved
> into eternal meanings, great shimmering waves of pure feeling
> which had no other expression than this, and these were so
> closely entwined and harmonized they formed one indivisible
> unity. . . . Like a mote of earthly dust becalmed in the still,
> dead center of an actual explosion, she continued to sit there
> after the blinding glare broke into gradations of color too in-
> finite and subtle to define, and slowly faded and died. Within
> her now she could feel a strange fusion of body, mind and spirit
> into a new and integrated entity that seemed apart from the
> gross elements from which it sprang.[14]

For the remainder of the novel, Chalmers will repeat this revelatory moment in a sequence of Emergences that climax with her death.

Initially, Diane in *Refuge* has a very different experience. At first, her ovarian cancer helps her focus on the here and now, and gives her a heightened sense of life's transitory beauty: "It doesn't matter how much time I have left. All we have is now. I wish you could all accept that and let go of your projections. Just let me live so I can die. . . . Terry, to keep hoping for life in the midst of letting go is to rob me of the moment I'm in."[15] Helen in *Otowi* also expresses this existential focus on the eternal present when she explains to Turner, "We've had everything wonderful that a man and a woman could have together. . . . Now let me go free! Don't spoil it with pain and regret!"[16]

However, Diane, like Helen, finally attains a riveting transcendent understanding as her cancer progresses. As John Tallmadge notes, "The story of *Refuge*, I would suggest, is that of true initiation."[17] For instance, a few weeks before her death, Diane has a moment that clearly parallels Helen's Emergence, right down to the description of feelings and color:

[Mother] held out her hand. "Something wonderful is happening. I'm so happy. Always remember, it is here, in this moment, and I had it."

I didn't understand.

"Something extraordinary is happening to me. The only way I can describe it to you is that I am moving into a realm of pure feeling. Pure color."

I took off my coat and folded it over the chair. Sitting down beside her, I replied, "Maybe that's what this business of eternal life is. . . ."

She took my hand again. "No, no, you're missing it — it's right here, right now. . . ."[18]

In both books, these Emergences produce a changed vision leading to a spiritual initiation. But why are these initiations taking place, and what is the world view to which they lead?

Waters' concept of Emergence derives from the Hopi Indian myth that humanity is on a vast journey towards spiritual perfection that will ultimately take us through seven complete worlds. We are currently in the fourth world, but Hopi elders have been predicting we will soon cross over into the fifth. Waters believed that this journey is both personal and planetary. In the prologue of *Otowi*, Chalmers writes in her journal, "Perhaps none of us really ever learn anything by degrees. We just keep on absorbing things unconsciously without realizing what they mean. Till suddenly, for no apparent reason, it all comes into focus with a blinding flash. Civilizations like people must evolve the same way."[19]

Although Williams does not refer to the Pueblo Emergence myth, she too believes we are preparing to enter a new consciousness, a concept she explores more fully in *Leap*, a meditation on Hieronymus Bosch's *Garden of Earthly Delights*. In *Leap*, Williams writes, "What happens when our institutions no longer serve us, no longer reflect the truth of our own experience. . . ? How can we learn to speak in a language that is authentic?" Her answer, "The ceiling is raised by our imagination. Authentic acts reform."[20] Later, she notes the parallels between our times and the moment when the Middle Ages were giving way to the Renaissance, when Bosch executed his painting: "The Reformation was a movement that broke the bubble that held the Middle Ages in place."[21]

Just as cancer serves as the force that breaks the quotidian bubbles for
Helen and Diane, propelling them into spiritual transcendence, Waters and
Williams believe that the creation of the atomic bomb is the primary crisis
pushing humanity into a new consciousness. In both books, this crisis manifests in nightmares. Helen dreams of the future hydrogen bomb the evening
the fission bomb drops on Hiroshima: "Then one night she had awakened
screaming. It was as if everything, house, mountains, the world, the heavens,
was enveloped in one apocalyptic burst of fire."[22] Terry has a recurring dream
about the atomic bomb she saw as a child, a dream she finally shares with her
father after her mother's death: "I told my father that for years, as long as I
could remember, I saw this flash in the night in the desert — that this image
had so permeated my being that I could not venture south without seeing it
again, on the horizon, illuminating buttes and mesas."[23] In a synchronistic
moment, Helen dies the night of the hydrogen bomb test, the bomb's illumination matching her own final burst of insight. The very A-bomb tests Terry
witnessed in *Refuge* kill her mother by causing the high rates of cancer suffered
by those who live downwind.

In both books, the atomic crisis leads to a reconciliation of dualities.
As Felicia Campbell states, "The largest unity in the novel is what is happening inside Helen Chalmers is also happening in the outside world."[24] After a
vision of the first atomic test, Helen knows a profound event is drawing near:
"If such a thing happened within her, it must in some way, sometime, happen in the world outside. . . ."[25] Another major duality healed in *Otowi* is the
gulf between science and mysticism, as physicist Gaylord notes in this parallel
between the atomic detonation and Helen's psychic detonation:

> The similarity of this implosive-explosive process objectively in
> the A-bomb and subjectively as it happened to Helen Chalmers
> is at once casually apparent. Fear, worry, guilt, dread, shame,
> financial failure — all this psychological dynamite accumulated
> within her, recalled with pain and anguish, and brooded upon,
> seemed suddenly on a quiet day to be detonated from all di-
> rections; to be driven in upon her, implosively, with immense
> psychological force.[26]

Or, as Waters states in *Of Time and Change*, "The cosmic energy is the same, viewed differently by those taking either an intuitive or a pragmatic approach to its totality."[27]

In *Refuge*, the reconciliation of dualities is subtler. Williams demonstrates the connection of the inner and the outer worlds through the link between the rising levels of the flooding Great Salt Lake and Diane's worsening cancer. Indeed, the lake peaks the day her mother is buried. Thus the flood destroys Williams' beloved Bear River Migratory Bird Refuge at the same time the cancer kills her mother, a calmer version of Helen's synchronous death just as the first hydrogen bomb detonates. As Brooke Libbey writes concerning *Refuge*, "Rather than recapitulating the age-old hierarchy of subject over object, such a strategy would account for the agency of the other through a positional reciprocity or transference between self and other, human and nature."[28]

Also, in *Refuge* Williams heals the dichotomy between a destructive masculine patriarchy and a nature-based matriarchal world view. As Cassandra Kircher notes, it seems at first that Williams sets up a simplistic duality in *Refuge*: male equals exploitive culture and female equals healing nature. But Kircher argues that Williams' work is not strictly binary.

> The ways that Williams problematizes both the female/nature and male/culture alliances and, more importantly, the way she moves beyond dichotomies to depict a circular notion of family keeps the book from being essentialist. . . . [S]he also moves women out of an exclusive collaboration with nature by linking them to non-destructive institutions, such as the Utah Museum of Natural History and the Mormon Church, which offer women a valuable community within a patriarchal framework.[29]

For Williams, the symbol of this gender unity is her essentially Gnostic call to place a "Motherbody" in heaven in the form of a female Holy Spirit to balance the male energy of God the father and Jesus the son.[30]

In *Masked Gods*, an examination of Navajo and Pueblo mythology, Waters describes his belief that a Jungian "reconciling symbol" will arise from the unconscious and act as our guide through our transition into the Pueblo Indian fifth world: "And in the past such reconciling symbols have arisen from the collective unconscious of mankind to lead whole races, nations, and civilizations in great bursts of creative energy to another Emergence, a new stage of consciousness."[31] Appropriately enough, nearly identical reconciling symbols occur in *Otowi* and *Refuge*.

In *Otowi*, Helen Chalmers enters a kiva, the Pueblo Indian circular place of worship. There she discusses with Facundo her dream of the four spirals of existence, representing the circle of life projected forwards through the four Pueblo worlds of ascending evolutionary existence.[32] In *Refuge*, Williams takes Mimi to the Sun Tunnels sculpture, four concrete tunnels aligned to the equinoxes and solstices to form a circle, as in a kiva: "In Nancy Holt's 'Sun Tunnels,' the Great Basin landscape is framed within circles and we remember the shape of our planet, the shape of our eyes, our mouth in song and in prayer."[33] Earlier, Williams uses her finger to trace a Fremont spiral petroglyph that embraces, like Helen's four spirals, the entire universe: "I placed the tip of my finger on the center and began tracing the coil around and around. It spun off the rock. My finger kept circling the land, the lake, the sky. The spiral became larger and larger until it became a halo of stars in the night sky above Stansbury Island."[34]

But the most important reconciling symbol in both books is the world center, for Williams, like Waters, is a visionary hoping for a universal transformation. In *Refuge*, the symbol is the "Cosmic Egg . . . held within the pelvis of the ancient Bird Goddess" evoked by Mimi to explain Terry's sudden horror at the hollow wild birds' eggs collection at the Utah Museum of Natural History.[35]

In *Otowi* it is Mt. Meru, the Buddhist sacred mountain or world center, brought to the page as gentle Mr. Meru, parapsychologist and keeper of Helen's journal. Frances M. Malpezzi reveals Meru's importance when she states, "As Meru takes us into the myth and thus into ourselves he functions just as Eliade sees the mythical Mt. Meru functioning — as an *axis mundi* which links us to the sacred."[36] Alexander Blackburn goes further and proposes that Helen herself is the reconciling symbol: "Through an imperative of the unconscious, the protagonist breaks through to a mystical experience of timelessness, finds a solution to conflict, and emerges to an awareness which is, so to say, the paradigm for cultural transformation. Likened to a mandala-shaped kiva, the protagonist is herself a kind of personification of a reconciling symbol."[37]

Regardless, Meru has Helen's journal; and thus her voice, the journal, is at the world's center — Mt. Meru, the world egg, the *axis mundi* of initiation and transformation, and in that journal Chalmers pleads with Jack Turner to understand the natural journey of death, the inevitable realization of Emergence. They could be the words of Diane Tempest as well: "*So when your turn comes, Jack, don't be afraid. Be glad! It's our greatest experience, our mysterious voyage of discovery into the last unknown, man's only true adventure. . . .*"[38]

Gary R. Olsen
Escape from Time:
A Comparison of the Treatment of Time in Frank Waters'
The Woman at Otowi Crossing
and Hermann Hesse's *The Glass Bead Game*

What, then, is time? If no one asks me, I know what it is. If I wish to explain it to him who asks, I do not know. (Augustine, ca. A.D. 400)

There was a point in Western history during the halcyon days of the Enlightenment when Augustine's perplexity regarding time would have seemed quite naive, even unnatural. Isaac Newton had in 1687 published his *Principia*, a marvelously compelling picture of the natural world which seemed to encompass all aspects of the cosmos. Time, like space, was for Newton and his followers an absolute, an invariant phenomenon readily understood by man's reason. Space was viewed as the immobile frame of reference for all movements, while time was thought to run uniformly and simultaneously throughout the universe, without reference to anything beyond itself. The natural world was a spatial and temporal order reflective of the glorious order of man's reason.

As we look back from the vantage point of the late twentieth century, however, it is Newton rather than Augustine who seems naive. Time has once again become a puzzling and elusive phenomenon. Ever since Einstein published his remarkable theories early in the century, challenging Newton and shaking eighteenth-century assumptions, scientists, philosophers, and intellectuals in general have faced strange and troubling questions about the nature of temporality. Thinkers must now consider such concepts as the relativity of time, time dilation, and even time reversal. For those who follow science closely there are also such seemingly absurd notions as "black holes" and "wormholes" in the fabric of some strange stuff called "space-time," bizarre phenomena which seem to suggest such possibilities as "instantaneous" movement through the cosmos. This, in turn, calls into question cherished notions of common sense such as linear causality. Science has, in fact, become a Pandora's Box of strange and tantalizing possibilities regarding time.[1]

As might be expected, philosophers have not been untouched by these developments. In 1927, the year which brought Charles Lindbergh's heroic flight from New York to Paris in the then remarkable time of thirty-three and one-half hours, a German thinker, Martin Heidegger, published *Being and Time*, an abstruse yet penetrating meditation on man's relation to time. Whereas earlier German thinkers, notably Marx and Hegel, had placed man firmly in the context of historical time, viewing history as a kind of river which carries individuals and nations in its flow, like pieces of flotsam in a current, Heidegger brought time to the heart of human existence. *Being and Time* presents man as a creature of temporal distance, perpetually beyond himself in an effort to embrace and master his future, a future which mandates his inevitable death and permeates every aspect of his life. In Heidegger's vision, "Man is not, strictly speaking, in time as a body is immersed in a river that rushes by. Rather, time is in him; his existence is temporal through and through, from the inside out."[2] Simply put, man is time and time is man.

It is within this context that we must consider the works of Frank Waters and Hermann Hesse. Both writers, however different in other respects, give time pride of place in their works and wrestle mightily with the picture of time-bound existence presented by Heidegger and his disciples. They are preoccupied with the problem of time, and their writings reflect a deep and common need to deny it hegemony in human affairs. The easy acceptance of the eighteenth century has, for Waters and Hesse, been replaced by an urge to escape the grasp of time.

At first glance, *The Woman at Otowi Crossing* and *The Glass Bead Game* seem to have little in common. Waters' story is set in the shadows of the Jemez mountains of New Mexico during and after World War II, while Hesse's tale is futuristic, vaguely placed in a distant century to come and without geographical specificity. The chief protagonists of the novels differ greatly. Joseph Knecht, Hesse's Magister Ludi or Master of the Glass Bead game, is a man at the pinnacle of his world, a gentle and wise man charged with the awesome responsibility of governing the sacred game and Castalia, the province which houses and sustains the game's activities. He is the most important man in the hermetically secure world of the game players. On the other hand, Helen Chalmers, Waters' mystic, is a seemingly insignificant woman who spends her days meditating quietly at the edge of civilization, beneath the strikingly beautiful Los Alamos mesa, the focal point of America's effort to build atomic weapons during World War II. In no way can she be considered an important personage like Joseph Knecht. She lives in a world about to be torn asunder by man's perverted genius, the nuclear age, while Knecht sits comfortably atop a world of intellect and spirit in which man's baser instincts have been subverted by the great Glass Bead Game.[3]

In a deeper sense, however, the novels are related. Both Chalmers and Knecht see time as a major concern of their lives, though they approach the problem from very different perspectives. Knecht lives in Castalia, an artificial world of "eternal" verities where every effort is made to see the Glass Bead Game as a "timeless" expression of man's cultural genius. Chalmers, on the other hand, lives in a chaotic and time-bound world of war and confusion. But these differences are superficial; the stories of Chalmers and Knecht are about time and man's desire and ability to transcend its tyranny.

While this theme is not immediately evident in *The Glass Bead Game*, Waters leaves little doubt as to the central meaning of his story. The higher vision which sets Helen Chalmers apart from ordinary mortals is expressed in the first few words of *The Woman at Otowi Crossing*:

> There is no such thing as time as we know it. The entire contents of all space and time co-exist in every infinite and eternal moment. It is an illusion that we experience them in a chronological sequence of "time".[4]

It is this vision which sets Helen apart from her contemporaries and makes *The Woman at Otowi Crossing* clearly and manifestly an elaboration upon the premise: time, whatever ordinary mortals might think, is an illusion.

Hesse's novel, also known by the title *Magister Ludi,* presents us with a more ambivalent picture. Appearing first in Switzerland in 1943, the work, like that of Waters, is one of many meanings and dimensions. Ostensibly a historical study written around the year 2400 by an anonymous narrator, it can be read as a critique of excessive aestheticism and intellectual irresponsibility, matters that had troubled Hesse since his alienation from the German state during World War I. There are those who would emphasize the comic aspect of the story, and others who see in the vaguely defined game of beads some kind of prediction of the computer age. Or the work can be viewed as a commentary on recent German intellectual history, with clearly recognizable portraits of Jacob Burckhardt, Friedrich Nietzsche, and Thomas Mann. Naturally, given its setting in the pedagogical province of Castalia, the story is often considered in light of its utopian themes. Hesse's novel is complex, and the central theme of time is not immediately evident. But again, *The Glass Bead Game,* like Hesse's other stories, is about man's relation to time.

In order to put these otherwise disparate novels in perspective, it is useful to contemplate a theory of human existence which Hesse articulated early in his career. We are born, he believed, into a state of unity and connection with all Being. As children we are at one with the world around us and our experience is unconditioned by doubt. We accept and affirm the world around us, and time is of little concern. But then, as we mature, life brings awareness of good and evil, of loss and despair, of change, decay and suffering in the world. Time in particular washes hard upon us. This, according to Hesse, is the experience of all sensitive men, as it was of the Buddha, subject of his novel *Siddhartha.* Thereafter, they live at a level of individuation and alienation from the world and from others, having lost the child's capacity for open acceptance. Only humor and a sense of life's ironies offer solace to these unfortunates. Time weighs heavily upon their lives, and the inevitability of decay and death is ever-present.

But a special few, whom Hesse calls "the Immortals," manage to move on to a higher plane. These superior beings affirm all of existence, however disorderly and cacophonous. They "know nor day nor night nor time's dividing"[5] and achieve in their lives the state of awareness described in *Siddhartha:*

. . . the world itself, being in and around us, is never one-sided. Never is a man or a deed wholly Samsara or wholly Nirvana; never is a man wholly a saint or a sinner. This only seems so because we suffer the illusion that time is something real. Time is not real. . . . And if time is not real, then the dividing line that seems to lie between this world and eternity, between suffering and bliss, between good and evil, is also an illusion.[6]

It is clear, then. Waters and Hesse, at least in the latter's early stories, agree: man's immersion in time lies at the heart of his malaise, and spiritual health and well-being require transcendence of temporality. There is little doubt that Hesse would have found Helen Chalmer's sudden flash of mystical insight quite understandable. She is clearly one of the Immortals, and Waters' description of her awakening would hardly seem out of place in any of the German writer's stories:

> Then suddenly it happened.
>   A cataclysmic explosion that burst asunder the shell of the world around her, revealing its inner reality with its brilliant flash. In its blinding brightness all mortal appearances dissolved into eternal meanings, great shimmering waves of pure feeling which had no other expression than this, and these were so closely entwined and harmonized they formed one indivisible unity. A selfhood that embraced her, the totality of the universe, and all space and all time in one immortal existence that had never had a beginning nor would ever have an end.[7]

Helen's progress toward enlightenment is reminiscent of Hesse's Siddhartha:

> Every day now Helen's sense of reality sharpened: that one great unity of all creation, imbued with one consciousness and infused with one power, of which everything in the universe was an embodied part. Before its irreducible reality her illusions of temporal time, or individual separateness, vanished.[8]

But Hesse's position seems to have changed, a change reflected in *The Glass Bead Game*. Had he not written this last story, or if it was simply an extension of what came before, we could easily conclude that he and Waters shared the same view of time. The earlier stories, most notably *Siddhartha* and *The Journey to the East*, clearly reflect his sense of repugnance at Heidegger's view of the human condition. His major protagonists, as clearly as Helen Chalmers, seek a release from the despotism of time.

But there was a change of heart and mind. Joseph Knecht, who, like all Castalians, shares in a kind of institutional immortality by virtue of the Game of Beads, begins to doubt. Castalia and its game begin to seem stale and moribund. Ironically, the Magister Ludi, whose faith should have been greater than that of even the most fanatical players, begins to contemplate the unthinkable, an abandonment of Castalia and the game. He dreams of leaving the spiritual province, of immersing himself in life and time, regardless of the consequences. While Helen Chalmers moves inexorably toward transcendence, a "jelling of life and time into a composite now,"[9] Knecht moves in the opposite direction. He has come to understand that the timeless quality of the Game is an illusion and that his life as Magister Ludi amounts to an elaborate if unintended hoax. Unlike Helen Chalmers, he is privileged to live in a time of peace and stability, of mathematics and music, and in a place where spiritual fulfillment and contemplation of eternal verities is the mark of the good life. But it seems hollow and unfulfilling.

To a significant extent, Knecht's doubts arise out of his own experience. It is important, however, to note the role in his education played by a man who grants time its due, a brilliant Benedictine, Pater Jacobus. This historian and philosopher, whom Knecht encounters in the course of his official duties, plays a critical role in the Magister Ludi's enlightenment.[10] Their first meeting, and the prolonged conversations that follow from it, serve as the catalyst for profound changes in Knecht's perspective. Pater Jacobus casts a jaundiced but penetrating eye upon Castalia and the Glass Bead Game, arguing that, however beautiful they might seem, they are bound to pass away. They are bound to suffer the ravages of time, as everything must.

The anonymous narrator of *The Glass Bead Game* summarizes the view which results from Knecht's exposure to Pater Jacobus:

> Knecht was a great and exemplary administrator, an honor to
> his high office, an irreproachable Glass Bead Game Master. But
> he saw and felt the glory of Castalia, even as he devoted him-
> self to it, as an imperiled greatness that was on the wane. He
> did not participate in its life thoughtlessly and unsuspectingly,

as did the great majority of his fellow Castalians, for he knew about its origins and history, was conscious of it as a historical entity, subject to time, washed and undermined by time's pitiless surges. . . . Much of this was due to the influence of . . . Father Jacobus. . . .[11]

The ideals of Castalia and the Game are, of course, not without defenders in the novel. Fritz Tegularius, Knecht's friend and confidant, plays an important role as an intellectual who argues forcefully for the values and principles of Castalia.[12] Tegularius defends the Glass Bead Game against the criticisms of Pater Jacobus. He defiantly proclaims his refusal to descend into the muck of time and history, and his advice to Knecht is emphatic:

> To associate real history, the timeless history of Mind, with this age-old, stupid scramble of the ambitious for power and the climbers for a place in the sun . . . is in itself a betrayal of the living spirit. . . . World history is a race with time, a scramble for profit, for power, for treasures. What counts is who has the strength, luck, or vulgarity not to miss his opportunity. The achievements of thought, of culture, of art are just the opposite. They are always an escape from the serfdom of time, man crawling out of the muck of his instincts and out of his sluggishness and climbing to a higher plane, to timelessness, liberation from time, divinity.[13]

Knecht's story comes to a rather abrupt end when he takes the unprecedented step of resigning his post and departing Castalia. He has sought and found employment as a tutor for the son of his friend Plinio Designori, a man of the world who, earlier in his life, spent time at Castalia and became a close friend of the future Magister Ludi. One summer morning the teacher, following the wild impulse of his charge, abandons rationality and plunges headlong into the frigid waters of a high mountain lake. Not surprisingly, he drowns. The unexpected death, which serves as an inspiration for the boy, also becomes a source of wonder and enlightenment for the game players who survive him, and Knecht's departure from "timeless" heights of Castalia comes to serve a didactic purpose.

For Helen Chalmers, however, there is no compromise to be made, no descent from the high plane of mystical consciousness. She sees time as the very stuff of the civilization she has come to abhor, of this "dark age of materialism [that] is in such an advanced stage of decadence it can't last much longer. . . ."[14] In the midst of revelations about the horrors of Hiroshima and Nagasaki, of a world gone mad with a passion for destruction, she finds refuge and solace in her sense of the timeless. Like Facundo, the old Indian who faithfully tends her vegetable garden, she learns to find sustenance in magic moments that stand apart from time, in the strange, ineffable, eternal truth that lies beyond ordinary reason, beyond analysis and science, "beyond logic."[15]

Helen, of course, must also deal with death. Content to remain at Otowi Crossing until the end, she experiences the full ravages of time, both in herself and others. But she understands that time is a superficial attribute of human life, as is the delusion of individual existence. Pater Jacobus' history, which in her life manifests itself in the creation and detonation of great weapons of destruction, is for her but another repetition, "another cycle on that ceaseless round of birth, pain, and death which marked humanity's slow spiral crawl toward its only freedom."[16] Knecht might seek to find himself in the world and in time. But Helen Chalmers seeks to find the world in herself, and, finding a "texture impervious to time,"[17] joyfully loses herself in that world.

There are other characters of interest in Waters' novel. Jack Turner, for example, fits nicely into Hesse's scheme as one of the suffering souls who fail to achieve true understanding. While Helen is clearly one of the Immortals, her friend and frustrated admirer is, like most of us, condemned to live on the second level of existence, sustained mainly by the skepticism through which he filters oppressive reality and by his sense of humor. Helen feels sincere affection for Jack and seeks to ease his burdens, but she also pities him:

> . . . every word revealed how acutely he was suffering under the
> illusion of time rushing past; constricted to feelings and loves
> that must be grasped hurriedly and held tightly lest they be
> swept away and lost forever.[18]

For Jack, of course, Helen is a mystery, a woman whose "psychosis" leads her to delusions of grandeur. His life in time, with all of its existential messiness, is to be preferred to her unfathomable wisdom. "Come off your perch, Helen," he demands:

> You're living on this corrupt and rotten earth same's the rest of us. We're not noble souls puffed up with divine morality. We're weak and afraid . . . We're selfish and headstrong. . . . But by God, we're human![19]

One can imagine the enlightened Joseph Knecht directing a similar protest at Fritz Tegularius or any of the Glass Bead Game players who portray their efforts as timeless and beyond the "muck" of history. In this curious sense, Jack Turner and Joseph Knecht are similar. They are men of this world, of what they might call the "real" world. For Turner and Knecht, time is vitally and unavoidably real. There is no escaping its demands. Indeed, it is their life in time that makes them feel alive, which gives their lives meaning.

It is clear, then, that the problem of time is critical to the thinking of both Frank Waters and Hermann Hesse and that the two novels in question explore similar themes. Helen Chalmers and Joseph Knecht are spirit-mates wrestling with the same demon. It would be a mistake, however, to make too much of the parallels to be found in the two novels. Lying beneath the similarities of *The Woman at Otowi Crossing* and *The Glass Bead Game* are profound differences. The novels are very different in tone and structure. Waters' story has an emotional depth that seems lacking in *The Glass Bead Game*. Above all, Waters and Hesse approach the world and man's place in it from very different perspectives.

Hesse's story is best understood within the context of the German literary and philosophical tradition which spawned it. His intellectual roots are evident not only in his use of historical models for his characters, but also in the questions he poses and the answers he provides. Joseph Knecht's fate, though unusual in the context of the greater body of Hesse's work, can be readily understood in terms of existential commitment, a theme current in European and German thinking during and after World War II. It is misleading to simply label Hesse an existentialist and to view *The Glass Bead Game* in that context, but neither would it be appropriate to disassociate him from the literary and philosophical disputes which characterized the European intellectual community at mid-century. Theodore Ziolkowski places Hesse somewhere "between romanticism and existentialism,"[20] a designation that seems appropriate.

Hesse's existentialist proclivities are quite apparent in *The Glass Bead Game*. His emphasis is upon the ethical dimension of Knecht's life. How to live and act authentically, how to be true to one's innermost self? These are the questions that dominate the novel. And Knecht's death, coming as a result of his will to act, is legitimized by his very decisiveness. His willingness to throw caution to the wind in favor of commitment is the hallmark of his affirmation of life. Hesse's writings have always appealed primarily to readers for whom ethical concerns are paramount; *The Glass Bead Game* does not, in this respect, disappoint.

The focus in Waters' work seems altogether different. *The Woman at Otowi Crossing* and his other writings are clearly conditioned by non-Western philosophies and religions. They can also be understood, however, in the context of contemporary scientific thinking. There is no doubt that the story of Helen Chalmers has ethical implications, but, more significantly, it leads the reader to speculate about the true nature of reality and about man's capacity to perceive and understand what is ultimately real. It inspires the reader to contemplate the basic mysteries of the world as well as man's ability to penetrate these mysteries.

Waters is, it seems, part of an intellectual tradition which can be said to begin with Immanuel Kant in the late eighteenth century. For it is Kant who begins the modern process of defining man's place in the post-Newtonian world.

Shaken to the core by David Hume's critique of Newtonian concepts, Kant recognized that the human ability to know the basic causes of things had been called into question by the Englishman's philosophy. Despite his emotional reservations, Kant found quite persuasive Hume's argument that man cannot truly know or describe an objective reality of causal connections independent of his thinking about that reality. He was not content, however, to leave the matter at that point. We can, he concluded, draw from human experience a special kind of knowledge of the world; we can "know" in a limited sense. We can deduce that causality and other fundamentals of the physical world, such as three-dimensional space and linear time, will always be the framework within which human observations of the natural world must take place. This will always be the case because of the very nature of our minds and our senses; we are condemned to perceive reality in this limited way. Whether our human perception reveals "reality" or simply an elaborate illusion is, Kant believed, beside the point and something we can never truly know.

Time, viewed by Newton as an absolute, one of the basic and invariant features of the natural world, thus becomes, for Kant, dependent upon perception. No longer an attribute of the world itself, time is rather one of the basic parameters of human perception. Thus, in this new and limited sense time was an ever-present and necessary feature of reality, but only man's reality.

It is, of course, currently fashionable to disparage much of Kant's philosophy. We should not, however, neglect the implications of his philosophy for modern thinking, including that of Frank Waters. If the human mind is far from being a passive receiver of stimuli from the external world but is rather, as Kant teaches, an active and creative instrument which organizes and structures reality, the seemingly strange perceptions of mystics like Helen Chalmers take on a whole new significance. If there is no "real world," or if reality is what we make of it, then the "realism" of Jack Turner and others like him is quite hollow. It is no more or less than a structure imposed upon the world by the needs of the human mind, a mind, it can be argued, at a preliminary stage in its evolution.

Forced to stand alone, Kant's philosophy might well be easily dismissed. But his ideas are complemented by the concepts of modern science and not so easily dismissed. As previously noted, Einstein and his intellectual heirs have added considerably to our understanding of the world as well as to our confusion regarding the true nature of time. The special and general theories of relativity reveal a world in which time is a variable and inconstant phenomenon, dependent upon one's place and velocity in the universe. No longer a universal constant, time, even when it has nothing to do with man's mind or psyche, can only be measured and understood in relation to other "reference frames" and other motions. Time speeds up and slows down, it "dilates," it varies from place to place. Reality, says Einstein, is a chunky complex of relative reference frames and times. In the final analysis, as Helen Chalmers would have it, "there is no such thing as time as we know it."

Ultimately, of course, physical science has advanced well beyond Einstein's mind-shaking revelations. It is common now to view space and time not as discrete phenomena but rather as a singular stuff, "space-time." This substance, far from being uniform, is strangely "warped" by gravity and by other forces. Queer and fantastic theories abound in which "singularities," places from which time cannot escape, are said to exist throughout the universe. Such gravitational focal points are sometimes said to lead beyond the end of time, or into an altogether new time. Whatever the case, the dance of the cosmos as revealed by contemporary science, curiously reminiscent of ancient Hindu and Taoist views, is wild and beautiful to contemplate. Within that context, the prosaic protestations of the Jack Turners of the world seem quite naive.

Frank Waters studied engineering and philosophy of science but was not a scientist, and one should not turn to his novels for elaborate discussions of abstruse scientific theory. *The Woman at Otowi Crossing* is nevertheless a story best understood, however, within this context in which Helen's "peculiar" ideas seem almost commonplace. Her "awakening" and her sense of connection with the cosmos are best understood against the background of vistas revealed by science. "Within her now," writes Waters, "she could feel a strange fusion of body, mind and spirit into a new and integrated entity that seemed apart from the gross elements from which it sprang."[21] That "new and integrated entity" is the wondrous world of modern science.

So, while those about her languish in their illusions of linear time and individual uniqueness, the mystic at Otowi Crossing moves ever-closer to "the immemorial and rhythmic order"[22] of the cosmos. Her eventual death, attended by the birds and beasts of the forest, is more a coming home and an affirmation than it is an ending. "The inexorable rush of time," an illusion anyway, "had stopped"[23] and life was complete.

In *Mexico Mystique*, Waters summarizes the core of his thinking:

> The religious philosophies of the East assure us there is no first creation. Worlds come and go eternally. Infinity, the irreducible real, periodically finitizes itself into the reducible real of the worlds of material form, of time, space and causality. Then they are withdrawn again into the unmanifest alogical whole, only to be projected again; appearing and disappearing with the out-breathing and in-breathing of all Creation, the pulse of life itself.[24]

There is no need to escape from time for, as Helen understood, at a fundamental level there is no such thing as time.

Alexander Blackburn
Archetypal Promise from Apocalyptic Premise:
The Woman at Otowi Crossing

> It seems strange to me now that when I first arrived
> I was not conscious of the myth beginning to take
> form. Not only the myth of the Project on top of the
> mesa, but the myth at its foot, at Otowi Crossing.
> Only now can one realize they were two sides of the
> same coin, neither of which could have existed
> without the other. Both growing, as all myths must
> grow, with agonizing slowness and in secrecy.
> Forming one myth as we know it now — perhaps the
> only true myth of these modern times.
>
> [*Otowi,* 74][1]

This statement attributed to Dr. Edmund Gaylord, an atomic physicist who has awakened from his sleep in conscious will and instinctive behavior and who seeks a new world of the human spirit, is part of Waters' most original fictionalized attempt to resolve the apparent contradiction between science and mysticism, matter and mind, reason and intuition. The myth of the Project, which is based on the discovery of a New World of enormous physical energy locked inside the atom, is evidently one polarized to rationalism, materialism, and the concept of linear time. The myth of the Woman at Otowi Crossing, which is based on the discovery of a New World of enormous psychic energy locked inside the mind, is, on the other hand, evidently one polarized to the unconscious, with its powers of perception of and being within the wholeness and timelessness of Creation.[2] These myths are said to be "one myth," complementary and united or reconciled, "perhaps" a single psychophysical energy — Absolute Consciousness, or Irreducible Reality — that may be realized once humanity has evolved to a new and higher stage of awareness. *The Woman at Otowi Crossing* presents Waters' mature novelistic vision of Emergence.

What might be surprising is Gaylord's earlier misconception of his own intellectual powers and of the methods of science that he has applied in helping to bring about atomic and thermonuclear explosions. But it is a historical misconception deeply engrained in our thinking, not easily remedied; and it is shared by many scientists still today who, while conducting "mystical" experiments based on the matter-energy equation and on the relativity theory that events occur in a space-time continuum, are reluctant to discard the outmoded Newtonian view of a mechanistic universe. This situation, reported by such scientific philosophers as Arthur Koestler, Fritjof Capra, and F. David Peat, may well have its source in the Western idea of "mind."[3] When science is properly conceived, it is creative, its processes of thinking vividly intuitive, subjective, and irrational until after the experimental event. Science, like mysticism, depends on the unconscious mind. Scientific thought, properly conceived, is compatible with mysticism and a principal manifestation of individual, unenforced spiritual experience. But of course scientific thought, unless you're Einstein, who considered science a spiritual quest, is seldom so conceived: science is believed to be a branch of knowledge which operates predominantly with abstract symbols whose entire rationale is objectivity, logicality, and verifiability.

Whence arises this paradox, namely that the creative act emerging from unconscious mentation is regarded as depthlessly conscious? It arose with modern science itself under the influence of Descartes, who identified "mind" with consciousness alone, as if conscious and unconscious experiences belong to different, opposed, and irreconcilable compartments. Although the concept of the unconscious is an ancient one, it has for more than three centuries evoked a feeling of wary skepticism that in turn blocks the way to psychic integration with our individual selves and to comprehension of a worldview whereby everything in the universe is interrelated and interdependent. That has long been Eastern mysticism's worldview, and Einsteinian physics and Jungian psychology have only in the twentieth century begun to approximate it and to synthesize the insights of East and West. At the present time there are signs of change indicated in the titles of popular scientific books such as *The Tao of Physics*, *The Dancing Wu Li Masters*, and *Synchronicity: The Bridge Between Matter and Mind* — and in the characterization of an atomic physicist in *The Woman at Otowi Crossing*. For the most part, however, modern science has ignored and continues to ignore the grave and the constant in human affairs, the unconscious and its archetypes.

And now this same one-sided, materialistic, and hubristic science has bequeathed to the world since 16 July 1945, when the first atomic bomb was detonated in New Mexico, the apocalyptic premise to survival, the possibility of annihilation of all life as we know it.[4] Although Waters does not personally believe that such a dire catastrophe awaits us, the development of this power of destruction has occurred when, by all accounts, modern culture has reached a highly alarming stage of crisis of social, ecological, moral and spiritual dimensions.[5] Today there are no boundaries, and the old ethnically oriented mythologies which centered authority in gods "aloft" rather than in the individual human spirit are dying except in archaic cultures. So it seems that humanity faces man-made apocalypse at the very moment in history when the archetypal promise of myth, individually centered yet universal in meaning, has only begun to announce itself through creative minds as if urgently summoned to our aid, from the depths of the unconscious psyche, in the hour of dread.

Therein, I think, lies the prophetic greatness of *The Woman at Otowi Crossing*. Begun in 1953, though not published until 1966 and even then not brought out in a definitive edition until 1987, the novel carries forward and enlarges on a comparison-contrast developed in 1950 in *Masked Gods*: the atomic reactor at Los Alamos and the Sun Temple of Mesa Verde, considered as allegories about physical and psychic energies, reveal that "both the transformation of matter into energy, and the transfiguration of instinctual forces into creative energy depend upon the reconciliation of the primal dual forces of all life" (*Masked Gods*, 421-22). By preempting the fission-fusion language for nuclear energy as a metaphor for a psychological conflict resulting in release of new energy, Waters was prepared within a few short years after the

Hiroshima bombing on 6 August 1945 to accept the Atomic Age as a revelation of reality (albeit an age tragically introduced in a destructive form) and
to confront the apocalyptic premise — that one nuclear war forecloses the
future — with the archetypal promise of the creative myth of Emergence. If
we evaluate an author's achievement not only with respect to the ordinary
recalcitrance of his materials but also with respect to the magnitude of conflict
imaginatively confronted and artistically contained, *Otowi* will have to be considered as, arguably, the supreme visionary novel in world literature at present.
Although many modern novelists have confronted the facts of death in the
self and in the heart of culture, it is Waters who convincingly invigorates the
primal powers constituting hope.

While he was writing *Masked Gods*, Waters was influenced by aspects
of Jungian psychology and was in particular drawn to Jung's idea of a "reconciling symbol" as explained in M. Esther Harding's *Psychic Energy* (1947).
According to the theory, a solution to conflict will not appear in the form of
an intellectual conclusion or in a change in conscious attitude, such as might
be brought about by education or precept, but will develop spontaneously
in the unconscious, arising as an image or symbol which has the effect of
breaking the deadlock. The potency of the reconciling symbol "avails not
only to bring the impasse to an end but also to effect a transformation or
modification of the instinctive drives within the individual: this corresponds
in the personal sphere to that modification of the instincts which, at least in
some measure, has been brought about in the race through the ages of cultural effort."[6] Almost incredible as this proposition seems, the psychological
imperative to bring about a radical change in the instincts and a promotion
of human development has long been believed to be possible in the East, in
the various forms of yoga, for instance. The reconciling symbol leads, Waters
feels, "whole races, nations, and civilizations in great bursts of creative energy
to another Emergence, a new stage of consciousness" (*Masked Gods*, 410). He
speculates that such a symbol might be the circle: just as in relativity "a ray of
light-energy travelling from the sun at 186,000 miles per second will describe
a great cosmic circle," so the "evolutionary Road of Life completes its circuit
by returning to its source" (*Masked Gods*, 434). He further speculates that a
phenomenon such as telepathy points to the possibility of future emergence,
through the unconscious, to a psychological fourth dimension in which past,
present, and future are "coexistent" (*Masked Gods*, 431).

These speculations would help to shape the theme of *The Woman at Otowi Crossing*. Through an imperative of the unconscious, the protagonist breaks through to a mystical experience of timelessness, finds a solution to conflict, and emerges to an awareness which is, so to say, the paradigm for cultural transformation. Likened to a mandala-shaped kiva, the protagonist is herself a kind of personification of a reconciling symbol. By counterpointing the myth of the Project and the myth of the Woman at Otowi Crossing and unifying these in the myth of Emergence, Waters shapes for those who can respond to it a vision for the future in which world crisis is resolved on a higher plane of at-one-ment with the cosmos.

The rediscovery of the unconscious mind and of its capacity for spontaneously releasing the energy of archetypes as solutions to crisis is of the highest interest in contemporary consideration of the "death of mankind."[7] The unconscious mind has power to effect alteration of our inner life and of the outer forms in which life finds expression and support. The promise of the unconscious mind lies in its creativity.

But if creativity may free us from a plunge into world catastrophe, is it not also a form of human motivation? Early twentieth-century psychology, influenced by Freud, reduced motivation to escape from anxiety and tended to leave out of account activities that might be self-rewarding and urges that might be independent of such biological drives as hunger, sex, and fear. Nowadays, nonreductionist theories have dramatically revealed the deleterious effects of protracted stimulus starvation as well as the organism's need for more or less constant stimulation, or at least a steady flow of information — a hunger for experience and thirst for excitation probably as basic as hunger and thirst themselves. In other words, living organisms exhibit an exploratory drive and demonstrate an essential creativity. It follows that what is self-rewarding can be at the same time self-transcending and other-rewarding, and here, at the psychological rather than at the consciously ethical level, we encounter our gift for empathy and its power for global redemption. In the manifestations of the unconscious, such as in dreams, the boundaries of the self are fluid, and one can be oneself and somebody else simultaneously. The gift for empathy then activates our participatory emotions, those which answer the human need for meaning whereby the self is experienced as part of a totality, which may be God, nature, and mankind. Therefore, the full human self is a power for human survival because in its most developed representatives

— in mystics, for example — a whole new body of possibilities is brought into the field of experience, breaking the crust of closed societies and opening them to the perception of dimensions in which all life is timelessly incorporated as a unity.[8]

And so we come to see that a process or emergence to a higher consciousness, in which rational consciousness is reconciled with the unconscious, becomes the realization of a common humanity and an orientation in the direction of world culture.[9] Mankind's development is then not determined by catastrophe but by, in Waters' philosophy, "the periodic synchronization of human and cosmic rhythms" (*Mexico Mystique*, 274). As consciousness expands to relate the inner life of man to his material outer world, the cataclysmic changes that many people have predicted since the release of atomic energy may prove instead to be transformation into a new world of the mind, due to the release of psychic energy.

If we grant that transformation is validated by mystical experience, we may still think that visionaries are people close to the edge of neuroticism; and they are, in the sense that they have moved out of society into the area of original experience, where, freed from Literalism, they must interpret life for themselves. The actual crux of the matter where mysticism is concerned is not that it seems antisocial and not that all symbolic expressions of it are faulty but that mystical experience, awakened, is the *function* of life. Campbell makes this point in one of his television interviews with Bill Moyers:

> *MOYERS*: In classic Christian doctrine the material world is to be despised, and life is to be redeemed in the hereafter, in heaven, where our rewards come. But you say that if you affirm that which you deplore, you are affirming the very world which is our eternity at the moment.
>
> *CAMPBELL*: Yes, that is what I'm saying. Eternity isn't some later time. Eternity isn't even a long time. Eternity has nothing to do with time. Eternity is that dimension of here and now that all thinking in temporal terms cuts off. And if you don't get it here, you won't get it anywhere. The problem with heaven is that you'll be having such a good time there, you won't even think of eternity. You'll just have this unending delight in the beatific vision of God. But the experience of eternity right here and now,

in all things, whether thought of as good or as evil, is the function of life.[10]

What Campbell is saying in *The Power of Myth* (the interviews published posthumously in 1988) is what Waters has been saying in his visionary novels all along, but pointedly in *Otowi*: its protagonist is a mystic. It is she who is aware and enlivened lucidly, she who is functioning within the vision of eternity. The other characters — with the exception of an old Indian and eventually with the exception of Gaylord, who has a mystical experience of his own — only think of themselves as "normal," when in fact their thinking in temporal terms cuts them off from reality. So we have a protagonist who has been nudged into the realm of the paranormal but who is nonetheless truly normal, a paradox for those who haven't broken through into the mystery dimensions or been pushed into the interface between what can be known and what is never to be discovered.

Yet modern science itself has been pushed precisely into such an interface, unable, for example, to decide whether an atom is a wave or a particle, when it is both and therefore the manifestation of a transcendent energy source. Again, it is the thinking in temporal terms which creates the problem, for we are accustomed to regard events in nature as a causality of pushes and pulls to connect them. Now that scientists are beginning to postulate that events arise out of the underlying patterns of the universe, the similarities between the views of physicists and mystics are being acknowledged, and the possibility of relating subatomic physics to Jungian psychology and to parapsychology is being seriously studied. With such studies, the classical notion of causation is being modified to make room for what Jung called an "acausal connecting principle," or synchronicity.[11]

Synchronicity is the term employed by Jung to explain the coincidence in time of two or more causally unrelated events which have the same or similar meaning. According to the theory, archetypal energy could be manifested both in internal imagery and in external events, and the meaningfulness of this coincidence of a psychic state and a physical event is emphasized by the connection with archetypal processes. Synchronicities act as mirrors to the inner processes of mind and are thus to be associated with a profound activation of energy deep within the psyche. As described by F. David Peat, the very intensity of synchronistic happenings suggests their profile:

> It is as if the formation of patterns within the unconscious
> mind is accompanied by physical patterns in the outer world.
> In particular, as psychic patterns are on the point of reaching
> consciousness then synchronicities reach their peak; more-
> over, they generally disappear as the individual becomes con-
> sciously aware of a new alignment of forces within his or her
> personality.[12]

It seems that one cannot describe the advent of this psychic energy without using the language of explosiveness, of something that reaches a peak, like the critical mass within an atomic reactor, and then bursts, like a bomb. Indeed, Peat believes that synchronicities tend to occur during periods of person- al transformation, when there is a burst of psychic energy: births, deaths, intense creative work, falling in love, and the like. As we shall see, the synchro- nistic happenings that occur to the protagonist of *Otowi* fit into this profile exactly: as her old way of life is dying, as she herself is dying, she "explodes" into visions that are meaningfully precognitive of nuclear explosions, and then, as she becomes aware of a transformed personality, the synchronicities disappear and her Emergence — the myth made manifest — consolidates itself in the new world of consciousness.

Significantly, I think, Jung first contemplated synchronicity at the time when Einstein, a guest on several occasions for dinner in Jung's home, was developing his first (or special) theory of relativity.[13] In relativity theory we can never talk about space without talking about time and vice versa. When all things are seen as interdependent and inseparable parts or manifestations of an ultimate, indivisible reality, with opposite concepts unified in a higher dimension of space-time reality, there is no "before" and no "after" and thus no causation. Accordingly then, phenomena such as telepathy, clairvoyance, and precognition, all of which suggest an explanation beyond the merely coincidental, might also point to the unfolding of an order which is neither matter nor mind. Indeed, the theory of synchronicity leads to the proposal that "mind and matter are not separate and distinct substances but that like light and radio waves they are orders that lie within a common spectrum." What may be reflected in a synchronistic happening such as precognition are, according to Peat, "the dynamics of the macrocosm as it unfolds simultane- ously into the mental and material aspects of a person's life."[14] Synchronicity, in short, proposes a bridge between mind and matter and admits a spiritual element into the philosophy of science. Hence Erich Neumann wrote in 1955 in a eulogy to Jung, "If the premise of synchronicity . . . can be validated, this would mean no more nor less than that phenomena which have hitherto been described in theological terms as 'miracles' are in principle contained in the structure of our world."[15] Jean Bolen, another Jungian psychologist, declares in *The Tao of Psychology:*

> With the idea of synchronicity, psychology joined hands with parapsychology and theoretical physics in seeing an underlying "something" akin to what the mystic has been seeing all along. The important element that synchronicity adds is a dimension of personal meaning that acknowledges what a person intuitively feels when a synchronistic event is directly experienced. Theories and laboratory experiences make thinkable the idea of an underlying invisible connection between everything in the universe. But when it is an intuitively felt experience, a *spiritual* element enters. The human psyche may be the one receiver in the universe that can correctly apprehend the meaning underlying everything, the meaning that has been called the Tao or God.[16]

When Jung studied Richard Wilhelm's translation of the Taoist *I Ching* or "Book of Changes," he recognized that an acausal synchronistic principle had long been known in Chinese mysticism, which is primarily concerned with nature's Way, or Tao. The Chinese, like the mystics of India, believed that there is an Ultimate Reality which underlies and unifies the multiple things and events we observe, and Tao, in its original cosmic sense as the undefinable, Ultimate Reality, is thus equivalent of the Hinduist *Brahman* and the Buddhist *Dharma-Kāya.* The Tao differs from the Indian concepts, however, by virtue of its intrinsically dynamic character. As explained by Capra, the Chinese "not only believed that flow and change were the essential features of nature, but also that there are constant patterns in these changes." The Taoists, specifically, "came to believe that any pair of opposites constitutes a polar relationship where each of the two poles is dynamically linked to the other."[17] From this belief, so difficult for the Western mind to grasp, that contraries are aspects of the same thing, there was derived a further belief that any extreme development becomes its opposite within the limits for the cycles of change. When, for example, a culture consistently favors yang, or masculine, values and attitudes — analysis over synthesis, rational knowledge over intuitive wisdom, science over religion, and so on — and has neglected the complementary yin, or feminine, counterparts, such a one-sided movement reaches a climax and then retreats in favor of the other polarity. Thus, where synchronicity is concerned, the coincidence of events in space and time not only points meaningfully to a ground of unity but also suggests a dynamic web of patterns according to which the synchronistic event may signal a change of polarities of transpersonal significance.

We have reached the juncture where Jung's theory of synchronicity and Waters' myth of Emergence mingle to form the dynamic worldview of *The Woman at Otowi Crossing*. Waters, in 1950, had read Wilhelm's translation of the *I Ching* and Jung's foreword to it explaining synchronicity and realized "the universal significance of this profound book" (*Mountain Dialogues*, 114). It helped to confirm his speculations about the Mesoamerican symbology of life as a continuous transformation of opposites through movement, a movement mythologized in Indian America as Emergence through successive "worlds" when a civilization reaches a verge of extreme development and is replaced by another one on the Road (Tao, "Way") of Life. To Waters, that ancient myth of Emergence was and is an allegory for man's ever-expanding consciousness, and here in Jung's theory of synchronicity, although it represents phenomena on a lower temporal plane than Emergence, was a link; parapsychological phenomena occur mainly in the surroundings of an individual whom the unconscious wants to take a step in the expansion of consciousness. And so a fictionalized individual represented as having authentic mystical experiences, including synchronistic events, might be projected into the vanguard of a new age that is coming to birth as an old age has reached its climax in an apocalyptic premise. Assuming that every event in the visible world is the noncausally related effect of an archetype in the unseen world, one would have a fiction revelatory of a dynamic process in history. And that fiction is *The Woman at Otowi Crossing*.

On an immediate level *Otowi* is the story of an "ordinary" middle-aged woman, Helen Chalmers.[18] As the story opens, she and her lover, Jack Turner, are waiting at a railroad whistle stop for the arrival of Emily, Helen's twenty-year-old daughter by a previous marriage. It is soon apparent that Helen, who abandoned Emily in infancy, has accumulated psychological dynamite — guilt, shame, and fear of financial failure — during almost twenty years of lonely isolation in a remote area of northern New Mexico called Otowi Crossing, where she manages a tearoom in a small adobe house. Emily does not arrive that day, but an army colonel does, to inquire about a school called Los Alamos on the mesa above Otowi Crossing. Soon after experiencing a faint premonition, Helen discovers that she has breast cancer. Realizing that she cannot marry Turner, she contemplates the seeming futility of her life. Just then she has the first of her mystical visions, a "fusion" (21) of self into the complete pattern of the universe. After many misgivings and resentments about this awakening, she courageously accepts the power of destiny that drives her, commits herself to its fulfillment, and painfully sacrifices intimacy with the two persons she most loves, Turner and Emily. Doomed and yet reborn, with only Facundo, an old Indian from the nearby pueblo, to understand her integrity and psychic power, she has terrifying precognitive dreams, the content of which appalls her — nothing less, as we know through dramatic irony, than A-Bomb and H-bomb explosions, even planetary disappearance. She nevertheless grows in spiritual power and becomes a benevolent influence on many who know her, including physicists from the secret city of Los Alamos, who are experimenting with another, seemingly opposite kind of power. Helen influences one of these physicists, Gaylord, so much that, as he is observing the first H-bomb detonation over the Pacific, he has telepathic knowledge of the moment of her death and transfiguration, the triumph of spirit over matter.

That is the story on one immediate level. Waters never permits us to lose sight of Helen as a flesh-and-blood woman who suffers into wisdom; who swims in the nude and responds exuberantly to the natural world; who enjoys sex and friendship; who cooks and who nurses the afflicted. Waters, however, counterpoints the four parts of her myth — breakthrough to hidden reality, learning to live in a new world of freedom, exercise of released psychic energy, and its constructive influence on others — to the myth of science, whose hierophants successively break through to the new world of subatomic energy, release it, and victimize themselves and masses of humanity with radioactive fallout. So another immediate level of the story is a history of the Atomic Age from the Manhattan Project through the Trinity Site explosion, Hiroshima, experiments in the Nevada desert, and the H-bomb explosion in the Marshall Islands. The interaction of the immediate levels of the story leads to a distinction between Helen Chalmers, the vessel of worldly experiences, and the Woman at Otowi Crossing, the personification of the myth of Emergence. Lest the woman in her mythic role seem to impose on modern sensibilities, Waters allows various characters to raise our objections for us: a strategy of an ironist. Turner believes Helen is a neurotic recluse in danger of becoming a psychotic lost in a meaningless dream state. Emily, an anthropologist with intellectual pretensions, is upset by her mother's mythological interpretations of historical signs. Throckmorton, a rich but puerile politician, sees Helen as easy prey for his manipulation. All these characters get their comeuppance. Turner's pragmatism is a betrayal of trust that loses him any chance for a complete relationship with Helen. Emily's science is of no emotional help; after aborting her child by Gaylord, she comes to an academic dead end in a Mexican university. Throckmorton's goose is cooked when Turner tricks him into making public a proposal for bombing America's enemies. While the fates of these characters may not remove all objections to the myth of Emergence, they do indicate some validation of Helen's normalcy and moral wholeness.

The most convincing validation of Helen's mysticism comes from the story of Gaylord, to whom focus shifts in the last third of the novel. Repeating the pattern of Helen's emergence, but with a terraced crescendo, he inherits her archetype as a moving principle of life. Thenceforth his spiritual effort is to hold to the experience in loyalty, courage, and love beyond fear and desire. In mythological terms this "gay lord" is like the questing hero from Grail legends: an impotent Fisher King of the Atomic Waste-Land is cured of his wound and given reign over a regenerated world. When we first encounter him, he is dedicated to science at the expense of emotional development. He is little more than a dehumanized robot isolated from his Jewish family and the teeming life of New York City. In spite of his duty to science, though, he feels drawn to Emily shortly after his arrival at Los Alamos. Therein lies his dilemma, for security regulations strictly forbid courtship. When Emily becomes pregnant, Gaylord promises marriage but procrastinates, betraying the dictates of his heart at the very hour when a historical Klaus Fuchs is passing atom bomb secrets to Harry Gold — *that* big a betrayal. Gaylord gets his bomb at Trinity, *his* secret; Emily gets an abortion, *her* secret. Gaylord, unaware of the abortion and beginning to mature emotionally, no longer feels alienated from his family and neighbors in New York. When he is apparently sterilized by radioactivity during an accident at Los Alamos, the tragic irony of his apparently irreversible fate — as guilt-ridden as Helen's had been — is his belated feeling of compassion for humanity. The climax of Gaylord's story occurs in Nevada when a "shot" fails to explode after countdown, and it is his duty to climb the tower to defuse the bomb. At this moment he experiences disassociation from the instinctual pattern of fear and guilt which has constituted his emotional field. Having attained spiritual detachment, Gaylord disconnects the jinxed bomb and, later in Las Vegas, finds the courage to "connect" his presumably lost manhood with a willing "show-biz" goddess, allusively a lunar deity named Monday Willis. In a wonderfully comic scene, Monday breaks down the barriers of Gaylord's isolation and comments, "Jesus, but it's taken you a long time!" (278).

But it is Helen Chalmers who is at the center of the novel. It is Waters' narrative technique to convey the mystery of her character not only through her interactions with other characters but also through the compressed imagery of her mystical experiences, through the counterpointing of life and death forces, through her own words as expressed in a *Secret Journal*, through the symbolism of her death scene, and through the perceptions given by a Chorus, as I shall call it, of major and minor characters after her death. Out of this narrative complexity we finally perceive Helen's experience in the perspective of myth, the paradigm for humankind.

The novel highlights five mystical experiences of which three are incidents frozen in time and two are dreams. The first experience is one of totality:

> Then suddenly it happened.
>
> A cataclysmic explosion that burst asunder the shell of the world around her, revealing its inner reality with its brilliant flash. In its blinding brightness all mortal appearances dissolved into eternal meanings, great shimmering waves of pure feeling which had no other expression than this, and these were so closely entwined and harmonized they formed one indivisible unity. A selfhood that embraced her, the totality of the universe, and all space and all time in one immortal existence that had never had a beginning nor would ever have an end. [21]

This vision of the interpenetration of space and time in which an infinite, timeless, and yet dynamic present is experienced instead of a linear succession of instants is the basis of Helen's emergence, but it is also a basis of theoretical physics and of pueblo ceremonialism. Little wonder, then, that Helen comes to be admired by the Indians of San Ildefonso Pueblo. After telling Facundo about a strange dream, he takes her to a kiva, and the meaning of her dream is revealed by its symbolic architecture:

> In a flash she saw it all. The kiva, the whole multi-world universe, was at the same time the body of man. The whole of Creation already existed in him, and what he called an Emergence or a round of evolution was but his own expanded awareness of it. Once again with ecstatic intuition she glimpsed what she really was. Constellations ringed her head and waist; planets and stars gleamed on her fingers; the womb-worlds of all life pulsed within her. [62]

Since a kiva reconciles all opposites (see *Masked Gods*, 421), Helen's precognitive dream of it connotes her participation in the reconciliation to the point of a mutual embodiment of all parts of the universe. The dream reinforces her original experience of totality, and the bowl incident, the next of her psychic experiences to be dramatized, both consolidates her sense of a timeless reality and brings into focus the redemptive nature of Emergence.

In. one of the most powerful passages in the novel, Helen moves through three-dimensional time of past, present, and future to atonement with eternity. She has unearthed a piece of pottery on which is the thumb print of a Navawi'i woman (i.e., a woman from a local tribe of perhaps a thousand years ago) at the same time that wild geese in a V-formation fly overhead. A psychic experience results:

> At that instant it happened again: the strange sensation as of a cataclysmic faulting of her body, a fissioning of her spirit, and with it the instantaneous fusion of everything about her into one undivided, living whole. In unbroken continuity the microscopic life-patterns in the seeds of fallen cones unfolded into great pines. Her fingers closed over the splotch of clay on the bowl in her arms just as the Navawi'i woman released her own,

without their separation of centuries. She could feel the enduring mist cooling and moistening a thousand dry summers. The
mountain peaks stood firm against time. Eternity flowed in the
river below. . . . And all this jelling of life and time into a composite now took place in that single instant when the wedge of
wild geese hurtled past her — hurtled so swiftly that centuries
of southward migrations, generations of flocks, were con-
densed into a single plumed serpent with its flat reptilian head
outstretched, feet drawn back up, and a solitary body feather
displaced by the wind, which seemed to be hanging immobile
above her against the gray palimpsest of the sky. [124-25]

While the passage glances only figuratively at the fission-fusion experiments of
nuclear technology, the allusion to the plumed serpent, Quetzalcoatl, under-
scores Helen's experience of timelessness as the principle of all Creation and
the theme of all world religions: in Waters' interpretation, "the agonizing
redemption of matter by spirituality" and "the transfiguration of man into
god" (*Mexico Mystique*, 126). As the feather is arriving as a symbolic annunci-
ation of the way of redemption for humankind, the mythic Woman at Otowi
Crossing assumes the role of the Plumed Serpent, that of a Redeemer.[19] From
this moment, the nature of Helen's visions is shifted out of its initiating and
consolidating phase into an apocalyptic and synchronistic phase, and she herself is authorized, in the fullness of achieved identity, to suffer the anguish of
the forces of death and destruction in order to light the way to rebirth.

The mushroom incident and the candle nightmare illustrate this trend.
Once, while Helen and Jack are walking in the woods, they find a monstrous
mushroom, and Jack boots it into the air as Helen screams:

At that instant it happened. With all the minutely registered
detail of a slow-motion camera, and in a preternatural silence,
she saw the huge and ugly mushroom cap rise slowly in the air.
Unfolding gently apart, its torn and crumpled blades opening
like the gills of a fish, the fragmented pieces revolved as if in
a slow boil revealing a glimpse of chlorine yellow, a splotch of
brown and delicate pink. Deliberately it rose straight into the
air above the walls of the canyon, its amorphous parts balloon-
ing into a huge mass of porous gray. The stem below seemed to

rise to rejoin it; then, shattered and splintered, it settled slowly back to earth. . . . Now again she screamed. Crouching down in terror, she vainly covered her head with her arms against the rain of its malignant spores. Countless millions, billions of spores invisibly small as bacteria radiated down around her. They whitened the blades of grass, shriveled the pine needles, contaminated the clear stream, sank into the earth. Nor was this the end of the destruction and death they spread. For this malignant downpour of spores was also a rain of venomous sperm which rooted itself in still living seed cells to distort and pervert their natural, inherent life forms. There was no escape, now or ever, save by the miracle of a touch. [173]

Helen registers this experience while she is still ignorant of its synchronistic, deadly equivalent as atomic mushroom cloud. Similarly, she is prescient but untutored when her dream of a candle visits her just before the bombing of Hiroshima:

Then one night she had awakened screaming. It was as if everything, house, mountains, the world, the heavens, was enveloped in one brilliant apocalyptic burst of fire. . . . How horrible it was! That long narrow candle with a wick on top casting a tiny radiance. Then the wick suddenly erupted into flame, touching off a monstrous explosion that enveloped earth and sky, the whole world in a fiery flame. . . . Her dream had been more than a hellish illusion, but not another break-through like the first she'd experienced so long ago. That had opened to her the one creative wholeness with all its peace and plenitude. This last ghastly dream-vision, for all its overpowering brilliance, had been impacted with something negative, destructive, evil. [204]

Her visions of creative wholeness now countered by visions of apocalyptic destruction, Helen becomes the scale in which the forces of life and death are weighed in precarious balance.

The narrative art of *Otowi* tilts that balance in favor of life. It is of the utmost interest to observe how Waters goes about the business of validating the authenticity of Helen's emergence. For Waters knows exactly how large a stone he is casting into the shallow pond of modern civilization. In raising Helen to the Woman, to the level of transfiguring myth, he is also, as I have previously noted, careful to raise the possible objections. Just as in *Romeo and Juliet*, for example, we are convinced about love's beauty because we are given the cynical Nurse and Mercutio to set our threshold doubts at rest, so in *Otowi* our conviction of Helen's health and wisdom is heightened because we are given a cast that includes "tough-minded" characters who measure her for us but in the final analysis are themselves measured and usually found wanting. Emily Chalmers is one of these. Always guided by the rational and scientific assumptions of archaeology and anthropology, Emily disdainfully recalls her mother as having "come from a middle-class family distinctly commonplace compared to the Chalmers" and as having "had no advantages and little education" (36). But this certified expert on the Indians is frightened by the primitivism of naked Navajos during a fire ceremony, is disturbed by the hoofbeats of a wild stallion, and considers the Indian myth of Emergence not as a parable of the evolutionary journey of mankind but as the literal record of ancient migratory routes. In a fit of narcissistic rage, Emily aborts her child, and the sterility of her life thus subverts her opinions about Helen.

Another and tougher character is Jack Turner. This honest newspaper editor and reporter loves Helen and is himself lovable, so when he scouts her mystical experiences as the result of a mental breakdown, he clearly represents a majority opinion in American culture and is doing the "right" thing by trying to lure Helen to the couch of a Freudian analyst. But Turner's limitations are revealed in a number of ways: his love of Western Americana is tainted with nostalgia, symptomatic of his addiction to thinking in terms of linear time (the Chile Line railroad a symbol here); he has a habit of doing harm through good intentions, such as when he helps Emily to find an abortionist; and he lugs around his own repressed guilt for having fathered an illegitimate daughter with an Indian woman. At the end of the novel he confesses to Meru, an investigator of psychic phenomena, that he has considered destroying Helen's *Secret Journal* because he feared it was the "product of an unbalanced mind" (312). Even though he has made some amends in life by setting up his daughter in a New York apartment, Turner's interest in promoting Helen's legend makes it doubtful that he ever understood her at all, for she has no wish for celebrity status or to impose her will on others. Of those closest to her, then, only Facundo initially and Gaylord finally comprehend her and feel compassion for a person visited by all the joys and terrors of the unseen life. One might think that an old Indian cacique and an atomic physicist would present the most formidable obstacles to acceptance of a mystic who is a white woman. Accept her they do, however, because each in his own way considers as valid Helen's emergence.

Further validation is accomplished through techniques of counterpointing and of witness bearing.

In American literature, structural, symbolic, and thematic counterpointing traditionally leads to simplistic juxtapositions of individual and society, nature and civilization, intuition and reason, timelessness and temporality, and the like. *Huckleberry Finn* and *Go Down, Moses*, for example, are developed by counterpointing, and the characters of Huck Finn and Ike McCaslin, once exposed to experience of absolutes, are isolated in the ideal. But Huck's idyll on the river and Ike's initiating encounters with wilderness and the bear represent nostalgic and negative reinforcements of American pastoralism; that is, the dream of a better way of life is seen by Twain and by Faulkner as doomed, as powerless to link past with present, individual with society. *The Woman at Otowi Crossing* breaks with this tradition by means of a reconciliation of opposites at "the still point of the turning world," as Eliot in his *Four Quartets* famously described this interplay.[20] Living at the "crossing" between counterpointed territories (Los Alamos versus San Ildefonso Pueblo), cultures (modern-scientific versus primal-mythopoetic), psychic polarities (rational consciousness versus unconscious), values (materialistic versus humanistic-ecological), and rituals (science with laboratory rituals enforced by a priesthood of intellectuals versus mysticism with tribal rituals enforced by a priesthood of hierophants), Helen dissolves differences by superseding them, in herself, in a higher state of awareness. She seems to be isolated, like the classic American boy-man protagonists; unlike them, however, as a Chorus figure remarks, she is at the hub of time:

> "She had it all right, a glimpse of the universal whole.
>
> "What a spot she was in to receive it! At the birth place of the oldest civilization in America and the newest. Probably in no other area in the world were juxtaposed so closely the Indian drum and the atom smasher, all the values of the prehistoric past

and the atomic future. A lonely woman in a remote spot with few friends, she felt herself at the hub of time." [179]

Instead of being an outcast, exile, or rebel, Helen becomes an open individual, and her openness will, through its power, open society to transformation.

Counterpointing is a valid way of seeing opposites as two sides of the same coin, *if* contrasting images and symbols are meaningfully connected. They are in *Otowi* through the myth of Emergence. The reader of this novel not only has to question his or her habit of categorizing situations as either-or, but also has to participate in the myth of the Woman in order to perceive that it is *our* myth and that in judging her in her mythic role we are in effect evaluating life and death forces in our own spheres of being. We can understand well enough the contrast of a kiva and a nuclear reactor, though it's unlikely we've actually seen either one, but once we've synthesized these images as representing energies, we are no longer ignoring the esoteric and unconscious forces but *admitting* these to consciousness. And that is a pointer to Emergence. On the one hand, the sun is associated with creativity, fertility, Facundo (as sun-priest), the face of Gaylord's mother, the temple at Mesa Verde, the plumed serpent and rhythmic order; on the other hand, the sun is associated with atomic and thermonuclear destruction, the power of the sun having been usurped. Once we recognize that the sun has both constructive and destructive power, we have increased our moral awareness of the necessity of controlling excessive human intervention in the processes of a primal source. And that is a pointer to Emergence, too. Chronological time imagery links the Chile Line's whistle, Turner's guilty memories, and nuclear-test countdowns, whereas the imagery of eternity links stones, mountains, pools, circles, kachina forces, magnetic fields, a cooking pot, Earth, ancient America, and the Mother Goddess in her archetypal aspect as the Woman. When we perceive spiritual reality, it is then possible for us to be aware of living in a world of linear time, yet capable of experiencing the timelessness of an eternal reality of which we are a part. Our consciousness is then experienced as moving, rather than fixed.[21] And that is also a pointer to Emergence. In sum, life and death forces in *Otowi* both oppose each other and interact, and our "explanation" of the interaction turns out to be a mode of mythic consciousness.

Otowi has the power — and *power* is an oft-repeated word at the heart of this novel — to unsettle our sense of the self in its relationship to an "external" world and to recall us to a deeper mode of awareness beneath this self-consciousness which remains mythic in its overall patterns. The dualism of subjectivity and objectivity is not given with the human condition. What *is* given with the human condition, in the words of Falck, "may be an integrated mode of vision which comprises both the perceptual and the subjective or spiritual, and which we can recapture from the viewpoint of a later cultural stage only through a unifying and metaphorical effort of poetic imagination."[22] There is, so to speak, a mode of vision which accommodates as self-validating the emergence of Helen Chalmers.

Helen herself bears witness to her experience in the excerpts from her *Secret Journal* (1, 145-46, 250, 314) that frame the novel as prologue and epilogue and also appear at the novel's approximate midpoint, like a fulcrum by means of which vital powers are exercised. The myth she reveals is not dogmatically privileged, as would occur in the approach of traditional religion, and the questions of truth have not been prejudged. Like a piece of music, the novel gives us an immediate presence and presentation of ontological meaning, and the truth or satisfyingness of myth remains open to critical question. Helen questions it too; the fragments of her journal are not reiterations of her mystical experiences (though by implication these form part of an undisplayed journal) but philosophical reflections upon the meaning of the experiences. The reflections, moreover, are addressed to Turner in a spirit of love and bewilderment: "*I don't know, Jack. I don't know why this happened to me when it did*" (1, italics in original). To her, Emergence is "*a normal, natural experience that eventually comes to every one of us*," the import of which is that "*we're not separate and alone*" but "*part of one vast interconnected, living, conscious whole*" (146, italics in original). Moreover, psychic forces, "vast projections from the soul of humanity," have "the cosmic authority" (250) to deter nuclear war. The key passage of the journal, however, is not conveyed in the style of argumentation but in that of exaltation:

> So all these scribbled pages, Jack, are to help you understand that
> an awakening or Emergence, as the Indians call it, is more than
> a single momentary experience. It requires a slow painful process
> of realization and orientation. Just like a newborn child, you get
> it all and instantaneously in the blinding flash of that first break-
> through — the shattering impact of light after darkness, of freedom
> after confinement. Then the rub comes. The learning how to live

> *in this vast new world of awareness. The old rules of our cramped*
> *little world of appearances won't work. You have to learn new ones.*
> *The hard way, too, because everything you've known takes on new*
> *dimensions and meanings. This process of awakening with new*
> *awareness, a new perspective on everything about you, of perceiving*
> *the 'spherical geometry of the complete rounded moment' as Gaylord*
> *once called it — this is the wonderful experience I've been going*
> *through. . . . So when your turn comes, Jack, don't be afraid. Be*
> *glad! It's our greatest experience, our mysterious voyage of discovery*
> *into the last unknown, man's only true adventure. . . .* [314, italics
> in original]

The passage is a summation of the process already dramatized in the novel as a whole: realization and orientation of the inner self are the dynamics of characterization in a novel which must break with conventional form in order to be a disclosure or revelation of the true nature of the world in which we live, or at least of a meaningful world. It has been meaningful to Helen Chalmers, and her hard-won exultation is the song of life.

We are also given the testimony of ten individuals who have a wide range of responses to Helen. Most of these individuals are interviewed by an unidentified omniscient narrator. The interviews, interspersed throughout the present time of the novel, are "flashforwards"[23] (most take place in the future) effecting a sense that three-dimensional time (past, present, future) is an illusion from which few escape. Some of those interviewed are major characters in the novel — Emily (35-38; also author of a letter, 152-53), Turner (58-59), and Gaylord (73-74, 269-72; also author of reminiscences, 309-11) — while some are characters whose roles are minor or whose only appearance in the novel is through the interview — Dr. Gottman, Freudian psychologist in California, who rejects Jungian ideas as occult and considers Helen's "case" to be abnormal and morbid (132-34); Kaminsky or Kerenski, New York bookseller specializing in mysticism, who believes in the authenticity of Helen's experience (179-80); Alice Person, conventional Chicago matron once resident at Los Alamos, who is offended by Helen's lack of vanity as a "psychic" (207-09); Verna Taylor, shopkeeper in Cuernavaca, who discredits Emily's character and academic pretensions (241-43); Guy Alvord, big-time media reporter, who has popularized Helen's legend and who reveals Turner's self-interest in the same promotion (272-74); Milton P. Jasper, former political campaign manager now a Washington executive, who attests to Helen's power in transforming Throckmorton from a dangerous demagogue to a philanthropist (293-96); and M. Meru, New York authority on psychic phenomena, who accepts Helen's *Secret Journal* as the most complete record of a valid mystical experience in modern times (312-14).

Taken together, these ten characters form a Chorus with differing viewpoints. Emily, Turner, Gottman, and Alvord are dubious witnesses; Person, Taylor, and Jasper are a mixed lot; Kaminsky, Gaylord, and Meru are authoritative, Gaylord because he has mystical experiences of his own, including a telepathic "witnessing" of Helen's "death and transfiguration" (311), Meru because he has the privileged last word about her in the epilogue, understands the significance of myth, and is himself mythical. M. Meru, as his name implies, signifies Mt. Meru in Hindu and Buddhist cosmography, a metaphysical hub of the universe whose final judgment of Helen's spirituality is clearly to be heeded. Frances M. Malpezzi summarizes Meru's authority:

> Standing at his office window in his blue serge suit, enhaloed
> by fluttering white birds, bearing the name of a sacred moun-
> tain of Eastern mythology, Meru represents the amalgamation
> of reason, Christian mysticism, harmony with nature, Eastern
> mysticism. He is a synthesis of the sacred and the profane. As
> the *axis mundi* connecting the secular world with the divine, he
> authenticates the Emergence of Helen Chalmers.[24]

Malpezzi believes that Meru is central to *Otowi*. Although I believe that he should more properly be considered as a coda to the novel, introduced after the natural conclusion to its movement, I agree to the extent that Meru joins Gaylord in placing Helen's experience in the perspective of myth. For it is Gaylord, we recall, who, at the instant of a thermonuclear explosion over the Pacific, knows that Helen has become assimilated to indescribable light, her life energy suddenly liberated as a symbol of absolute inner unassailability and of life that survives death — a resurrection like a new sunrise.[25]

There is no actual death scene (though I have called it that); rather, there is a quiet vigil, a tableau, in which Emily, Turner, and Facundo wait for Helen's death. The focus is on Facundo, who is outside in the chill of night. Suddenly a band of seven deer becomes visible beyond the fence. To Facundo, the deer are her emblem, their celestial counterparts in the Pleiades, and this symbolic amalgamation of a living universe provides an eerie sensation of an Absolute Consciousness interpenetrating time and space. When Facundo taps a drum and sings a death song, the deer bound away, then slowly turn about, "and with quick delicate steps" (306) come back to wait at the fence. This tableau of the deer calls up various associations, all with the same meaning. As the Pleiades, they are glimpsed as the highest stage beyond the ascendant architecture of the kiva. Buddhism postulates seven stages for evolutionary development, the seventh stage ending the Road of Life, with man now divine and perfected. Whereas Western medical science recognizes seven physical centers ascending upward from the base of the spine to the brain, Eastern mysticism postulates seven centers (chakras) of psychic energy, with the seventh and most important chakra lying just below the crown of the head and regarded as the seat of universal consciousness. In Kundalini yoga the serpent power rises from the lowest physical center to the highest psychic center, pictured on Buddhist temples as the horned antelope. What all these representations of seven have in common is emergence to divinity.[26] But it is the superb feeling and decorum of the tableau with Facundo and the deer that may surpass its esoteric meaning and accomplish in one powerful image more than the reflective testimony of characters accomplishes. Waters approaches the mystery of death as John Donne does the mystery of love in "A Valediction: Forbidding Mourning":

> Our two souls therefore, which are one,
> Though I must go, endure not yet
> A breach, but an expansion,
> Like gold to airy thinness beat.[27]

The quick delicate steps of Helen's deer foretell a death which will not bring about a separation from life but a triumphant expansion of her essential spirit into the golden radiance of a larger sky.

Notes and Citations

The authors in this collection have used a variety of styles and methods for documentation, making conformity to a single style such as M.L.A. or Chicago too difficult a task to undertake. Consequently, notes and citations appear here as in the original manuscripts. The Tanner bibliography can be consulted for works by Waters up to the mid-1980s. Source materials since then are readily available, and most of Waters' works remain in print.

-The Editors

John Nizalowski: "Preface"

Blackburn, Alexander. Interview with John Nizalowski. Taos, New Mexico June 28, 2003.

—. *A Sunrise Brighter Still: The Visionary Novels of Frank Waters*. Athens: Swallow Press/Ohio University Press, 1991.

Deloria, Jr., Vine. "Frank Waters: Prophet and Explorer." In *Frank Waters: Man and Mystic*, edited by Vine Deloria, Jr. (Athens: Swallow Press/ Ohio University Press, 1993) 166-173.

Kishbaugh, Alan. Interview with John Nizalowski. Los Angeles, California. June 14, 2007.

Kraft, James. *Who is Witter Brynner?: A Biography*. Albuquerque: University of New Mexico Press, 1995.

Rudnick, Lois Palken, *Mabel Dodge Luhan: New Woman, New Worlds*. Albuquerque: University of New Mexico Press, 1984.

Waters, Barbara. Interview with John Nizalowski. Arroyo Seco, New Mexico. July 2, 2003.

Waters, Frank. Interview with John Nizalowski. Arroyo Seco, New Mexico. July 22, 1989.

— . *The Lizard Woman*. Athens: Swallow Press, 1930. Rpt. 1995.

— . *Masked Gods*. Athens: Swallow Press, 1950. Rpt. 1984.

— . "A New Look at an Old World View." Lecture. College of Santa Fe. July 29, 1989.

— . "Notes on Los Angeles." In *Pure Waters: Frank Waters and the Quest for the Cosmic*, edited by Barbara Waters (Athens: Swallow Press/Ohio University Press, 2002) 22-30.

— . *Of Time and Change*. Denver: MacMurray & Beck, 1998.

— . *Pike's Peak: A Family Saga*. Chicago: Swallow Press, 1971.

Thomas J. Lyon. "Introduction"
From Thomas J. Lyon, ed., *A Frank Waters Reader: A Southwestern Life in Writing* (Athens: Swallow Press/Ohio University Press, 2000) xi-xxviii.

Vine Deloria, Jr. "Frank Waters: Prophet and Explorer"
From Vine Deloria, Jr. in *Frank Waters: Man and Mystic*, edited by Vine Deloria, Jr. (Athens: Swallow Press//Ohio University Press, 1993) 166-73.

1. Frank Waters, *The Man Who Killed The Deer* (Athens: Swallow Press/Ohio University Press, 1985) 133.

2. Frank Waters, *Masked Gods: Navaho and Pueblo Ceremonialism* (Albuquerque: University of New Mexico Press, 1950) 271.

3. Ibid., 450.

4. Ibid., 457.

5. John G. Neilhardt, *Black Elk Speaks* (Lincoln: University of Nebraska Press,1979) 4.

⸺⸻⸺

John R. Milton. "The Question of Frank Waters' Mysticism"
In John R. Milton, *The Novel in The American West* (Lincoln: University of Nevada Press, 1980) 264-67, 269, 271-74.

⸺⸻⸺

Charles L. Adams. "On Pike's Peak and the Life of Frank Waters"
In *Writers' Forum* 11 (1985) 195-208.

⸺⸻⸺

Quay Grigg. "Masking the Self"
In Vine Deloria, Jr., ed., *Frank Waters: Man and Mystic* (Athens: Swallow Press/Ohio University Press, 1993) 156-65.

⸺⸻⸺

Alexander Blackburn. "The Interior Country"
In *The Interior Country: Stories of the Modern West*, edited by Alexander Blackburn with Craig Lesley and Jill Landem (Athens: Swallow Press/ Ohio University Press, 1987) ix-xvii.

1. Theodore Roethke, "The Rose," in Theodore Roethke, *The Far Field* (Garden City, N.Y.: Doubleday & Company Anchor Books, 1971) 31.

2. Waters' novel, *Pike's Peak* (1971), is a revision of a trilogy of his novels, *The Wild Earth's Nobility* (1935), *Below Grass Roots* (1937), and *The Dust Within the Rock* (1940).

3. See Thomas J. Lyon, *"The Man Who Killed the Deer," Writers Forum 11* (1985) 180-194.

4. A psychological theme of rightness with the land is dramatized in many of the novels of Frank Waters but especially in *People of the Valley, The Man Who Killed the Deer*, and *Pike's Peak*.

5. Wallace Stegner, *The Sound of Mountain Water: The Changing American West* (Garden City, N.Y.: Doubleday & Company, Inc., 1964) 10.

6. Gerald W. Haslam, "Western Writers and the National Fantasy," in *Western Writing*, edited by Gerald W. Haslam (Albuquerque: University of New Mexico Press, 1974) 4.

7. Genocide defined as the forced relocation of native people is studied in Jerry Kammer, *The Second Long Walk: The Navajo-Hopi Land Dispute*, Albuquerque: University of New Mexico Press, 1980.

8. For this summary view of tragedy I am indebted to John Wain, *The Living World of Shakespeare* (Harmondsworth: Penguin Books, 1966) 163-64, 167.

9. See Peter Wiley and Robert Gottlieb, *Empires in the Sun: The Rise of the New American West*, Tucson: University of Arizona Press, 1985.

10. Frederick Jackson Turner, *The Frontier in American History* (New York: Holt, Rinehart and Winston, 1962) 212-13. Turner introduced his thesis at a meeting in Chicago in 1893, just three years after Hotchkiss guns, firing a shell a second, massacred a group of Indians at Wounded Knee (a fact never mentioned by Turner). According to the thesis, the American character was formed on the frontier over a period of hundreds of years of in-migration, by people motivated by the existence of "free" lands. By 1893, however, free lands no longer existed in the West to give individuals a chance to improve their lot in life. Retiring from Harvard in 1924, Turner moved to Pasadena, California, where he died in 1932, just a few years before completion of Hoover Dam – symbol both of the marriage of public money with free enterprise and of the rise of a metropolitan West that has destroyed the frontier.

11. On the relevance of Ancient America to Modern America, see Frank Waters, *Masked Gods: Navaho and Pueblo Ceremonialism*, Albuquerque: University of New Mexico Press, 1950.

12. Roethke, *The Far Field*, 28.

13. Will Gatlin is the soul-searching protagonist in Edward Abbey's novel *Black Sun*.

14. Barry Lopez, "Winter Count 1973," in *The Interior Country*, 205.

Joseph Gordon. "Shining Mountains"
In *Rekindling the Inner Light: The Frank Waters Centennial*, edited by Barbara Waters (Taos/Tucson: Frank Waters Foundation Press, 2003) 117-27.

1. Frank Waters, *People of the Valley* (Athens: Swallow Press, 1984) 133-34.

2. Frank Waters, *The Man Who Killed The Deer* (Athens: Sage Books/Swallow Press, 1985) 80.

3. Frank Waters, *The Woman at Otowi Crossing* (Athens: Swallow Press, 1981) 32-33.

4. Ibid., 116.

5. Ibid.

6. Ibid.

7. Ibid.

8. Frank Waters, *Pike's Peak: A Family Saga* (Chicago: Swallow Press, 1971) 311-12.

9. Frank Waters, *Mountain Dialogues* (Athens: Swallow Press/Ohio University Press, 1981) 35.

10. Frank Waters, *The Colorado* (New York: Holt, Rinehart and Winston, 1974) 172-73.

11. Ibid., 188.

12. Waters, *Mountain Dialogues*, 135.

13. Frank Waters, *Midas of the Rockies* (Athens: Swallow Press/Ohio University Press, 1989) 106.

14. Waters, *Mountain Dialogues*, 36.

15. Waters, *Colorado*, 17.

16. Ibid.

17. Ibid., 18.

18. Waters, *Mountain Dialogues*, 50.

19. Waters, *Colorado*, 22.

20. Ibid., 22-23.

21. Ibid., xiii.

22. Waters, *Mountain Dialogues*, 48.

23. Waters, *Colorado*, 36.

24. Ibid., 40.

25. Waters, *Pike's Peak*, 191.

26. Waters, *Mountain Dialogues*, 49.

⟨⟩

John Nizalowski. "Frank Waters: Prophet of the Sixth World Consciousness"
In *Reading Under the Sign of Nature: New Essays in Ecocriticism*, edited by John Talmadge and Henry Harrington (Salt Lake City: The University of Utah Press, 2000) 148-62.

1. Frank Waters, *Masked Gods: Navajo and Pueblo Ceremonialism*. Athens: Swallow Press/Ohio University Press, 1989.

2. Alexander Blackburn, *A Sunrise Brighter Still: The Visionary Novels of Frank Waters*. Athens: Swallow Press/Ohio University Press, 1991.

3. Thomas J. Lyon, *Frank Waters*. New York: Twayne, 1973.

4. Charles L. Adams, "Frank Waters: Western Mystic," *Studies in Frank Waters* (1982) 1-2.

5. Frank Waters, *The Dust Within the Rock*. New York: Liveright, 1940.

6. Frank Waters, *Pike's Peak: A Family Saga*. Chicago: Swallow Press. 1971.

7. Frank Waters, *People of the Valley*. Chicago: Swallow Press, 1969.

8. Matthias Schubnell, "Toward the Sixth World: Frank Waters and the New Environmental Consciousness," *Studies in Frank Waters* 13 (1991) 1-21.

9. Frank Waters, *The Man Who Killed the Deer*. Chicago: Swallow Press, 1970.

10. Thomas J. Lyon, "Does the Land Speak? Frank Waters and the Southwest," in *Sundays in Tutt Library with Frank Waters*, edited by Katherine Scott Sturdevant (Colorado Springs: The Hulbert Center for Southwestern Studies, The Colorado College, 1988) 13-25.

11. Frank Waters, *The Woman at Otowi Crossing*. Athens: Swallow/Ohio University Press, 1987.

12. Frances M. Malpezzi, "The Emergence of Helen Chalmers," in *Women and Western American Literature*, edited by Helen Winter Stauffer and Susan J. Rosowski (Troy, N.Y.: Whitston Publishing, 1982) 100-133.

13. Frances M. Malpezzi, "Meru: the Voice of the Mountain," *South Dakota Review* 27: 2 (1989) 27-35.

14. Frank Waters, *The Colorado*. Athens: Swallow Press/Ohio University Press, 1984.

15. Frank Waters, *Mexico Mystique: The Coming Sixth World of Consciousness.* Chicago: Swallow Press, 1975.

16. Frank Waters, *Mountain Dialogues*. Athens: Swallow Press/Ohio University Press, 1981.

17. Frank Waters, *Pumpkin Seed Point: Being Within the Hopi.* Chicago: Swallow Press, 1969.

18. Frank Waters, "The Hopi Prophesy and the Chinese Dream: An Interview with Frank Waters by Tom Tarbet," *East/West* (May 1977) 52-64.

19. Vine Deloria, Jr., "Frank Waters: Prophet and Explorer," in *Frank Waters: Man and Mystic*, edited by Vine Deloria, Jr. (Athens: Swallow Press/Ohio University Press, 1993) 166-173.

20. Rudolfo Anaya, "Migrating Eagle," in *Frank Waters: Man and Mystic*, edited by Vine Deloria, Jr. (Athens: Swallow Press/Ohio University Press, 1993) 33-38.

Mathias Schubnell. "Toward the Sixth World: Frank Waters and the New Environmental Consciousness"
In *Studies in Frank Waters* 13 (1991) 11-21.

Berry, Thomas. *The Dream of the Earth*. San Francisco: Sierra Club, 1988.

Lyon, Thomas J. *Frank Waters*. New York: Twayne, 1973.

Southwestern Writers, edited by John F. Crawford, William Balassi, and Annie O. Eysturoy (Albuquerque: University of New Mexico Press, 1990) 15-25.

Waters, Frank. *People of the Valley*. Chicago: Swallow, 1969.

—. *The Man Who Killed the Deer*. New York: Pocket Books, 1975.

—. *Mountain Dialogues*. Chicago: Swallow, 1981.

—. "This Sacred Land," *Arizona Highways* (Nov. 1987) 38-44.

—. "Frank Waters: Interview by Charles Adams," in *This Is About Vision: Interviews With Southwestern Writers*, edited by John F. Crawford, William Balassi, and Annie O. Eysturoy (Albuquerque: University of New Mexico Press, 1990) 15-25.

❧

Vine Deloria, Jr. "Reflections from a Dusty Road: Frank Waters, Time, and the Indians"

In *Rekindling the Inner Light: The Frank Waters Centennial*, edited by Barbara Waters (Taos/Tucson: Frank Waters Foundation Press, 2003) 37-47.

1. Frank Waters, *The Man Who Killed the Deer* (Athens: Swallow Press/ Ohio University Press, 1985) 40.

2. Ibid., 18.

3. Frank Waters, *Book of the Hopi*. New York: Penguin Books, 1977.

4. Frank Waters, *Masked Gods: Navaho and Pueblo Ceremonialism* (Albuquerque: University of New Mexico Press, 1950) 432.

5. Waters, *Deer*, 113.

6. Waters, *Masked Gods*, 434-35.

7. Waters, *Deer*, 59.

❧

Alexander Blackburn. "The Mythology of the Planet"

In *Rekindling the Inner Light: The Frank Waters Centennial*, edited by Barbara Waters (Taos/Tucson: Frank Waters Foundation Press, 2003) 93-104.

1. Joseph Campbell, *The Power of Myth* (New York: Doubleday, 1988) 22.

2. Michel de Montaigne, *The Complete Essays*, trans. M. A. Screech (New York: Penguin Books, 1991) 122.

3. Frank Waters, "The Regional Imperative," in *Sundays in Tutt Library with Frank Waters* (Colorado Springs: The Colorado College, 1988) 50. The essay is reprinted in *Pure Waters* (Athens: Swallow Press/Ohio University Press, 2002) 121-28.

4. Pierre Teilhard de Chardin, *The Future of Man*, trans. Norman Denny (New York: Harper Torchbooks, 1969) 124.

5. Sir Julian Huxley, "Introduction" to *The Phenomenon of Man*, by Pierre Teilhard de Chardin (New York: Harper Torchbooks, 1961) 22.

6. Ibid.

7. Teilhard de Chardin, *Future of Man*, 57.

8. Frank Waters, *Mexico Mystique: The Coming Sixth World of Consciousness* (Athens: Swallow Press/Ohio University Press, 1989) 283.

9. Frank Waters, *Mountain Dialogues* (Athens: Swallow Press/Ohio University Press, 1981) 7.

10. Ibid., 69.

11. Joseph Campbell, *The Masks of God: Creative Mythology* (London: Secker and Warburg, 1968) 6-7.

12. Ibid., 7. Italics in original.

꧁ ꧂

John Nizalowski. "Borderlands and Transfiguration: Desert Mysticism in Frank Waters' *The Lizard Woman*"
In *Interdisciplinary Studies in Literature and Environment* 13.2 (Summer 2006) 93-101.

Blackburn, Alexander, *A Sunrise Brighter Still: The Visionary Novels of Frank Waters*. Athens: Swallow Press/Ohio University Press, 1991.

Chávez, Denise, "Passion, Obsession, and Enlightenment in the Desert: Frank Waters' *The Yogi of Cockroach Court* and *The Lizard Woman*." In *Rekindling the Inner Light*, edited by Barbara Waters (Taos: The Frank Waters Foundation Press, 2003) 138-151.

Conrad, Joseph, "The Secret Sharer" in *The Portable Conrad*, edited by Morton Dauwen Zabel (New York: Viking, 1947) 648-699.

Jung, Carl, *The Portable Jung*, edited by Joseph Campbell, New York: Penguin, 1971.

Lyon, Thomas J, *Frank Waters*. New York: Twayne, 1973.

Manchester, John, "Frank Waters," *South Dakota Review* 15.3 (1977) 73-80.

Plec, Emily, "Frank Waters' Ecofeminist Sensibility." In *Rekindling the Inner Light*, edited by Barbara Waters, (Taos: The Frank Waters Foundation Press, 2003) 167-182.

Waters, Frank, "The Changing and Unchangeable West." In *Growing up Western*, edited by Clarus Backes. (New York: Harper Perennial, 1997) 193-220.

—. *The Dust Within the Rock*. Athens: Swallow Press/Ohio University Press, 2002.

—. *The Lizard Woman*. Athens: Swallow Press/Ohio University Press, 1995.

—. *Pumpkin Seed Point*. Athens: Swallow Press/Ohio University Press, 1981.

<hr />

Denise Chávez. "Passion, Obsession, and Enlightenment in the Desert: Frank Waters' *The Yogi of Cockroach Court* and *The Lizard Woman*"
In *Rekindling the Inner Light: The Frank Waters Centennial*, edited by Barbara Waters (Taos/Tucson: Frank Waters Foundation Press, 2003) 138-51.

1. Frank Waters, *Mountain Dialogues* (Athens: Swallow Press/Ohio University Press, 1981), 91.

2. Ibid., 105.

3. The Four Noble Truths: *duhka* (suffering) exists; *duhka* has an identifiable cause; that cause can be terminated; the means by which that cause may be terminated. The Noble Eightfold Path: right understanding; right thought, right speech; right action; right livelihood; right effort; right mindfulness; right concentration.

4. Frank Waters, *The Yogi of Cockroach Court* (New York: Rinehart, 1947) 26.

5. Ibid., 25.

6. Ibid., 75.

7. Frank Waters, *The Lizard Woman* (Austin: Thorp Springs Press, 1984) 76.

8. Waters, *Yogi of Cockroach Court*, 113.

9. Ibid., 218-19.

10. Ibid., 268.

11. Ibid., 275.

12. Waters, *Lizard Woman*, vi.

13. Ibid., vii.

14. Ibid., vi.

15. Ibid., 7.

16. Ibid., 26.

17. Ibid., 47-48.

18. Ibid., 90.

19. Ibid., v.

⸺⸙⸺

Linda Lizut Helstern. "Mixedbloods: Stereotypes and Inversions in *The Yogi of Cockroach Court*"
In *Rekindling the Inner Light: The Frank Waters Centennial*, edited by Barbara Waters (Taos/Tucson: Frank Waters Foundation Press, 2003) 152-62.

1. Terence A. Tanner, *Frank Waters: A Bibliography* (Glenwood, Illinois: Meyerbooks, 1983) 93.

2. Ibid., 91.

3. Frank Waters, *The Yogi of Cockroach Court* (Chicago: Swallow Press, 1972) 21.

4. Ibid., 254.

5. Frank Waters, *Masked Gods: Navaho and Pueblo Ceremonialism* (Albuquerque: University of New Mexico Press, 1950) 49.

6. Waters, *Yogi of Cockroach Court*, 83.

7. Ibid., 87.

8. Ibid.

9. Gloria Anzuldua, *Borderlands/La Frontera: The New Mestiza* (San Francisco: Aunt Lute, 1987) 29.

10. Waters, *Yogi of Cockroach Court*, 19.

11. Ibid., 24.

12. Ibid., 19.

13. Ibid., 29.

14. Ibid., 30-31.

15. Ibid., 185.

16. Frank Waters, *The Colorado* (New York: Holt, Rinehart and Winston, 1974) 269.

17. Waters, *Yogi of Cockroach Court*, 69.

18. Deborah Miranda, "Native American Women's Love Poetry and Erotics," *MLA Newsletter* 34: 1 (Spring 2002) 7.

19. Mourning Dove (Hum-Ishu-Ma), *Cogwea: The Half Blood: A Depiction of the Great Montana Cattle Range* (Lincoln: University of Nebraska Press, 1981) 15.

20. Waters, *Yogi of Cockroach Court*, 24-25.

21. Ibid., 64.

22. Ibid., 66.

23. Ibid., 82.

24. Ibid., 188.

25. Ibid., 187.

26. Ibid., 186, 266.

27. Ibid., 274.

28. Ibid., 47.

29. Frank Waters, *The Man Who Killed the Deer* (New York: Farrar and Rinehart, 1942) 246.

30. Waters, *Yogi of Cockroach Court*, 64.

31. Ibid., 65.

32. Ibid., 109.

33. Ibid., 83.

34. Ibid., 133.

35. Ibid., 83.

36. Ibid., 12.

37. Frank Waters, *Pike's Peak: A Family Saga* (Chicago: Swallow Press, 1971) 726-27.

José R. Martinez. "El Abuelo of Hispanic Literary Characters"
In *Rekindling the Inner Light: The Frank Waters Centennial*, edited by Barbara Waters (Taos/Tucson: Frank Waters Foundation, 2003) 17-24.

1. Frank Waters, *People of the Valley* (Athens: Swallow Press, 1984) 159.

2. Ibid.,116-117.

3. Ibid., 156-157.

4. Ibid., 157-158.

5. Ibid. 158.

6. Ibid.

7. Frank Waters, *Mountain Dialogues* (Athens: Swallow Press/Ohio University Press, 1981) 54.

⊸≫⊶

Inés Dölz-Blackburn. "Imagery and Motifs in Frank Waters' *People of the Valley*"
In *Studies in Frank Waters 7* (1985) 57-73.

1. The edition I consulted for this study is Frank Waters, *People of the Valley*, (Chicago: Swallow Press, 1969).

2. A complete newcomer in the immense and complex Waters field, I soon came to realize the delicate nature of Waters' prose and ideas. Although some of the works listed in the bibliography are not directly quoted, they were all fundamentals in showing me "a way."

3. In reading the very favorable reviews of *People of the Valley* published in 1941–indebtedness to the excellent Terence A. Tanner, *Frank Waters: A Bibliography*, Glenwood, Ill., Meyerbooks, 1983, listing all the entries–I noticed that they fail to detect the poetry, mystery, and myth throughout the book and more or less give only, although enthusiastic, an over-simplistic appraisal (e.g., "a folk tale well taught" *Library Journal*). The possible exception is the review entitled "Engineer Reviews Engineer's Novel"–*Boston Transcript*, March 14, 1941, 2, in which the author refers to "a graphic tale of a portion of our Southwest unknown to most of us," to Waters as "a lover of humanity," his "earthy philosophy" in the text, the theme of "close relationship of man, the soil and the forces of change," and finally the "nonplused people" sustained by the "wisdom" of Maria del Valle.

4. Barbara Waters has taught *People of the Valley* for seven years to high school students in Tucson and states that, although the general appreciation of the book is enthusiastic, there are some problems with the understanding of the Hispanic way of being shown in the book–e.g., "love of the simple for the land"–and the acceptance of the colorful colloquial Spanish included ("Conversation with Barbara Waters," Tucson, March 26, 985). Even literary critics have this problem. Vernon Young bitterly criticizes the apparent contradiction in the presentation of Maria del Valle who may at times speak with "forensic elegance" (Young, 368) and

at other times might harangue her people calling them "Fools, burros" (Young, 441). I believe Young does not understand the idiosyncrasy of the Hispanic soul of the simple person who is "a chosen one," such as Maria del Valle, and who might combine timeless wisdom expressed conceptually at times with a pedestrian form of speaking: Don Quijote y Sancho, two sides of the Hispanic spirit. This quality I have been able to detect directly in my encounters with this type of Hispanic people –through long association with some people like Maria del Valle in my native country Chile and indirectly through my fifteen years in studying Hispanic literary folklore in Spain and Hispano America.

5. Some of the following implications have also been noted by Frances Malpezzi, "A Study of the Female Protagonist in Frank Waters' *People of the Valley* and Rudolfo Anaya's *Bless Me, Ultima,*" *South Dakota Review* 14: 2 (Summer, 1976) 104. On March 26, 1985, I visited the village of Mora, New Mexico, where the story takes place. I was rereading the book, and I wanted to compare my perspective with that of the artist. Just looking at nature I was able to grasp a glimpse of what Waters makes transparent and essential in his descriptions of boundless immensity and wild beauty. One Hispanic person to whom I addressed a question about *People of the Valley* informed me that Frank Waters was a fictitious name and that the *real* author of the book was someone called Rendon!

6. Maria is presented repeatedly rolling a cigarette, an act of authority of country women leaders who wish to assume "a macho role" (see pp. 120-148, 165, 176) and be respected.

7. It is "the moment" of Helen Chalmers in *The Woman at Otowi Crossing* (Chicago: Swallow Press, 1966) when she becomes one with the most hidden forces within herself and there is a fusion and diffusion (30, 67-68, 116).

8. He proves it in this book. He even has a keen control of colloquial Spanish. In a recent conversation, he affirmed so accurately that the Hispanic soul is the same from America to Chile after I told him that Maria del Valle also lives in the Chilean country and that I had frequently met her and observed her there along with her people (Tucson, March 27, 1985).

9. Roland F. Dickey in *New Mexico Village Arts* comments on the "old Chimayo sarapes reckoned among the most intricate examples of New Mexico weaving" (p. 112).

10. Miguel de Unamuno (1864-1936), a Basque writer, in *San Manuel Bueno, Martir*, a short story, develops a narration in which we also encounter a lake, mountains and "the people" led by a priest who does not believe but preaches Faith. The general feeling there, however, is that of disharmony, suffering, and agony. El Greco, a mystical 16th century Spanish painter, gives us in "View of Toledo" a spiritual setting analogous to the way I picture the one of "the blue valley."

<hr>

Thomas J. Lyon. "On *The Man Who Killed the Deer*"
In *Writers' Forum* 11 (1985) 180-94.

<hr>

Alexander Blackburn. "The Allegory of Emergence in *The Man Who Killed the Deer*"
In Alexander Blackburn, *A Sunrise Greater Still: The Visionary Novels of Frank Waters* (Athens: Swallow Press/Ohio University Press, 1991) 90-111.

1. Frank Waters, "*The Man Who Killed the Deer*: 30 Years Later," *New Mexico Magazine* 50 (January 1972) 17-20.

2. Joseph Campbell, *The Way of the Animal Powers* (London: Summerfield Press, 1983), 76.

3. Waters, "*The Man Who Killed the Deer*: 30 Years Later," 17.

4. Burton Rascoe, "Two Worlds in Conflict," *Saturday Review of Literature* (13 June 1942) 71.

5. "I had some vague idea while writing it [*Moby-Dick*], that the book was susceptible of an allegoric construction, & also that *parts* of it were–but the specialty of many of the particular subordinate allegories, were first

revealed to me, after reading Mr. Hawthorne's letter, which, without citing any particular examples, yet intimated the part-&-parcel allegoricalness of the whole." The quote is from Herman Melville's letter of 8 January 1852 to Sophia Hawthorne, cited in Edwin Honig, *Dark Conceit: The Making of Allegory* (New York: Oxford University Press, Galaxy Books, 1966) 193-94, italics in original.

6. A point made by Angus Fletcher, *Allegory: The Theory of a Symbolic Mode* (Ithaca: Cornell University Press, 1964) 73.

7. Martiniano may seem to some readers an unusual name for a Native American, as is the name Palemon. Whatever the source for these names, other than reality or imagination, Waters' choice of names sometimes heightens the effect of universality. This is especially true when a character named M. Meru in *Otowi* brings in associations with Mt. Meru, a metaphysical mountain in Hindu cosmography.

8. See Waters, "*The Man Who Killed the Deer*: 30 Years Later."

9. See Campbell, *The Way of the Animal Powers*, 129.

10. See Weston La Barre, *The Peyote Cult*, 4th ed., enl. (Hamden, Connecticut: Archon Books, 1975) xv-xvi, 228.

11. Jamake Highwater, *The Primal Mind: Vision and Reality in Indian America* (New York: Meridian Books, 1981) 135.

12. Fletcher, *Allegory*, 21.

13. Honig, *Dark Conceit*, 114.

14. The similarity between Waters' idea of Emergence and Jung's "individuation" is discussed by Christopher Hoy, "The Archetypal Transformation of Martiniano in *The Man Who Killed the Deer*," *South Dakota Review* 15 (1977) 51-57.

15. Waters was reading works by the mystic Georges Gurdjieff (1872?-1949) in the late 1930s, encouraged to do so by Mabel Dodge Luhan in Taos.

Although Waters had developed his idea of conscience prior to that time, he would have found a similar view of it in Gurdjieff's teaching, at the forefront of which is the contrast between morality, which is relative to time and place, and conscience, which is universal. In both Waters and Gurdjieff one finds the profound conception of conscience as a power in us that makes us sensitive to the workings of cosmic laws of interrelationship. See John Godolphin Bennett, *Gurdjieff: Making a New World* (London: Turnstone Books, 1973) 83-84, 257, 293, on Gurdjieff's concept of conscience.

16. Susanne K. Langer, *Philosophy in a New Key: A Study in the Symbolism of Reason, Rite, and Art*, 3rd ed. (Cambridge: Harvard University Press, 1963) 149. Langer's seminal work, first published in 1942, indicates the widespread interest at that time in literary symbolism.

17. Jack L. Davis views *Deer* as an "impressive forerunner of fiction ostensibly written from within the native consciousness" in "The Whorf Hypothesis and Native American Literature," *South Dakota Review* 14 (1976) 59-72. Although Waters himself had no intention of impersonating Native American "consciousness," Davis was not the last to find Waters guilty of such nonsense. For instance, Leslie A. Fielder in *The Return of the Vanishing American* (New York: Stein & Day, 1968) lumps *Deer* together with Oliver La Farge's *Laughing Boy* and condemns both for a "pretense of writing with the consciousness of Indians." Not only is Fielder's argument absurd, at least where *Deer* is concerned, but also it is inconsistent. The impersonation of Native American consciousness (if that's the word) in Ken Kesey's novel, *One Flew Over the Cuckoo's Nest*, is spared Fielder's scorn.

18. Martin Cyril D'Arcy, *The Sense of History: Secular and Sacred* (London: Faber & Faber, 1959) 33.

19. See Dorothy Lee, *Freedom and Culture* (Englewood Cliffs, N.J.: Prentice-Hall, 1959) 9-11, 20-24.

20. Page references to *The Man Who Killed the Deer* are to the readily available Pocket Books edition. Italics in original.

21. See Hightower, *The Primal Mind*, 69-74.

22. Henry James, *The Art of the Novel: Critical Prefaces* (New York: Charles Scribner's Sons, 1934) 45.

23. For some of the ideas and phrasings in this paragraph I am indebted to John Wain, *The Living World of Shakespeare* (Harmondsworth: Penguin Books, 1966) 163-68.

24. That *Deer* reflects some of the thinking in *Lizard Woman*, which Waters began to compose in 1926 if not sooner, strengthens the contention that he arrived early and independently at views parallel to Jung's.

25. See Carl G. Jung, "Answer to Job," in *The Portable Jung*, edited by Joseph Campbell (New York: Penguin Books, 1976) esp. 626-27.

26. Honig, *Dark Conceit*, 53.

<hr/>

Benjamin S. Lawson. "The Men Who Killed the Deer: Faulkner and Frank Waters"
In *Faulkner Journal* 18.1/2 (2002) 179-89

Anaya, Rudolfo A. "Migrating Eagle" in Vine Deloria, Jr., ed., *Frank Waters: Man and Mystic* (Athens: Swallow Press/Ohio University Press 1993) 33-38.

Blackburn, Alexander: *A Sunrise Brighter Still: The Visionary Novels of Frank Waters*. Athens: Swallow Press/Ohio University Press, 1991.

Blevins, Win. "A Tribute to *The Man Who Killed the Deer*" in Deloria, Frank Waters, 149-55.

Brinkmeyer, Robert H. Jr. *Remapping Southern Literature: Contemporary Southern Writers and the West*. Athens, Georgia: University of Georgia Press, 2000.

Carter, Forrest. *The Education of Little Tree*. Albuquerque: University of New Mexico Press, 1990.

Cather, Willa. *The Professor's House*. New York: Random House, 1973.

Crane, Hart. *The Complete Poems and Selected Letters and Prose of Hart Crane*, edited by Brom Weber, New York: Doubleday, 1966.

Dabney, Lewis M. *The Indians of Yoknapatawpha: A Study in Literature and History*. Baton Rouge: Louisiana State University Press, 1974.

Davis, Jack L., and June H. Davis. "Frank Waters and the Native American Consciousness," *Western American Literature* 9 (1974) 33-44.

Deloria, Vine, Jr., ed. *Frank Waters: Man and Mystic*. Athens: Swallow Press/ Ohio University Press, 1993.

Deloria, Vine, Jr. "Frank Waters: Prophet and Explorer" in Deloria, *Frank Waters*, 166-73.

Eastlake, William. "The Word Trader," in Deloria, *Frank Waters*, 3-5.

Faulkner, William. *Go Down, Moses*. 1952. *William Faulkner: Novels 1942-1954* (New York: Library of America, 1994) 1-281.

Fielder, Leslie. *The Return of the Vanishing American*. New York: Stein & Day. 1968.

Grey, Zane. *Riders of the Purple Sage*. New York: Pocket Books, 1980.

Horsford, Howard C. "Faulkner's (Mostly) Unreal Indians in Early Mississippi History," *American Literature* 64.2 (1992) 311-30.

Hoy, Christopher. "The Archetypal Transformation of Martiniano in *The Man Who Killed the Deer*," *South Dakota Review* 13 (1975-76) 43-56.

—. "The Conflict in *The Man Who Killed the Deer*," *South Dakota Review* 15 (1977) 51-57.

Krefft, James Harvey. "The Yoknapatawpha Indians: Fact and Fiction." Diss. Tulane University, 1976.

La Farge, Oliver. *Laughing Boy*. Boston: Houghton Mifflin, 1929.

Lyon, Thomas J. *Frank Waters*. New York: Twayne, 1973.

Milton, John, ed. *Conversations with Frank Waters*. Chicago: Swallow Press, 1971.

Plec, Emily, "Narrative as an Instrument of Folk Psychology in Frank Waters' *The Man Who Killed the Deer*," *Studies in Frank Waters* 18 (1997) 23-37.

Powell, Father Peter J. "The Presence of the Sacred" in Deloria, *Frank Waters*, 174-82.

Taylor, J. Golden, ed. *The Literature of the American West*. Boston: Houghton Mifflin, 1971.

Wall, Stephen. "In the Spirit of Wholeness: An Appreciation of the Writings of Frank Waters" in Deloria, *Frank Waters*, 101-05.

Waters, Barbara. "The Final Task" in Deloria, *Frank Waters*, 63-85.

Waters, Frank. T*he Book of the Hopi*. New York: Viking, 1963.

—. *The Man Who Killed the Deer*. Chicago: Swallow Press, 1970.

—. *Masked Gods: Navaho and Pueblo Ceremonialism*. Albuquerque: University of New Mexico Press, 1950.

<hr />

John Nizalowski. "Journey to the World Mountain: Frank Waters' *The Woman at Otowi Crossing* and Terry Tempest Williams' *Refuge*"
In *Rekindling the Inner Light: The Frank Waters Centennial*, edited by Barbara Waters (Taos/Tucson: Frank Waters Foundation Press, 2003) 204-214.

1. Vine Deloria, Jr., "Frank Waters: Explorer and Prophet," in *Frank Waters: Man and Mystic*, edited by Vine Deloria, Jr. (Athens: Swallow Press/Ohio University Press, 1993) 171.

2. Alexander Blackburn, *A Sunrise Brighter Still: The Visionary Novels of Frank Waters* (Athens: Swallow Press/Ohio University Press, 1991) 138.

3. Terry Tempest Williams, *Refuge: An Unnatural History of Family and Place* (New York: Vintage Books, 1992) 127.

4. Ibid., 242.

5. Ibid., 127.

6. Frank Waters, *The Woman at Otowi Crossing* (Athens: Swallow Press/Ohio University Press, 1987) 198.

7. Ibid., 8.

8. Williams, *Refuge*, 79.

9. Waters, *Otowi*, 124.

10. Williams, *Refuge*, 189.

11. Mickey Pearlman, "Terry Tempest Williams," in *Listen to Their Voices* (New York: W. W. Norton, 1993) 123.

12. Waters, *Otowi*, 312.

13. Ibid., 314.

14. Ibid., 21.

15. Williams, *Refuge*, 161.

16. Waters, *Otowi*, 303.

17. John Tallmadge, "Beyond the Excursion: Initiatory Themes in Annie

Dillard and Terry Tempest Williams," in *Reading the Earth: New Directions in the Study of Literature and the Environment*, edited by Michael P. Branch, et al. (Moscow: University of Idaho Press, 1998) 205.

18. Williams, *Refuge*, 217.

19. Waters, *Otowi*, 7.

20. Terry Tempest Williams, *Leap* (New York: Pantheon Books, 2000) 118.

21. Ibid., 143.

22. Waters, *Otowi*, 204.

23. Williams, *Refuge*, 282-83.

24. Felicia Campbell, "Helen and Facundo: A Unity," *Studies in Frank Waters* 10 (1998) 65.

25. Waters, *Otowi*, 174.

26. Ibid., 252-53.

27. Frank Waters, *Of Time and Change* (Denver: MacMurray and Beck, 1998) 272.

28. Brooke Libbey, "Nature Writing as *Refuge*: Autobiography in the Natural World," in *Reading Under the Sign of Nature: New Essays in Ecocriticism*, edited by John Tallmadge and Henry Harrington (Salt Lake City: University of Utah Press, 2000) 260.

29. Cassandra Kircher, "Rethinking Dichotomies in Terry Tempest Williams' *Refuge*," in *Ecofeminist Literary Criticism: Theory, Interpretation, Pedagogy*, edited by Greta Gaard and Patrick D. Murphy (Urbana: University of Illinois Press, 1998) 161.

30. Williams, *Refuge*, 240-41.

31. Frank Waters, *Masked Gods: Navaho and Pueblo Ceremonialism* (Athens: Swallow Press/Ohio University Press, 1984) 410.

32. Waters, *Otowi*, 60.

33. Williams, *Refuge*, 269

34. Ibid., 189-90.

35. Ibid., 262.

36. Frances Malpezzi, "Meru: the Voice of the Mountain," *South Dakota Review* 27: 2 (Summer 1989) 32.

37. Blackburn, *Sunrise*, 115.

38. Waters, *Otowi*, 314. Italics in original.

⚬ ⚬

Gary R. Olsen. "Escape from Time: A Comparison of the Treatment of Time in Frank Waters' *The Woman at Otowi Crossing* and Hermann Hesse's *The Glass Bead Game*"
In *Studies in Frank Waters* 11 (1989), 69-89.

1. For a brief but provocative discussion of the latest theories and discoveries in this area of science, see David H. Freedman, "Cosmic Time Travel," *Discovery* (June 1989) 58-64.

2. William Barrett, *Irrational Man: A Study in Existential Philosophy* (Garden City: Doubleday Anchor Books, 1962) 227.

3. Hesse does not clearly define the nature of the Glass Bead Game in his novel or elsewhere. For an interesting discussion of a computer program which uses *The Glass Bead Game* as its inspiration and model, see James R. Lee, "The Chinese House Game," *Academic Computing* (April 1989) 26-27.

4. Frank Waters, "Prologue," *The Woman at Otowi Crossing*, rev. ed. Athens: Swallow Press/ Ohio University Press 1987.

5. Hermann Hesse, *Steppenwolf*, trans. Basil Creighton (New York: Holt, Rinehart, and Winston, 1963) 211.

6. Hermann Hesse, *Siddhartha*, trans. Hilda Rosner (New York: New Directions, 1951) 115.

7. Waters, *Otowi*, 21.

8. Ibid., 82.

9. Ibid., 124.

10. The character of Pater Jacobus is based upon the distinguished nineteenth-century historian and philosopher Jacob Burckhardt, a man for whom Hesse had tremendous admiration and respect.

11. Hermann Hesse, *The Glass Bead Game*, trans. Richard and Clara Winston (New York: Holt, Rinehart and Winston, 1969) 265.

12. The character of Fritz Tegularius is based upon Friedrich Nietzche, a younger contemporary and colleague of Burckhardt at Basel.

13. Hesse, *Game*, 278.

14. Waters, *Otowi*, 179.

15. Ibid., 310.

16. Ibid., 249.

17. Ibid., 314.

18. Ibid., 139.

19. Ibid., 236.

20. Theodore Ziolkowski, *The Novels of Hermann Hesse: A Study in Theme and Structure* (Princeton: Princeton University Press, 1965) 341-61.

21. Waters, *Otowi*, 21.

22. Ibid., 125.

23. Ibid., 310.

24. Frank Waters, *Mexico Mystique: The Coming Sixth World of Consciousness* (Chicago: Swallow Press, 1975) 283.

⊶ ⤳⋘ ⊷

Alexander Blackburn. "Archetypal Promise from Apocalyptic Premise: *The Woman at Otowi Crossing*"
In Alexander Blackburn, *A Sunrise Brighter Still: The Visionary Novels of Frank Waters* (Athens: Swallow Press/Ohio University Press, 1991), 112-131.

1. Page references are to the revised edition of *The Woman at Otowi Crossing* (Athens: Swallow Press/Ohio University Press, 1987).

2. The "discovery" of psychic energy has only recently been accredited. For instance, Dr. Joseph Banks Rhine and his wife Dr. Louisa E. Rhine spent some fifty years at Duke University trailblazing (over academic objections) and then doing the work of establishing the scientific foundation for parapsychology (E.S.P., or extrasensory perception, was one of their famed contributions), but final respectability was not granted to parapsychology by the scientific establishment until 1969 when the prestigious American Association for the Advancement of Science accepted, after rejecting two previous applications, the Parapsychological Association as a member organization.

3. See Arthur Koestler, *The Act of Creation* (New York: Macmillan, 1964); Fritjof Capra, *The Tao of Physics: An Exploration of the Parallels Between Modern Physics and Eastern Mysticism*, 2d ed. rev. (Boulder, Colorado: Shambhala, 1983); and F. David Peat, *Synchronicity: The Bridge Between Matter and Mind* (Toronto: Bantam, New Age Books, 1987).

4. The concept is surveyed in Ernest W. Lefever and E. Stephen Hunt, eds., *The Apocalyptic Premise*, Washington, D.C.: Ethics and Public Policy Center, 1982.

5. In "Prelude to Change," Waters' commencement address at the University of Nevada, Las Vegas, on 23 May 1981, he reviews the Hopi prophecy about world destruction and then rejects the view that cataclysmic changes will overtake the planet.

6. M. Esther Harding, *Psychic Energy: Its Source and Goal* (New York: Pantheon Books, 1947) 8.

7. See Jonathan Schell, *The Fate of the Earth* (New York: Alfred A. Knopf, 1982) 115. Scientific knowledge, Schell writes, has brought us face to face with the "death of mankind" and in doing so has "caused a basic change in the circumstances in which life was given to us, which is to say that we have altered the human condition."

8. In summarizing some conclusions about motivation I have consulted Koestler, *The Act of Creation*, 495-508.

9. Waters' novel *Flight from Fiesta* emphasizes the theme of "common humanness" (102).

10. Joseph Campbell, *The Power of Myth,* with Bill Moyers, edited by Betty Sue Flowers (New York: Doubleday, 1988) 67.

11. Synchronicity was a concept long incubated. In 1930 Jung introduced the "synchronistic principle" in a memorial address to his friend Richard Wilhelm. The best-known references are Jung's Foreword to the *I Ching* (1950), "On Synchronicity" (1951), and "Synchronicity: An Acausal Connecting Principle" (1952).

12. Peat, *Synchronicity*, 27.

13. In a letter to Dr. Selig dated 25 February 1953 Jung wrote, "It was Einstein who first started me off thinking about a possible relativity of time as well as space, and their psychic synchronicity." See June Singer, *Boundaries of the Soul: The Practice of Jung's Psychology* (Garden City: Doubleday, Anchor books, 1973) 398.

14. Peat, *Synchronicity*, 186-87.

15. Erich Neumann, *Creative Man: Five Essays*, trans. Eugene Rolfe (Princeton: Princeton University Press, 1979) 254.

16. Jean Shimoda Bolen, *The Tao of Psychology: Synchronicity and the Self* (New York: Harper & Row, 1979) 84, italics in original.

17. Capra, *The Tao of Physics*, 104-105.

18. A source for the characterization of Helen Chalmers is the life of Edith Warner, who lived at Otowi bridge and befriended J. Robert Oppenheimer and other physicists from nearby Los Alamos, New Mexico. Himself acquainted with Warner, Waters began composition of *Otowi* in 1953, according to Terence A. Tanner, *Frank Waters: A Bibliography, with Relevant Selections from His Correspondence* (Glenwood, Illl.: Meyerbooks, 1983) 190. Because a book by and somewhat about Peggy Pond Church, *The House at Otowi Bridge: The Story of Edith Warner and Los Alamos* (Albuquerque: University of New Mexico Press) was not published until 1959, the gossip about a Waters' indebtedness of his *Otowi* to Church's book has little or no basis in fact. Moreover, Helen Chalmers is a fictional creation only slightly patterned after Warner (in spite of some "blending" of the two in Paulus' opera *Otowi* in 1995). On Waters' use of details from Warner's life, see Frances M. Malpezzi, "The Emergence of Helen Chalmers," in *Women in Western American Literature*, edited by Helen Stauffer (Troy, N.Y.: Whitson Publishing 1982) 100-113.

19. Waters consistently views Quetzalcoatl as a Redeemer figure – see *Pumpkin* (101, 161-63, 167), *Mexico Mystique* (57-59, 124-26, 133, 139, 193), and *Mountain Dialogues* (143) – and believes that the original transcendental myth was distorted by the Aztecs into a secular, materialistic ideology. It was this vulgarized Quetzalcoatl that D.H. Lawrence fictionally restored to Mexico in his novel *The Plumed Serpent*, according to Waters in "Quetzalcoatl versus D.H. Lawrence's *Plumed Serpent*," *Western American Literature* 3 (Summer 1968) 103-13.

20. In any edition of "Burnt Norton" this is part of line 64.

21. This point is made by Bolen, *The Tao of Psychology*, 9.

22. Colin Falck, *Myth, Truth, and Literature: Towards a True Post-Modernism* (Cambridge: Cambridge University Press, 1989) 121.

23. The term *flashforwards* for the interviews in *Otowi* is used by Thomas J. Lyon, *Frank Waters* (New York: Twayne, 1973) 128.

24. Frances M. Malpezzi, "Meru, the Voice of the Mountain," *South Dakota Review* 27 (1989) 33.

25. The archetypal image of light as life energy suddenly liberated by the "explosion" of death is discussed in Marie-Louise von Franz, *On Dreams and Death: A Jungian Interpretation*, trans. Emmanuel Xiploitas Kennedy and Vernon Brooks (Boston: Shambhala, 1987) 84. Waters uses light imagery in this sense not only for the death of Helen Chalmers in *Otowi* but also for that of Tai Ling in *The Yogi of Cockroach Court*.

26. Waters discusses some representations of the number seven in *Masked Gods* (2222-23), *Pumpkin* (137-38), and *Mexico Mystique* (175, 191). There are allusions in Otowi to Amerindian myths of seven womb-caves (51, 95, 151), which Emily believes are references to the seven traditional kivas within a pueblo, but which Helen considers a parable of Emergence. The tableau with seven deer obviously supports Helen's interpretation.

27. In any edition of "A Valediction: Forbidding Mourning" these are lines 21-24.

FRANK WATERS

Born on July 25th, 1902, in Colorado Springs, Frank Waters began his twenty-eight book career in 1930 with *The Lizard Woman*, a novel set on the Mexican border. For the next six decades, he would go on to write many classics of fiction and non-fiction, including *The Man Who Killed the Deer* (1942), *Masked Gods* (1950), *Book of the Hopi* (1963), *Pike's Peak* (1971), and *Mountain Dialogues* (1981). Along the way, Waters engineered the first phone lines across the Mojave, wrote film scripts for Hollywood, edited a bilingual newspaper in New Mexico, penned public relations releases for Nevada's nuclear test range, and taught university level creative writing classes in Colorado. Waters received numerous honors in his lifetime, including the New Mexico Arts Commission Award for Achievement and Excellence in Literature, seven honorary doctorates, and the declaration of "Frank Waters Day" by New Mexico Governor Bruce King in 1993. Frank Waters died in his home in Arroyo Seco, New Mexico on June 3, 1995.

ALEXANDER BLACKBURN

Alexander Blackburn was born in Durham, N. C., in 1929 and carried a passion for writing across his academic training at Yale and Cambridge and his teaching of creative writing at Pennsylvania and Colorado/Colorado Springs. For his work as educator, novelist, critic and editor he has received the prestigious Frank Waters Award for Excellence in Literature. He lives in Colorado Springs with his wife, Dr. Inés Dölz-Blackburn, Chilean-born author and Professor of Spanish and Latin American Languages and Literature.

JOHN NIZALOWSKI

Born and raised in upstate New York, John Nizalowski moved to Santa Fe in the mid-1980's and has ever after lived west of the 100th meridian. He is the author of five books: the multi-genre work entitled *Hooking the Sun*; two collections of poetry, *The Last Matinée* and *East of Kayenta*; and two volumes of essays, *Land of Cinnamon Sun* and *Chronicles of the Forbidden*. Nizalowski has also published widely in a variety of literary journals, most notably *Under the Sun*, *Weber Studies*, *Puerto del Sol*, *Slab*, *Measure*, *Digital Americana*, and *Blue Mesa Review*. Currently, he teaches mythology, creative writing, and composition at Colorado Mesa University. His blog, Dispatches from the Land of Cinnamon Sun, can be found at http://johnnizalowski.blogspot.com/

CPSIA information can be obtained
at www.ICGtesting.com
Printed in the USA
FSHW011617031220
76407FS